TEACHING APTITUDE & Attitude Test

Useful for B.Ed Entrances and Other Teacher Recruitment Exams

Compiled & Edited by
Arihant 'Expert Team'

ARIHANT PUBLICATIONS (INDIA) LIMITED

ॐ **Administrative & Production Offices**

Regd. Office

'Ramchhaya' 4577/15, Agarwal Road, Darya Ganj, New Delhi -110002
Tele: 011- 47630600, 43518550

ॐ **Head Office**

Kalindi, TP Nagar, Meerut (UP) - 250002
Tel: 0121-7156203, 7156204

ॐ **Sales & Support Offices**

Agra, Ahmedabad, Bengaluru, Bareilly, Chennai, Delhi, Guwahati, Hyderabad, Jaipur, Jhansi, Kolkata, Lucknow, Nagpur & Pune.

ॐ **ISBN** 978-93-25792-76-0

PO No : TXT-XX-XXXXXXX-X-XX

Published by Arihant Publications (India) Ltd.

For further information about the books published by Arihant, log on to www.arihantbooks.com or e-mail at info@arihantbooks.com

Follow us on   

The book entitled 'Teaching Aptitude and Attitude Test' has been designed to meet the requirements of candidates preparing for all the prestigious B.Ed. Entrance Examinations conducted by different universities of our country. Teaching is a noble profession and needs to be given its due credit. A good teacher is expected to have certain qualities like confidence, patience, compassion for students, dedication to excellence, unwavering support, willingness to help student achieve, pride in students accomplishments and passion for life. To meet all these criteria, a candidate willing to choose teaching as a profession, need to undergo a prior assessment test so that he or she could do justice to the profession as well as enjoy and get true satisfaction.

The present book is a novel attempt to meet the standards of this esteemed profession and help the candidates appearing in the entrance examinations. The language of book is simple and easy to understand. The wide coverage of topics, provides it a complete solution for the purpose. It can be presumed that the 'book' will be a boon for the aspirants.

All attempts are made to make the 'book' error free and authentic. However, despite of all our efforts some errors may crept in. Criticism, reviews are welcome from all the respectable teachers, students and all other readers. We assure you to improve the 'book' in further editions to meet your satisfaction and accuracy.

Publisher

CONTENTS

Chapter 01

Teaching Aptitude and Attitude

People always differ from one another in their performance in one or the other fields of human activity like music, art, mechanical work, teaching, leadership, etc. Many individuals under same circumstances perform out well from others and prove themselves to be more suitable and efficient in certain jobs. Such capability is very important for a teacher to be a successful teacher which can be developed through proper training.

Concept of Teaching

Teaching is a methodology in which various activities are involved. The word 'teaching' is derived from the word 'to teach' which means 'to instruct'.

Teaching is a process in which one individual gains knowledge or learn something from a more knowledgeable person. Teaching can be better understood by understanding teaching behaviour at three levels, i.e.,

 (i) First level—Teaching skill
 (ii) Second level—General teaching behaviour
 (iii) Third level—Specific teaching behaviour

All these three levels are inter-related. At the first level, teaching can be defined as a set at component teaching skills. Such teaching skills are necessary to bring about the realisation of set of instructional objectives. These instructional objectives are the set of goals which a teacher set to achieve at the end of his class.

Definitions of Teaching

According to **N.L. Gage**, "Teaching is a form of interpersonal influence aimed at changing the behaviour potential of another person. It is a personal relationship between the teacher and the taught causing behaviour modification."

According to **H.C. Morrison** "Teaching is a disciplined social process in which the teacher influences the behaviour of the less experienced pupil and helps him develop according to the needs and ideas of the society."

According to **Jackson**, "Teaching is a face to face encounters between two or more persons, one of whom (teacher) intends to effect certain changes in other participants (students)."

Clarke defined the scope of teaching and included all those organised activities as teaching that may result in modifying the behaviour of the learner.

According to **J.B. Hongh and James K Duncan**, "Teaching is an activity with four phases, i.e., a curriculum phase, a planning phase, instructing phase and an evaluating phase."

According to **Amidon**, "Teaching is a process of interaction between the teacher and the taught as a cooperative enterprise, a two way traffic."

According to **Dewey**, "Teaching and learning are not separated processes and learning comes through doing."

According to **Rabindranath Tagore**, "Teaching is a natural process and it should be done in natural environment, close to nature."

Concept of Aptitude

The word 'aptitude' is defined in various ways by psychologists. An aptitude is not the same thing as ability or interest. It is more specific, measuring only certain aspects of functioning within a limited range. A person with a verbal ability cannot have aptitude for all the different tasks or vocations connected with verbal ability. Aptitude is only in part of born or native.

According to **Bingham** (1937) "A condition or set of characteristics regarded as symptomatic of an individual's ability to acquire with training some (usually specified) knowledge, skill or set of responses, such as ability to speak, a knowledge to produce music, etc."

Bingham states that aptitude is a measure of probabilities of success of an individual with training is certain type of situation, such as playing piano.

Thus, aptitude is something more than the ability. It is ability plus suitability of performance. For example, a person may be a good scholar, as he possesses high verbal ability, but it does not mean that he must be good teacher.

The Bingham's definition also found support from Freeman (1955) as he defines aptitude as a combination of characteristics which connotes an individual's capacity to acquire (with training) some specific knowledge, skill or set of organised responses, such as ability to speak a language, to become a musician, to do mechanical work, teaching, etc.

According to **George K. Bennett, Harold G. Seashore** and **Alexander G. Weisman** (1959), "Aptitude embraces any characteristics which is pre-disposed to learning including intelligence, achievement personality, interests and special skills."

Thus, we can say that definition of Bingham (1937) is the most acceptable definition as it covers the majority of the views expressed in other definitions.

Characteristics of Aptitude

- It is symptomatic or suggestive of one's ability for a particular work or job.
- It is a present condition with a future reference to person's potential ability to do something.
- It connotes more than potential ability in performance and implies fitness and suitability for the activities in question.
- It is innate capacities resulted from the interaction of heredity and environment.
- Aptitude embraces any characteristics which pre-disposes learning which includes intelligence, achievement, personality, interest and special skills.

Types of Aptitude

Generally, aptitude is of two types

1. **Positive Aptitude** People with positive aptitude view life challenges, religion, institutions and the situations they go through with confidence are sure that they can deal with them. They do not dwell on the problems and difficulties of the past and does not let them dictate his life. They would rather learn from the past mistakes and move on.

2. **Negative Aptitude** People with negative aptitude do not seek solution and progress. They always have negative thoughts about the society, religion, politics, community, etc. They lack self-esteem and positivity. These affect their thinking procedures and actions.

Teaching Aptitude

Teaching aptitude is the capacity to acquire proficiency with a given amount of training in teacher education. It refers to the capacity of an individual to be skilled in teaching by receiving formal or informal training. Thus, teaching aptitude is helpful in predicting the future success of an individual in teaching field after providing appropriate opportunities and training.

Many factors are involved with teaching aptitude and it depends upon certain personal traits, intellect and temperament. Research studies revealed that many factors have dominant roles in teaching aptitude.

Teaching mainly needs three qualities, i.e., knowledge, communication skills and aptitude. A teacher with good aptitude must be aware of the essential components of teaching like lesson planning, motivating students, teaching-learning strategies, comprehensive evaluation, effective communication and interaction, etc.

Concept of Attitude

Attitude refers to a set of emotions, beliefs and behaviours towards a particular object, person, thing or event. Attitudes are often the result of experience or upbringing and they can have powerful influence over behaviour. Psychologists define attitudes as learned tendency to evaluate things in a certain way. This can include evaluation of people, issues, objects or events.

Definitions of Attitude

According to **Gordon Allport,** "An attitude is a mental and neural state of readiness, organised through experience, exerting a directive or dynamic influence upon the individual's response to all objects and situation with which it is related."

According to **Thurstone,** "An attitude denotes the total of man's inclinations and feelings, prejudice or bias, pre-conceived notions, ideas, fears, threats and other any specific topic."

According to **N.L. Munn**, 'Attitudes are learned pre-dispositions towards aspects of our environment.

They may be positively or negatively directed towards certain people, service or institution."

Characteristics of Attitude

- Attitudes are complex combination of things, we call personality, beliefs, values, behaviours and motivations.
- An attitude exists in every person's mind. It helps to define our identity, guide or actions, and influence how we judge people.
- Attitude helps us define how we see situations and define how we behave towards the situation or object.
- It provides us with internal cognitions or beliefs and thoughts about people and objects.
- It can also be explicit and implicit. Explicit attitude is that we are consciously aware of and implicit attitude is unconscious, but still affects our behaviour.
- Attitude causes us to behave in a particular way toward an object or person.
- An attitude is a summary of a person's experience. Thus, an attitude is grounded in direct experience predicts future behaviour more accurately.
- It includes certain aspects of personality as interests, appreciation and social conduct.
- It indicates the total of a man's inclinations and feelings.
- An attitude is a point of view, substantiated or otherwise, true or false, which one hold towards an idea, object, or person.
- It has aspects, such as direction, intensity, generality or specificity.
- It may be positive or negative and may be affected by age, position and education.

Teaching Attitude

Teaching is a dynamic activity which requires a favourable attitude and certain specific competencies from its practitioners. Teacher's proficiency depends on the attitude he possesses for the profession. The positive attitude helps the teacher to develop a conductive learner-friendly environment in the classroom.

Infact, the teacher's roles and responsibilities have found extension outside his classroom. The implementation of educational policies, transaction of curricula and spreading awareness are the main areas which keep a teacher in the forefront.

Changing times have added new dimensions to teaching profession. Thus, it requires specified competencies and right attitude.

Attitude is defined as a state of readiness shaped through the experience and influences the response of individual towards the stimuli. It is a deciding factor of the teacher's performance. Through the right attitude, the teacher can do justice to his profession.

Importance of Positive Attitude

- A positive attitude towards learning is very necessary for being a successful learner.
- Formal classroom learning is very important and valuable for positive attitude.
- All kinds to learning opportunities need a positive attitude.
- A positive attitude and a belief in our ability will help us to enjoy the learning process and discover many opportunities for learning.

Ways to Develop Positive Attitude

There are different ways to develop positive attitude, such as

Utilise the most important hours of the day Make the most of the early morning hours of the day more productive. We must practice reading and writing at early hours because with the passing of time, we are involved in other activities as well.

Prioritise the goals and duties We should not exhaust our available time in doing the least priority jobs and leave a very little time for doing the most important work in our life that matters a lot.

Open for learning Open for learning anything and everything that looks complex and critical for the first time. This will help us breaking out from our comfort zone and trying something different rather than spending time on doing same routine work. We will be empowered to deal with the difficult and challenging emotions required for growth and evolution.

Upgrade yourself intellectually, emotionally and spiritually Set yourself apart from the ordinary crowd and upgrade yourself intellectually, emotionally and spiritually. Quickly we will realise that we can work with people much more effectively, solve problems easily and create an amazingly satisfied lifestyle.

Nourish your mind and soul We must enhance our current mental situation and improve our current priorities, goals, choices and daily behaviours. We should learn from our mistakes, and elevate ourselves with no regrets and repents.

Exercise

1 Teaching is a skillful application of
  (a) Knowledge
  (b) Experience
  (c) Scientific principles
  (d) All of the above

2 Teaching can be better understood by understanding teaching behaviour at .... levels.
  (a) two   (b) three   (c) four   (d) five

3 .... are necessary to bring about the realisation of set of instructional objectives.
  (a) Teaching skills   (b) Teaching methods
  (c) Both (a) and (b)   (d) None of these

4. Teaching can be analysed in terms of teacher behaviour at least at three levels, they are
  (a) teaching skills, learning behaviour and teaching behaviour
  (b) general teaching behaviour, specific teaching behaviour and learning skills
  (c) teaching skills, general teaching behaviour and specific teaching behaviour
  (d) learning skills, teaching skills and specific teaching behaviour

5 Following the analysis at what level, teaching can be defined as a set of component skills for the realisation of a specified set of instructional objectives?
  (a) First level   (b) Second level
  (c) Third level   (d) None of these

6 At which level teaching skills can be defined as a set of inter-related teaching behaviours for the realisation of specific instructional objectives?
  (a) Specific teaching skills
  (b) General learning behaviour
  (c) Specific teaching behaviour
  (d) General teaching behaviour

7 Who has/have defined the term 'teaching skills' as "a set of related teaching behaviours which in specified types of classroom interaction situations tend to facilitate the achievement of specified types of educational objectives"?
  (a) McIntyre
  (b) White
  (c) McIntyre and White Both
  (d) None of the above

8 Who of the following consider 'teaching as a personal relationship between teacher and taught causing behaviours modification'?
  (a) Gage   (b) Clarke
  (c) Green   (d) Amidon

9 Teaching is a process of interaction between teacher and taught-who states this?
  (a) Amidon   (b) Green
  (c) Clarke   (d) None of these

10 Who of the following stated that teaching should be done in natural environment?
  (a) Tagore   (b) Amidon
  (c) Green   (d) Clarke

11 What is the first and foremost objective of teaching?
  (a) To impart knowledge only
  (b) To develop skills that can help learners to solve their real life problems
  (c) To give lectures in the class
  (d) None of the above

12 Specific teaching behaviour can be brought about by
  (a) specific teaching skill
  (b) by reading from a book
  (c) imitating other
  (d) All of the above

13 Teaching aptitude means
  (a) devotion towards teaching work
  (b) the desire to become a teacher
  (c) all the requisite abilities to do the job of a teacher
  (d) None of the above

14 Important aspect of teaching aptitude is
  (a) the capability of the teacher to let the students realise the truth
  (b) the capability of the teacher to check the creativity of his students
  (c) the capability of the teacher to make student vocation oriented
  (d) the capability of the teacher to make teaching student oriented

15 Our attitude towards knowledge should be
  (a) to accept what is proved by science on the basis of empirical evidence
  (b) not to accept anything that is not personally verified
  (c) to accept as the final truth
  (d) to accept believing in the scope for improvement

16 Which of the following statements is most reasonable?
  (a) Teachers motivate students to acquire knowledge
  (b) Teachers are born
  (c) Teachers are capable of teaching
  (d) Interpretation of a complex theory is very useful for development of thinking process in students

17 The most beneficial aspect of the teaching profession is
  (a) an opportunity to dominate the children
  (b) an opportunity to express yourself
  (c) sufficient number of holidays in a year
  (d) hefty earnings from tuition work, besides earnings through salary

18 "Aptitude is a condition or set of characteristics regarded as symptomatic of an individual's ability to acquire with training some (usually specified) knowledge, skill or set of responses, such as ability to speak a knowledge, to produce music, etc." .... is the speaker.
  (a) Bingham   (b) Macclean
  (c) Taxler   (d) Freeman

19 .... said that "aptitude embraces any characteristics which is pre-disposed to learning including intelligence, achievement personality, interests and special skills."
  (a) George K. Bennett
  (b) Harold G. Seashore
  (c) Alexander G. Weisman
  (d) All of the above

20 .... is symptomatic or suggestive of one's ability for a particular work or job.
  (a) Knowledge
  (b) Aptitude
  (c) Attitude
  (d) None of the above

21 Aptitude is of .... types.
  (a) two   (b) three
  (c) four   (d) six

22 .... is the capacity to acquire proficiency with a given amount of training in teacher education.
  (a) Knowledge
  (b) Power of reasoning
  (c) Teaching aptitude
  (d) None of the above

23 Aptitude test is used to
  (a) measure success
  (b) measure proficiency
  (c) to indicate success in any task
  (d) measure the capacity/capability

24 Psychologists define .... as a learned tendency to evaluate things in a certain way.
  (a) Attitude
  (b) Aptitude
  (c) Knowledge
  (d) None of the above

25 According to ...., "An attitude is a mental and neural state of readiness organised through experience, exerting a directive or dynamic influence upon the individual's response to all objects and situation with which it is related."
  (a) Gordon Allport
  (b) Frank Freeman
  (c) Thur Stone
  (d) None of the above

26 "Attitude can be described as a learned pre-disposition to respond in a consistently favourable or unfavourable manner for a given object". Who is/are the speaker(s)?
(a) Martin Fishbein   (b) Icek Ajzen
(c) Milton Rokeach   (d) Both (a) and (b)

27 An attitude may be positive or negative and may be affected by ....
(a) age   (b) positive
(c) education   (d) All of these

28 By adopting which method we can develop our learning attitude?
(a) Utilise the most important hours of your day
(b) Prioritise your goals and duties and open for learning
(c) Upgrade yourself intellectually, emotionally and spiritually and nourish your mind and soul
(d) All of the above

Answers

1 (d)	2 (b)	3 (a)	4 (c)	5 (a)	6 (d)	7 (c)	8 (a)	9 (a)	10 (a)
11 (b)	12 (a)	13 (c)	14 (d)	15 (a)	16 (a)	17 (b)	18 (a)	19 (d)	20 (b)
21 (a)	22 (c)	23 (c)	24 (a)	25 (a)	26 (d)	27 (d)	28 (d)		

Chapter 02

Aptitude Towards Education

Educations is a process that continues throughout life. It is comprised of knowledge, experience, skills and attitudes.

It is helpful in the development of a society as it develops good citizens for future. Due to education, the socio-economic, cultural and political development of students can be possible.

Concept of Education

The word 'education' has been derived from the Latin word 'Educatum' which means 'to educate'. It is a systematic system as education has its set aims, objectives, curriculum and teaching methods as per the learner's attitude and abilities.

Following are the views of some prominent scholars regarding education

According to **J.S. Mill**, "Through education, people of one generation transfer culture to the people of another generation, so that they can preserve it and if possible can also progress in it."

According to **Tagore**, "The meaning of education is to enable the mind to discover the truth and to express it while making it its own".

According to **Vivekananda**, "Education is the display of the perfection embodied in man".

According to **Kant**, "Education is the development of the completeness of the individual to which he is capable".

According to **Froebel**, "Education is the process by which the child's innate powers come out".

According to **Aristotle**, "Education is the creation of a healthy mind in a healthy body".

Characteristics of Education

- Education is a continuous process. It starts with the birth of the individual and continues till death.
- It is not only limited within the educational institutes, but individual can get it from any sphere of his life.
- It helps to develop the inner qualities and powers of an individual.
- Education should ensure adequate preparation for immediate life. This will encourage the pupil to learn.
- The aim of education is self-realisation of the individual.
- It solves the problems of students and helps them to choose the right path in their life.
- Properly educated society will become a civilised society. Thus, the importance of education is immense for human society.

Objectives of Education

- Education has a great social significance. Thus, educational philosophers and outstanding teachers have given education a high place in their works.
- Education helps develop a mentally and physically strong individual.
- Education aims at the transmission of cultural heritage through history text books. Through education we become aware of our past, its art, literature, philosophy, religion and music.
- It helps to develop overall growth of an individual. Education helps to discover the God given talents of individual and work towards their fullest development.
- It educates the individual and inspires the child to learn more for life.
- The educational institutes must take a lead to imbibe in the young minds the true education, which includes not only academic excellence, but also the development of the complete personality.
- With the right mixture of academics and personal care, education gives a sure footing for a great future. Thus, the aim of education is to prepare every child to face the challenges of the world in a positive manner.
- Education instills in the pupils, the values of love, freedom, forgiveness, honesty and justice.
- 'Total Education' implies a holistic approach to education and which is concerned with the total development of an individual. It aims at developing the body, mind and spirit to the greatest extent.
- Proper education develops feelings of nationalism among students. It also helps to develop leadership ability among them.
- It nurtures creative potential in students which will make them fit for a better livelihood.
- Education must bring out the great caliber of every child. It makes every child to apply his theoretical knowledge in the practical field.

Types of Education

1. **Formal Education** The education which is given regularly and formally is known as formal education.

   It is intentional, organised and structured form of learning, imparted in educational institutions like school, college and university in order to modify the behaviour of an individual. It is facilitated by a teacher or trainer, intentional on the part of the learner and leads to certification.

2. **Informal Education** The system of education which is always going on random basis, which has no specific plan is known as informal education. It has no specific aims and no teaching methods.

   It is learning that goes on in daily life and can be received through daily experiences, such as from family, peer group, the media and other influences in a person's environment. It covers a vast array of learning that all people take part in, in their lives every day.

   In this type of education, the learner picks up knowledge from the television, radio, even from conversations with friends and family members.

3. **Non-Formal Education** After seeing the shortcomings of formal and informal education, a new system of education was developed which is known as non-formal education. It has an adopted strategy where the students' attendance is not fully required. Here the educative progress has a more flexible curricula and methodology.

   The activities or lessons of the non-formal education take place outside the institutions or schools. Here the needs and interest of the students are taken into consideration. It meets the individual needs better.

Other Types of Education

1. **General Education** General education is also called Liberal education. In this education, efforts are made to develop the child at a normal level. According to the educationists, this education should be compulsorily adopted by the human, because it motivates the man from animal like behaviour to human behaviour. The aim of this education is to prepare the child for a normal life.

2. **Special Education** Special education is that type of education which is conducted for a particular purpose.

In this education, special care is taken so that education should be according to child's interests, abilities and capabilities, because this education prepares the child for a particular field or profession. Through this education, opportunities are given to the child in such a way that he can develop his creativity and to reach his life's goal.

1 Which of the following elements is involved in the education process?
(a) Knowledge
(b) Skill
(c) Attitude
(d) All of the above

2 The word 'education' is derived from which of the following languages?
(a) Latin   (b) English
(c) French   (d) None of these

3 Which of the following development of students is possible through education?
(a) Social   (b) Economic
(c) Political   (d) All of these

4 Education has its set
(a) Teaching methods
(b) Aims
(c) Curriculum
(d) All of the above

5 Who said that "Education is the development of the completeness of the individual to which he is capable"?
(a) Tagore   (b) Kant
(c) JS Mill   (d) None of these

6 Who said that "Education is the display of the perfection embodied in man"?
(a) Kant   (b) J.S. Mill
(c) Tagore   (d) Vivekanand

7 According to whom, "Education is the process by which the child's innate powers come out"?
(a) Aristotle   (b) Tagore
(c) Froebel   (d) None of these

8 Which of the following is the characteristic of education?
(a) It is a continuous process
(b) It starts with birth and continues till death
(c) It is not limited within the educational institutes
(d) All of the above

9 Which of the following is true about education?
(a) It helps to develop inner qualities and powers of an individual
(b) The aim of education is self-realisation of the individual
(c) It solves problems of students
(d) All of the above

10 Which of the following is the objective of education?
(a) To develop physical and mental development of students.
(b) It aims to transmission of cultural heritage through history textbooks.
(c) It helps to develop overall growth of an individual.
(d) All of the above

11 The education which is given regularly is known as
   (a) Formal education
   (c) Non-formal education
   (c) Informal education
   (d) None of the above

12 The system of education which is always going on random basis and has no specific plan is known as
   (a) Formal education
   (b) Informal education
   (c) Non-Formal education
   (d) None of the above

13 Which is the aim of Informal education?
   [Chhattisgarh BEd 2016]
   (a) To reduce education budget
   (b) To end the autonomy of schools
   (c) To provide formal education
   (d) To impart education to common people

14 After seeing the shortcomings of formal and informal education, which new system was developed in education?
   (a) Non-formal education
   (b) Group education
   (c) Direct education
   (d) Indirect education

15 General education is also known as
   (a) Formal education
   (b) Liberal education
   (c) Informal Education
   (d) None of the above

16 In general education efforts are made to develop the child at
   (a) Normal level   (b) Specific level
   (c) Social level   (d) Psychological level

17 Which education is conducted for a particular purpose?
   (a) Special education
   (b) Informal education
   (c) Non-formal education
   (d) Democratic education

18 Teacher aim to help children to develop their abilities through education
   [Rajasthan BEd 2016]
   (a) Individually
   (b) Individually and in socially desirable ways
   (c) Only in socially desirable ways
   (d) The way the children want

19 Education should be such that the student should be
   (a) Well cultured
   (b) Professionally self-reliant
   (c) Endowed with moral virtues
   (d) All of the above

20 On what basis will you determine whether your education is successful or not?
   (a) If it increases your respect
   (b) If it gives you self-satisfaction
   (c) If it benefits others also
   (d) If it gives you a job

Answers

1 *(d)*	2 *(a)*	3 *(d)*	4 *(d)*	5 *(b)*	6 *(d)*	7 *(c)*	8 *(d)*	9 *(d)*	10 *(d)*
11 *(a)*	12 *(b)*	13 *(d)*	14 *(a)*	15 *(a)*	16 *(a)*	17 *(a)*	18 *(b)*	19 *(d)*	20 *(b)*

Chapter 03

Inclusive, Child Centered and Progressive Education

Inclusive Education

Inclusive education means all children in the same classroom irrespective of their diverse background are in the same school to get proper education.

Inclusive education is about looking at the ways our schools, classrooms, programmes and lessons are designed so that all children can participate and learn. Inclusion is also about finding different ways of teaching so that classrooms activity involve all children. It also means finding ways to develop friendships, relationships and mutual respect between all children and between teachers in the school.

Inclusive education is a way of thinking about how to be creative to make our schools a place where all children can participate. Creativity in inclusive education means teachers learn to teach in different ways or design their lessons in an appropriate way so that all children can be involved.

As a value, inclusive education reflects the expectation that we want all of our children to be appreciated and accepted throughout life.

Features of Inclusive Education

- Accepting unconditionally all children into regular classes.
- Providing as much support to children, teachers and classrooms as necessary to ensure that all children can participate in their schools and classes.
- Developing education goals according to each child's abilities.
- This means that children do not need to have the same education goals in order to learn together in regular classes.
- Designing schools and classes in such a way that help children learn and achieve to their fullest potential.
- Having teachers who have knowledge about different ways of teaching so that children with various abilities and strengths can learn together.
- Having principals, teachers, parents and others work together to determine the most affective ways of providing a quality education in an inclusive environment.

Benefits of Inclusive Education

- Through inclusive education, all children would be able to be a part of their community and develop a sense of belongingness and be better prepared for life as good citizens.
- It provides better opportunities for learning. Children with varying abilities are often better motivated when they learn in classes with other children.
- It provides all children with opportunities to develop friendship with one another. Friendships provide role models and opportunities for growth.
- It encourages the involvement of parents in the education of their children and the activities of their local schools.

Types of Inclusive Children

On the basis of individual differences, under inclusive education, children have been divided into three types - normal child, special child and deprived child, which can be understood in the following ways

1. Normal Children

The children who are of average physical and mental level and having an IQ level 90-100, are known as normal children. Normal children do not experience any obstacle in performing tasks involving normal physical and mental exertion, like most children in the class, they are also average in academic achievement. Their learning speed is also average or normal.

Whereas on the contrary, children with special needs are uncomfortable and unable to do such tasks, because they are deprived of physical defects or society.

2. Special Children

Such children who are physically, mentally and emotionally different from normal children are called special children.

Types of Special Children

Gifted Children Generally such children, whose IQ level is 120 or above, are called gifted children. Therefore, it is clear from this point that a gifted child is identified on the basis of his intelligence.

Mentally Retarded Children Mentally retarded children are called such children, who are suffering from mental retardation. Generally, mental retardation refers to the child's intelligence which is less than normal or average children.

But psychologists have considered the criterion of mental retardation not only in intelligence, but also in accommodative behavior. That is, such a child whose intelligence level (IQ) is less than 90 as well as there is a decrease in accommodative behavior, then he is known as a mentally retarded child.

Visually Impaired Children Such children who are affected by visual impairment are known as visually impaired children. Visual impairment is such a disability of the child which creates a hindrance in the child's vision. Visually impaired children do not see the letters written on the blackboard in the classroom properly, due to which they are not able to concentrate and study in the class.

Hearing Impaired Children Such children who are affected by hearing impairment are known as Hearing Impaired Children.Such a disability that causes hearing impairment in a person is called hearing impairment. Hearing impairedness separates the child from the society, due to which the language development of the child gets hampered.

Language Impaired Children Language is the only medium through which we exchange our thoughts. Through language one person communicates his thoughts to another person and understands the thoughts of others and responds appropriately to them. Children who have language-related defects have more adjustment difficulties in school and children's academic achievement and social development are severely affected.

Education of Special Children in India

The National Policy of Education, 1986 has been an important initiative in the direction of education in India. In this, provision has been made for education for the disabled children in the implementation program presented by the **Acharya Ramamurthy Committee**, which are as follows

- Provision of special school, and integrated education for disabled children.
- To arrange for vocational training and for training of teachers for innovation.
- Appointing specialised teachers, training educational administrators and simplifying the curriculum and its process.
- To arrange special learning materials, equipments, etc., in the schools.

3. Deprived Children

The general meaning of the word 'deprived' is 'to be left unaffected by the normal comforts of life'. In this sense every child can be said to be a deprived child; because every child remains unaffected by some or the other comforts. Psychologically deprived child means such children who come from socio-economically and culturally disadvantaged community.

Types of Deprived Children

Socially Deprived Children It includes those children who are disadvantaged in the society and are deprived of the facility of education due to many reasons. Several measures are being taken for these reasons.

For example; Opening more schools, providing residential facilities, providing free education facilities, etc.

Economically Deprived Children It includes those children who are backward from the economic point of view, due to which educational facilities are not available adequately to such children.

Children of Scheduled Castes and Scheduled Tribes In India, about 90% of the families in the Scheduled Castes and Scheduled Tribes community are those who are socio-economically and culturally backward and the children of such families are called deprived children.

Child Centered Education

Child centered education consists of education in which the child is the focal point of learning. Teaching is provided keeping in mind the interest, tendencies and abilities of the child. It gives importance to individual learning.

Child centered learning is one aspect of progressive education because it considers learning as a natural process for a child in which he/she learns from carrying out day-to-day activities.

Here, the teacher focuses on a child's learning, not on what the teacher teaches. The teacher must act as a guide who encourages, instructs and stimulates a child as per its needs, because every child has different capabilities and needs.

Characteristics of Child Centered Education

The characterstics of child centered education are as follows

- It considers the growth of a child as a priority.
- It makes the child's learning interesting and meaningful.
- It recognises the child's potential and utilises effectively.
- It leads to overall development of the child in physical moral and spiritual areas.

Principles of Child Centered Education

The basic principles of child centered education can be understood through various aspects as given below

1. **Understanding of Child Psychology** The teacher/educator must understand that the children's behaviour is governed by their requirements, social cognitive abilities, etc. Thus, shifting the focus of instruction from teacher to the student. Thus for instance, teacher will need to adopt different strategies educating the high intelligence, average intelligence and poor intelligence children.

2. **Evaluation and Testing** Evaluation of learning is important to understand that the learning is effective or not. Traditional testing techniques replaced the child centered learning by Continuous and Comprehensive Evaluation (followed by CBSE since 2010).

3. **Syllabus** This needs to be upgraded periodically. It must be based on a psychological analysis of the children's needs, values and variety required. It should be flexible to take care of all types of learners.

4. **Managing Discipline** Child psychology is used to manage discipline in a child centered classroom. The teacher will need to have a flexible response to various kinds of indiscipline indulged in by the learners.

5. **Practical Orientation** Learners should be oriented towards practical aspects of the topic being taught to them. They must learn the value of experimentation to solve problems. As research in child psychology gives new knowledge of the psychology of children. The teacher should try to implement this knowledge in the classroom.

6. **Diagnosis and Dismantling of Problems** Various kinds of problems occur in the classroom. The teacher must understand how to categorise each problem and find a solution to it by using his knowledge of child psychology.

Progressive Education

Progressive education is a reaction against the traditional style of teaching. It is pedagogical movement which includes experience over learning facts at the expense of understanding what is being taught. It is based on the idea that we should teach children how to think and that a test cannot measure whether or not a child is an educated person.

The process of 'learning by doing' is at the heart of this style of learning. It uses 'hands-on' projects as a means of learning.

Definitions of Progressive Education

Locke believed that "truth and knowledge arise out of observation and experience rather than manipulation of accepted or given ideas." He further mentioned that children need to have concrete experiences in order to learn.

Rousseau continued in Locke's line of thinking by saying that "Sub-ordination of students to teachers and only memorisation of facts would not lead to an education."

Frobel laid the foundation for modern education based on his understanding that children have unique needs and capabilities. He believed in 'self-activity' and play essential role in child education.

Dewey was a principal figure in the 'Progressive Education Movement' from the 1880s to 1904, and developed the philosophy of education as well as concrete school reforms. In beginning of 1897, Dewey published a summary of his theory on progressive education.

Dewey's Theory of Progressive Education

According to Dewey, progressive education consists of the following five aspects

1. **Education** It is participation of the individual in the social consciousness of the race. The educational process has two sides, the psychological and the sociological, with the psychological forming the basis. A child's own instincts will help develop the material that is presented to it. This forms the basis of Dewey's assumption that one cannot learn without motivation.

2. **School** It must represent the current life; thus, parts of the student's home life (such as moral and ethical education) should take part in the schooling process. The teacher is a part of this, not as an authoritative figure, but as a member of the community who is there to assist the student.

3. **Curriculum** The curriculum in schools should reflect the development of humans in society. The study of the core subjects like languages, science, history, etc., should be coupled with the study of practical skills like cooking, sewing and manual training. Dewey also felt that progress is not in a succession of studies but in the development of new attitudes towards and new interests in actual experiences.

4. **Method of Education** This must be focused on the child's powers and interests. Information presented to the student will be transformed into new forms, images and symbols by it so that the information fits with its development and interests. The development of this is natural.

5. **Social Progress as Related to the School** Education is the most fundamental method of social reconstruction for progress and reform. Thus, Dewey understood that schools were a means to reconstruct society and so, educationists must be given the proper equipment to help perform this task and guide their students.

Importance of Progressive Education

Learners have different capabilities and interests, so they develop in different ways. Thus, progressive education is important, because it takes care of this variation by

- giving children full opportunity to develop by providing an environment for development.
- not allowing any discrimination between learners.
- educating learners by cooperative learning.
- developing democratic values in the students.
- making education more practical with emphasis on self-learning.
- asking teachers to permit learners to design their own learning experiences according to their interests and capabilities.
- making children work on projects, so that they development self-confidence, maturity and independence.
- making children learn how to work together with others which instills discipline in their personalities.
- developing their moral character.

Characteristics of Progressive Education

- Curriculum is designed according to the interests of children.
- The approach to education is developmental, meaning that each child has unique needs for its own development.
- Collaborative learning is used for developing social values and skills.
- The teacher works as a facilitator.
- Rote learning is discouraged and there is less emphasis on textbooks.

Types of Progressive Education

Progressive education can be humanistic (focusing on arts and social sciences), constructivist (focusing on the child's creativity) or Montessori (teachers act as facilitators of learning in this type developed by the Italian doctor and educationist Maria Montessori).

These are discussed below

1. Humanistic

This is also called person- centered education. It is an approach to education based on the work of humanistic psychologists like Abraham Maslow and Carl Rogers.

Here empathy, caring about students and genuineness on the part of the learning facilitator (i.e. teacher) were found to be the key traits of the most effective teachers. Important objectives include developing children's self-esteem, their ability to set and achieve appropriate goals, and their development toward full autonomy.

2. Constructivist

This is a philosophy of learning founded on the premise that, by reflecting on our experiences, we construct our own understanding of the world we live in. Its guiding principles are as follows

- Learning starts with the issues around which students are actively trying to construct its meaning.
- The learning proces focuses on primary concepts and the educators focus on making connections between facts and fostering new understanding in students.
- The educators understand the mental models that students use to perceive the world and the assumptions they make to support those models.
- The only effective way to measure learning is to make the assessment a part of the learning process, so that it provides students with information on the quality of their learning.

3. Montessori

The Montessori philosophy is child-directed approach for primary level school children that is based on scientific observation of individuals from birth to adulthood.

It is focused on allowing children to make their own choices in learning, with a teacher guiding the process rather than leading it.

Differences between Traditional Education and Progressive Education

Parameter	Traditional Education	Progressive Education
School	Institution for preparing children for life	A part of life
Learners	Absorb information and obey rules	Actively participate in problem-solving
Parents	Treated as outsiders	Considered as the primary (first) teachers
Society	Separate from school	Extension of the classroom
Knowledge	Given by lectures and assignments	Constructed through direct experience and social interaction

Exercise

1 The quality of education depends upon .... of teachers.

(a) ability (b) efficiency
(c) interest (d) Both (a) and (b)

2 There are generally .... types of education.

(a) two (b) three
(c) four (d) five

3 Education starts with the birth of the individual and continues till death, thus it is ....

(a) a continuous process
(b) a rational process
(c) a common process
(d) None of the above

4 .... provides better opportunities for learning as children with varying abilities are often better motivated when they learn in classes surrounded by other children.

(a) Inclusive education (b) School education
(c) Proper education (d) None of these

5 Inclusive education develops a sense of belonging and better preparation for life in the .... as children and adults.

(a) school (b) higher institutions
(c) community (d) None of these

6 In order to solve the problem of aimlessness in education, we should develop **[MP Pre BEd 2016]**

(a) democratic citizenship
(b) centralised education
(c) straight and forward aims
(d) reform the administrative set-up

7 When a child fails in class, then it means **[UK BEd Entrance Exam 2017]**

(a) child is not able to study
(b) child has not memorised the answer
(c) child should take tuition
(d) system is failed

8 Inclusion of children with special needs **[CTET Sep 2016]**

(a) is detrimental to children without disabilities
(b) will increase the burden on schools
(c) requires a change in attitude, content and approach to teaching
(d) is an unrealistic goal

9 Successful inclusion requires all except **[KVS TGT 2017]**

(a) appropriate techniques and procedures for monitoring individual student progress
(b) teachers accept responsibility for the learning outcomes of students
(c) teachers have the knowledge and skills needed to select and adapt curricula and instructional methods according to individual student's need
(d) a competitive learning environment that focuses on individual's achievement

10 Inclusive education includes **[UK BEd Entrance Exam 2017]**

(a) the special school that encourage the special child through education
(b) only the girl students education
(c) disabled child
(d) the child who are differently abled at the physical, intellectual, social, language, etc.

11 In inclusive education which one of the following is least important trait? **[UK BEd 2017]**

(a) Sensitive regarding students
(b) Attachment and patience for students
(c) Knowledge of student's incompetence
(d) Socio-economic level of teacher

12 The concept of 'Inclusive Education' as advocated in the Right to Education Act, 2009 is based on **[CTET Dec 2019]**

(a) the behaviouristic principles
(b) a sympathetic attitude towards disabled
(c) a rights based humanistic perspective
(d) mainstreaming of the disabled by offering him/her primarily vocational education.

13 The term 'inclusion' means educating child with special need in the regular classroom for **[MP Pre BEd 2010]**
(a) sometime
(b) most of the time
(c) full time
(d) during social activities in the school

14 In an inclusive classroom, a teacher .... individualised education plans. **[CTET Dec 2019]**
(a) should not prepare
(b) should occasionally prepare
(c) should actively prepare
(d) should discourage the preparation of

15 An inclusive school reflects on all the following questions except **[MP Pre BEd 2019]**
(a) Do we believe that all students can learn?
(b) Do we work in teams to plan and deliver learning enabling environment?
(c) Do we properly segregate special children from normal to provide better care?
(d) Do we adopt strategies catering for the diverse needs to students?

16 In an inclusive classroom with diverse learners, cooperative learning and peer-tutoring **[MP Pre BEd 2019]**
(a) should be actively discouraged and competition should be promoted
(b) should be used only sometimes, since, it promotes comparison with classmates
(c) should be actively promoted to facilitate peer-acceptance
(d) should not be practised and students should be segregated based on their abilities

17 In diverse inclusive classroom the coeval and cooperative learning is **[UK BEd Entrance Exam 2017]**
(a) discourage effectively and should encourage competition
(b) practice sometime because it encourages the comparibility to peers
(c) effectively encourage in which coeval should be encourage
(d) not implement and should separate students as per their capacity

18 Which of the following is not a feature of child-centered education?
(a) Learning by doing
(b) Learning by living
(c) All of the above
(d) None of the above

19 Which of the following is not a feature of child-centered education?
(a) It makes learning interesting and meaningful
(b) It stresses on timely completion of the syllabus
(c) It provides complete freedom to the child to grow naturally
(d) It considers growth of a child as a priority

20 The emphasis from teaching to learning can be shifted by **[CTET Jan 2012]**
(a) focusing on examination results
(b) adopting child-centered pedagogy
(c) encouraging rote learning
(d) adopting frontal teaching

21 Child-centered education involves **[CTET Sept 2015]**
(a) children sitting in a corner
(b) learning in restricted environment
(c) activities that do not include play
(d) hands on activities for kids

22 Child-centered pedagogy means **[CTET Feb 2016]**
(a) giving moral education to the children
(b) asking the children to follow and imitate the teacher
(c) giving primacy to children's voices and their active participation
(d) letting the children be totally free

23 Which one of the following situations is illustrative of a child-centered classroom? **[CTET Feb 2016]**
(a) A class in which the teacher dictated and the students are asked to memorise the notes
(b) A class in which the textbook is the only resource the teacher refers to
(c) A class in which the students are sitting in groups and the teacher takes turns to go to each group
(d) A class in which the behaviour of students is governed by the rewards and punishments, the teacher would give them

24 Child-centered education refers to
[UK 2017]
(a) encourage the experience and learning of a child
(b) communicate the child what to do by the teacher
(c) encourage the child to adopt the prescribed notice
(d) teacher centric class

25 Which one of the following situations is illustrative of a child-centered classroom?
[CG Pre BEd 2018]
(a) A class in which the teacher dictates and the students are asked to memorise the notes
(b) A class in which the textbook is the only resource the teacher refers to
(c) A class in which the students are sitting in groups and the teacher takes turns to go to each group.
(d) A class in which the behaviour of students is governed by the rewards and punishments the teacher would give them

26 Child-centered pedagogy means
[CG Pre BEd 2018]
(a) giving moral education to the children
(b) asking the children to follow and imitate the teacher
(c) giving primacy to children's voices and their active participation
(d) letting the children to be totally free

27 Child-centered education refers to
[UP BEd Joint Exam 2019]
(a) encourage the experience and learning of a child
(b) communicate the child what to do by the teacher
(c) encourage the child to adopt the prescribed notice
(d) teacher centric class

28 A teacher can encourage children to become effective problem solver by
[CTET July 2019]
(a) encouraging children to make guesses and to look at multiple solutions to the problem
(b) writing step-by-step solution to all the questions in the textbook
(c) giving them plenty of opportunities to answer similar kinds of questions from the textbook
(d) emphasising on rote memorisation of the information given in the textbook

29 Children should.........questions in the class.
[CTET 2019]
(a) be stopped from asking
(b) be encouraged to ask
(c) be discouraged to ask
(d) not be allowed to ask

30 A teacher, because of his/her democratic nature, allows students to sit all over the class. Some sit together and discuss or do group reading. Some sit quietly and read by themselves. A parent does not like it. Which of the following may be the best way to handle the situation?
(a) Parents should complain against the teacher to the parents
(b) Parents should request the principal to change the section of the ward
(c) Parents should show trust in the teacher and discuss the problem with the teacher
(d) Parents should take away the child from that

31 Who created the concept of the kindergarten?
(a) Montessori
(b) Dewey
(c) Rosseau
(d) Frobel

32 A school founded on the progressive ideology will expect all students to
(a) actively construct knowledge by participation and collaboration
(b) follow the teachers' instructions faithfully
(c) get good marks in all exams
(d) learnt what the teachers teach without questioning

33 Sarla, a Hindi teacher, never answers directly a question raised by a student in class. Instead, she gives other students time to think of the answer, discuss in group, etc., before leading them to the correct answer. She is following which of the following approaches to teaching?
(a) Behaviourist
(b) Traditional
(c) Progressive
(d) None of these

34 A 'progressive' teacher should always motivate her students to
(a) ask all the queries they have
(b) accquire knowledge of the content given
(c) interact actively in any discussion in the classroom
(d) participate occasionally

35 Which one of the following is not a basic feature of progressive education?
(a) It considers each child as the same
(b) Integrated curriculum approach is used
(c) Less emphasis is laid on textbooks
(d) curriculum is designed as per the interests of children

36 Montessori education is basically for
(a) women's education
(b) teenage children
(c) older students
(d) young children

37 The best learning is that in which
(a) it is given by a knowledgeable teacher
(b) the pupils learns themselves
(c) it is given by using educational technology
(d) None of the above

38 Which of the following is a feature of progressive education?   [CTET Jan 2012]
(a) Flexible timetable and seating arrangement
(b) Instruction based solely on prescribed textbooks
(c) Emphasis on scoring good marks in examinations
(d) Frequent tests and examinations

39 In the Progressive Model of Education as implemented by CBSE, socialisation of children is done in such a way, so as to expect them to   [CTET Feb 2014]
(a) give up time-consuming social habits and learn how to score good grades
(b) be an active participant in the group work and learn social skills
(c) prepare themselves to conform to the rules and regulations of society wihout questioning
(d) accept what they are offered by the school irrespective of their social background

40 In context of progressive education, which of the following statements is true, according to Dewey?   [CTET Feb 2014]
(a) There should not be a place for democracy in a classroom
(b) Students should be able to solve social problems themselves
(c) Curiosity does not belong to the inherent nature of students rather it is to be cultivated
(d) Students should be observed and not heard in the classroom

41 Teachers, in order to help learners construct knowledge, need to focus on   [CTET Feb 2015]
(a) making sure the learner memorises everything
(b) scores/marks obtained by the learner
(c) involving the learner for active participation
(d) mastering learning of concepts by the learner

42 Children have the potential to create knowledge and make meaning. From this perspective the role of a teacher is that of a   [CTET Sept 2015]
(a) communicator and lecturer
(b) facilitator
(c) director
(d) negotiator

43 In a progressive classroom set-up, the teacher facilitates learning by providing an environment that   [CTET Sept 2016]
(a) is restrictive
(b) discourages inclusion
(c) encouages repetition
(d) promotes discovery

44 Which one of the following options best describes progressive education?   [CTET Dec 2018]
(a) Project method, ability grouping, ranking
(b) Learning by doing, project method, cooperative learning
(c) Thematic units, regular unit test, ranking
(d) Personalised learning, ability grouping, labelling students

45 Which one of the following statements about progressive education explains 'Education is life itself'? [CTET 9 Dec 2018]
 (a) Life is the true educator
 (b) School education should continue as long as possible
 (c) Schools are not required, children can learn from their life experiences
 (d) Education in schools should reflect the social and natural world

46 Children are most creative when they participate in an activity
 [UK BEd Entrance Exam 2018]
 (a) to escape their teacher's scolding
 (b) under stress to do well infront of others
 (c) out of interest
 (d) for rewards

47 Progressive education is associated with which of the following statements?
 [IGNOU BEd Entrance Exam 2019]
 (a) Teachers are the originators of information and authority
 (b) Knowledge is generated through direct experience and collaboration
 (c) Learning proceeds in a straight way with factual gathering and skill mastery
 (d) Examination is norm-referenced and external

48 In progressive education children are seen as [CTET July 2019]
 (a) blank slates   (b) miniature adults
 (c) passive imitators   (d) active explorers

49 If a child's educational achievement is deteriorating day by day, which of the following may be the most probable reason for this? [BHU BEd Entrance Exam 2020]
 (a) He/She is earning money
 (b) He/She is in bad company
 (c) Teachers are not teaching properly
 (d) Lack of concentration

50 In a progressive classroom setup, the teacher facilities learning by providing an environment that [CTET Sept 2016]
 (a) is restrictive
 (b) discourages inclusion
 (c) encourages repetition
 (d) promotes discovery

Answers

1	(d)	2	(b)	3	(a)	4	(a)	5	(c)	6	(b)	7	(d)	8	(c)	9	(d)	10	(d)
11	(d)	12	(b)	13	(c)	14	(c)	15	(c)	16	(d)	17	(d)	18	(c)	19	(b)	20	(b)
21	(d)	22	(c)	23	(c)	24	(a)	25	(c)	26	(c)	27	(c)	28	(a)	29	(b)	30	(c)
31	(d)	32	(a)	33	(c)	34	(c)	35	(a)	36	(d)	37	(b)	38	(a)	39	(b)	40	(b)
41	(c)	42	(d)	43	(d)	44	(d)	45	(c)	46	(c)	47	(a)	48	(a)	49	(c)	50	(d)

Aptitude Towards Learner

Teaching is an art of giving knowledge to students in an effective way. As a profession, it can be described as an occupation, which provides highly specialised intellectual services. It is a set of attitude and a technique which refers to the capacity of an individual to be skilled in teaching by receiving formal or informal training.

Since the late 19th and early 20th centuries, aptitude tests have been used to measure abilities, talents, motor skills, reasoning and even artistic abilities. Schools use aptitude tests to measure the abilities of a child.

Learning is the process of assimilation of knowledge resulting from the interaction between the teacher and the child or learner. According to **Skinner**, "Learning is a process of progressive behaviour through experience and training."

Teaching Approach

Teaching approach is a set of principles, beliefs or ideas about the nature of learning which is used for classroom instruction. Before taking the class, the teacher prepares himself with the subject matter and the technique. Teaching technique is a well-defined procedure used to accomplish a specific activity or task. Teachers take different approaches. Some important approaches are as follow

1. **Teacher-Centered Approach** Teacher-centered approaches are more traditional in nature, focusing on the teacher as instructor. They are sometimes referred to as direct instruction, deductive teaching or expository teaching and are typified by the lecture type presentation.

   In these methods of teaching, the teacher controls what is to be taught and how students are presented with the information. Sometimes, the teaching method is purely based on his own wish and procedure. This arbitrary approach is not regarded as proper approach.

2. **Child-Centered Approach** Student-centered teaching approaches place a much stronger emphasis on the learner's role in the learning process. Sometimes, it is also referred to as discovery learning, inductive learning or inquiry-based learning.

   When teacher is using student-centered approaches to teaching, he sets the learning agenda. Sometimes, teachers participate with the students in the whole learning procedure. This is also known as Participative Approach.

3. **Non-Interfering Approach** In this approach, teacher tries to avoid his responsibility. He wants to involve other teacher to do his work. But the other teacher cannot take his own decision. It is considered as negative approach.

4. **Democratic Approach** This approach is considered as the best approach of teaching. In this approach, the teacher uses methods to encourage creative and critical thinking of every student. It aims to empower students to exercise self-determination in terms of their education. Students are allowed to ask questions, give suggestions and their own views.

5. **Static Approach** In this teaching approach, teacher follows a static or fixed method. He does not bother about the students, their aptitudes, etc. In this approach, only the teacher's voice is heard, students are inactive. This is not regarded as proper methodology.

6. **Dynamic Approach** In this approach, teacher makes his method according to the learner. The teacher facilitates the learning process by allowing the learner to be engaged in the learning process with his guidance. In this method, student remains very active.

Learner

A learner is someone who is learning about a particular subject or how to do something. In other words, a learner is a person who is trying to gain knowledge or skill in something by studying, practising, or being taught.

Classification of Learner

1. **Visual Learner** Visual learners learn best when information is presented using patterns, shapes and other visual aids in place of written or spoken words. One way teachers can differentiate their instruction for visual learners is by using graphs and organisers to teach a lesson.

2. **Auditory Learner** To help auditory learners, teachers can post audio recordings of lessons on the class website and can incorporate group activities that require students to explain concepts. Various aspects of sound, for example pitch, volume, tempo, rhythm, resonance, etc. are important for auditory learners.

3.. **Motor Learner** These learners learn through motor activity. Various aspects of action e.g. frequency, duration, intensity, pressure, etc. are important for them.

4. **Kinesthetic Learner** These learners learn best when they use tactile experiences and carry out physical activity to practice by applying new information.

   People who prefer this mode are connected to reality either through concrete personal experiences, for example, practices or simulations.

5. **Logical Learner** These learners are the ones who are always making list, getting organised and trying to find the link between one piece of the puzzle and another. Logical learners are a natural fit for mathematics, science and other logic based subjects in schools.

Types of Learner

1. Child Learner

Babies are born ready to learn and their brains develop through use. They need a stimulating environment with lots of different ways to play and learn. He needs plenty of chances to practice what he is learning.

Child learns best by activity engaging with her/his environment. This includes

- Observing things, watching faces and responding to voices.

- Listening to sounds, making sound and singing.
- Exploring—e.g. putting things in her/his mouth, shaking things and turning things around.
- Asking questions.
- Experimenting with textures, objects and materials like water, sand and dirt.
- Doing things that stimulate all her/his senses e.g. touch, taste, smell, vision and hearing.

Characteristics of Child Learner

The main characteristics of child learner are

1. **Child learners get bored quickly** If the activities are not interesting and engaging enough, young learners get bored easily. This is because they have a limited attention span. Generally, after ten minutes, they can get disinterested in the activities at hand.

2. **Child learners are meaning-oriented** They may understand what is being said without necessarily understanding every individual word. They may not only guess and interpret what is being uttered, but they also respond to it with whatever language resources they have at their disposal.

3. **Child learners like to discover things** They are characterised by curiosity and enthusiasm. They like to make sense of the world around them through engaging and motivating activities where they have to discover by themselves rather than being told.

4. **Child learners prefer concrete activities** According to Piaget's Cognitive Development theory, young learners are still developing. They are making their own way from concrete to abstract thinking. Unlike adults who are more analytical, they are not yet well equipped to learn abstract concepts such as grammar rules.

5. **Child learners are more ego-centric** They prefer to talk about themselves. Children under the age of 12 need individual attention and approval from the teacher.

6. **Child learners are imaginative** Young learners are imaginative. Activities that are full of imagination is a source of enjoyment for them. It is sometimes difficult for them to distinguish reality from imagination.

7. **Child learners imitate** They learn by imitating adults. It is amazing how humans imitate and discover things from a very young age. Children acquire communication skills through social interactions. As imitation functions as a learning tool in children, it is rewarding to use it to teach children new skills and knowledge.

Role of Teacher Towards Child Learner

The teacher should follow some rules to teach the children. These are as follow

- The content should be interesting and motivating.
- Praising the children's performance is of paramount importance.
- Since children try to imitate teacher, the latter should be a good model of language use and social behaviours. The teacher's pronunciation, for instance, matters enormously, children imitate it perfectly well.
- The classroom should be ideally colourful and spacious enough to be able to move around without any problem. Teacher should supervise these.
- The teacher must be careful that the activities of children should take place in stress and anxiety-free atmosphere when they work in groups.

2. Adolescent Learner

Adolescence is a period of transition between childhood and adulthood that involves number of changes in body and mind.

Adolescence is a phase of life between 12 and 18 years of age.

Now, we will discuss the characteristics of adolescent learners from the point of view of academic, social, emotional and cognitive.

Characteristics of Adolescent Learner

(i) Academic or Intellectual Development

- Moving from concrete to abstract thinking.
- Prefers active over passive learning experiences.
- High achievement when challenged and engaged.
- An ability to be self-reflective.
- Demand relevance in learning and what is being taught.
- An intense curiosity and a wide range of intellectual pursuit, few of which are sustained over the long term.

(ii) Social Development

- As interpersonal skills are being developed, fluctuates between demand for independence and a desire for guidance and direction.
- Seeking approval of peers and others with attention-getting behaviours.
- Experimenting with ways of talking and acting as part of searching for a social position with peers.

(iii) Emotional and Psychological Development

A desire to become independent and to search for adult identity and acceptance.

- Mood swings marked by peaks of intensity and by unpredictability.
- Self-consciousness and being sensitive to personal criticism.
- Concern about physical growth and development.

(iv) Moral Development

- An understanding of the complexity of moral issues like question values, cultural expressions, etc.
- Being influenced by adult role models.

- Show compassion and are vocal for those who are downtrodden sections.
- Impatient nature regarding the pace of change.

Role of Teachers Towards Adolescent Students

Teacher can take some important steps for the teaching of adolescent students. These include

- Adopting brain-storming sessions.
- Developing hope of success by telling stories of great men.
- Framing different committees in the school.
- Creating debate, writing, cultural clubs for adolescent students.
- Introducing remedial and coaching classes for needy students.
- Arranging excursions and field trips.
- Making continuous comprehensive evaluation.
- Mention reasonable teacher-people ratio.

3. Adult Learner

Adult Learner (mature student) is a person who is older and is involved in forms of learning. Adults learner falls in a specific criteria of being experienced and does not always have a high school diploma. Many of the adults learners go back to school to finish a degree, or earn a new one.

Characteristics of Adult Learner

(i) Academic Development

- The adult learners are more autonomous and self-directed. They are goal oriented and practical.
- Relevancy-oriented and see reasons for learning something. They are not dependent on the others for direction.
- They appreciate in educational programmes that are organised and have clearly defined elements.
- They evaluate learning in terms of result and its utility to their life situations.

(ii) **Social Development**
  - Adult person is well aware about the social environment in which he lives.
  - He is bound by social customs, traditions, rituals, etc. He gives his own criticism and views on social customs.
  - He carries out his social responsibilities efficiently and effectively and also capable of carrying out his teaching work.

(iii) **Emotional Development**
  - Adult learner is able to make emotionally correct decision. He understands ideas and facts through proper reasoning rather than taking decisions emotionally.
  - The learning process helps them in the development of their emotional instincts.

(iv) **Cognitive Development**
  - It focuses learning in the mental and psychological process of mind and not on behaviour.
  - They are concerned with perception and the process of information. He is capable of taking right decision with regard to resolving factual, psychological and argumentative factors.
  - The adult learners are efficient enough to analyse moral, social and religious values of teaching.

Differences between Adolescent and Adult Learners

On the basis of learning, the differences between Adolescent and Adult Learners are discussed below

Elements	Adolescents	Adults
Learner	They are in search for personal identity.	Adults are more disciplined than adolescents.
Role of Learner's Expectation	They are in need of activities that meet their needs and learning expectations.	They have a clear understanding of their learning objectives.
Orientation to Learning	They become disruptive when they lose interest in the lesson or feel bored.	They need to be involved in choosing what and how to learn.
Motivation for Learning	They need help and support from the teacher and to be provided with constructive feedback.	They prefer to rely on themselves and work on their own pace.
Demand for Learning	They can draw upon a variety of resources in the learning environment, including personal experience, the local community, and the Internet.	They come to the classroom with a wide range of knowledge, expectations, and experiences.
Environment	They need the teacher to build bridges between the syllabus and their world of interests and experiences.	They are able to do a wide range of activities.
Activities of Learning	They can learn abstract issues and do challenging activities.	Adults learn at various rates and in different ways according to their intellectual ability, educational level, personality, and cognitive learning styles.
Evaluation	Their personal initiative and energy are moved into action through meaningful involvement with relevant and current content.	They come into the classroom with diverse experiences, opinions, thoughts, and beliefs which need to be respected.

Exercise

1 .... approaches are direct instruction, deductive teaching and lecture type presentation.
(a) Teacher-centered
(b) Child-centered
(c) Non-interfering
(d) None of the above

2 Which of the following strategies of teaching-learning is obstacle in developing creativity?   **[CG Pre BEd 2019]**
(a) Help students to think in flexible ways
(b) Encourage students to take risk
(c) Over control students during teaching-learning
(d) Guide students to be persistent and delay gratification

3 The classroom activities must suit the specific abilities of the students in the class, the responsibilities for this lies with the   **[IGNOU BEd Entrance Exam 2019]**
(a) class teacher to translate curriculum as she/he expects/judges appropriate for students
(b) curriculum development to make it flexible for each and every learner
(c) systemic factors must take note of the needs to the diverse learners
(d) textbook developers must keep in mind the difficulty level of the learners

4 Child-centered teaching approach is also known as .... approach.
(a) Non-interfering
(b) Democratic
(c) Traditional
(d) Participative

5 Which teaching approach is regarded as the best approach?
(a) Teacher-centered
(b) Child-centered
(c) Democratic
(d) Traditional

6 Why does the child get bored easily?
(a) If the activities are not interesting
(b) If the activities are engaging enough
(c) They have a limited attention span
(d) All of the above

7 The children under the age of 12 need .... from the teacher.
(a) individual attention (b) approval
(c) moral values   (d) Both (a) and (b)

8 Children try to imitate teacher, thus the teacher should be
(a) good model of language use and social behaviours
(b) pronounce correctly
(c) soft spoken
(d) Both (a) and (b)

9 Which of the following skills are needed for present day teacher to adjust effectively with the classroom teaching?
I. Knowledge of technology
II. Use of technology in teaching-learning
III. Knowledge of students' needs
IV. Content mastery
Codes
(a) I and III   (b) II and III
(c) II, III and IV   (d) II and IV

10 To cater the individual differences in his classroom, a teacher should
[CTET Sep 2016]
(a) segregate and label children based on their marks
(b) engage in a dialogue with students and value their perspectives
(c) impose strict rules upon his students
(d) have uniform and standard ways of teaching and assessment

11 "Having a diverse classroom with children from varied social, economic and cultural backgrounds enriches the learning experiences of all students."
This statement is   **[CTET Sep 2016]**
(a) correct, because children learn many skills from their peers
(b) correct, because it makes the classroom more hierarchical
(c) incorrect, because it leads to unnecessary competition
(d) incorrect, because it can confuse the children and they may feel lost

12 Which of the following statements about children are correct? [KVS TGT 2017]
   I. Children are passive recipients of knowledge.
   II. Children are problem solvers.
   III. Children are scientific investigators.
   IV. Children are active explorers of the environment.
   Codes
   (a) II, III and IV
   (b) I, II, III and IV
   (c) I, II and III
   (d) I, II and IV

13 Which of the following is the most important for teachers?
   [MP Pre BEd Entrance Exam 2017]
   (a) Maintaining good discipline
   (b) To solve the difficulties of students
   (c) Punctuality
   (d) Have a good time

14 The purpose of education should be
   [BHU BEd Entrance Exam 2017]
   (a) developing business skills in students
   (b) developing social awareness in students
   (c) preparing students for examination
   (d) preparing students for practical life

15 Moral values can be effectively inculcated among the students when the teacher
   (a) frequently talks about values
   (b) himself practices them
   (c) tells stories of great persons
   (d) talks of Gods and Goddesses

16 When a normal student behaves in an erratic manner in the class, you would
   (a) pull up the student then and there
   (b) talk to the student after the class
   (c) ask the student to leave the class
   (d) ignore the student

17 For an efficient and durable learning, learner should have
   (a) ability to learn only
   (b) requisite level of motivation only
   (c) opportunities to learn only
   (d) desired level of ability and motivation

18 Which of the following is/are the cause(s) of individual differences among learners?
   (a) Differences in Attitude
   (b) Differences in Intelligence
   (c) Differences in Age
   (d) Differences in Achievement

19 The students learn best by
   (a) listening
   (b) reading
   (c) doing
   (d) seeing

20 Some students in a class exhibit great curiosity for learning. It may be because such children
   (a) are gifted
   (b) come from rich families
   (c) show artificial behaviour
   (d) create indiscipline in the class

21 The learners always appreciate
   (a) a well-researched and informative lecture
   (b) a well-organised and presentable lecture
   (c) a concise and stimulating lecture
   (d) All of the above

22 Learners can learn more effectively by
   (a) listening
   (b) taking detailed written notes
   (c) actively participating
   (d) All of the above

23 Learners should not be encouraged to
   (a) ask as many questions as possible both inside and outside the class
   (b) actively interact with other learners in group work
   (c) participate in as many co-curricular activities as possible
   (d) memorise all the answers to questions which the teacher may ask

24 Students can be classified into four types on the basis of their learning. Which one of the following seeks meaning and reasoning to the learning?
   (a) Innovative learner
   (b) Analytic learner
   (c) Common sense learner
   (d) Dynamic learner

25 The period of adolescence is known as the period of stresses and strains. What type of behaviour is unwanted from the learners at that period?
   (a) Silence and hush-hush policy
   (b) Attitude of independence
   (c) Sympathetic understanding
   (d) Individual thought process

26 The ability to learn by an individual is
(a) acquired by the individual
(b) developed by the teacher
(c) absorbed from environment
(d) occurred from within

27 Which among the following is type of individual differences?
(a) Difference in attitudes
(b) Difference in achievement
(c) Physical difference
(d) All of the above

28 Difference in children's interests, tendencies and character are which differences?
(a) Personality differences
(b) Emotional differences
(c) Racial differences
(d) Economic differences

29 Which of the following factors would help students improve their academic performance? **[KVS TGT 2017]**
    I. Frequent evaluation of performance
    II. Positive teacher-student relationships
    III. Close teacher-parent interactions
    IV. Instruction at a higher level
    Codes
    (a) I and III   (b) II and IV
    (c) I and IV   (d) II and III

30 Every learner is unique means that
[IGNOU BEd Entrance Exam 2017]
(a) no two learners are alike in their abilities, interests and talents
(b) learners do not have any common qualities, nor do they share common goals
(c) a common curriculum for all learners is not possible
(d) it is impossible to develop the potentials of learners in a heterogeneous class

31 Primary school children will learn most effectively in an atmosphere
[IGNOU BEd Entrance Exam 2017]
(a) where the teacher is authoritative and clearly dictates what should be done
(b) where the focus and stress are only on mastering primarily cognitive skills of reading, writing and mathematics
(c) where the teacher leads all the learning and expects students to play a passive role
(d) where their emotional needs are met and they feel that they are valued

32 Doing activities with children will be effective only if
[Bihar BEd Entrance Exam 2018]
(a) the teacher conducts them to complete her 'Lesson Plan'
(b) the teacher does them as a pretense to obey her principal's directions for activity-based learning
(c) she believes that activity-based education will help the child in understanding the concepts
(d) the teacher does not know why she is doing it

33 In the constructivist framework, learning is primarily **[CTET Dec 2019]**
(a) based on rote-memorisation
(b) centered around reinforcement
(c) acquired through conditioning
(d) focused on the process of meaning making

34 The best place for a child's cognitive development is **[UK BEd Entrance Exam 2019]**
(a) playground
(b) auditorium
(c) home
(d) school and class environment

35 A teacher can identify a stressed child when the child shows the following behaviour. **[UP BEd JEE 2020]**
(a) Aggressive behaviour
(b) Full concentration in studies
(c) Excessive talking
(d) Hyperactivity

36 "These learners learn best when they use textile experiences and carry out physical activity to practice by applying new information." They are which type of learners?
(a) Auditory learners
(b) Kinesthetic learners
(c) Visual learners
(d) Motor learners

37 The academic characteristics of the adolescents are
  (a) they show a wide range of intellectual development
  (b) they tend to be curious
  (c) they favour active or passive learning
  (d) All of the above

38 Which quality do you consider the most important among students?
            [IGNOU BEd Entrance Exam 2017]
  (a) Expressing views independently
  (b) Modesty
  (c) Obedience
  (d) Hard working

39 Which one of the following questions invites children to think critically?
            [CTET Dec 2018]
  (a) What are the different ways in which we can solve this?
  (b) Do you know the answer to this?
  (c) What is the right answer?
  (d) Can you think of a similar situation?

40 Which quality is most important for students?   [BHU BEd Entrance Exam 2019]
  (a) Good behaviour
  (b) Independent thinking
  (c) Obedience
  (d) Hard work

41 When teachers have positive beliefs about students and their abilities, the students   [CTET July 2019]
  (a) are not affected in any way
  (b) are eager and motivated to learn
  (c) become relaxed and stop putting any efforts to learn
  (d) become demotivated and stressed

Answers

1. (a)	2. (c)	3. (a)	4. (d)	5. (c)	6. (a)	7. (d)	8. (d)	9. (c)	10. (b)
11. (a)	12. (a)	13. (b)	14. (d)	15. (b)	16. (b)	17. (d)	18. (c)	19. (c)	20. (a)
21. (c)	22. (c)	23. (d)	24. (b)	25. (a)	26. (d)	27. (d)	28. (a)	29. (a)	30. (a)
31. (d)	32. (c)	33. (d)	34. (d)	35. (a)	36. (b)	37. (d)	38. (a)	39. (a)	40. (b)
41. (b)									

Curriculum

A curriculum is basically a set of guidelines for different academic contents and chapters that are covered in a specific program offered by a particular school or college.

However, it covers the attitude, manner, knowledge, behaviour, performance, manner and the different skills that students will develop throughout the academic period.

Generally, a curriculum is well-planned and carefully designed by educational institutions or the government. Focusing on the overall learning experience provided by a course, it emphasises essentially on the mental and physical development of the students.

It does not mean only academic subjects, traditionally taught in schools but it includes the sum total of experiences that pupil receives through the manifold activities that go on in the school, classroom, library, laboratory, workshop, playgrounds and in the numerous informal contacts between teachers and pupil. In this sense, curriculum touches the life of the students at all points and helps in the evolution of a balanced personality.

Thus, a curriculum is a systematic arrangement of the sum total of selected learning experiences planned by a school for a defined group of students to attain the aim of particular educational programme. It is commonly formed as a Programme of Studies.

Definitions of Curriculum

While an education is a process, curriculum is a means of the process. While an education is learning, curriculum signifies situation for learning.

According to **Tanner** and **Tanner**, "Curriculum is the reconstruction of knowledge and experience systematically developed under the auspices of the school (or university), to enable the learner to increase his or her control of knowledge and experience."

According to **Coles**, "Curriculum is the sum of all the activities, experiences and learning opportunities for which an institution takes responsibility either deliberately or by default."

Objectives of Curriculum

Objectives for a good and ideal curriculum are as follows

- The curriculum should be such that the all-round development of the students should be possible.
- The aim of the curriculum is to develop the interests, attitudes, abilities and capabilities of the students.

- To develop social qualities in the students.
- To develop the sense of duty in the students.
- To develop the spirit of democracy in the students, so that they can become an ideal citizen in the future.
- To develop the imagination, thinking, decision-making and reasoning skills of the students.

Characteristics of Curriculum

- It must be continuously evolving from one period to another, to the present. For a curriculum to be an effective, it must have continuous monitoring and an evaluation. It must adapt its educational activities and services to meet the needs of modern and dynamic community.
- It is based on the needs of the people. It should be in proper sequence in order to meet the challenges of time and to make an education more responsive.
- It comprises of complex details as it includes guidance and counselling, health services, projects and also provides the proper instructional equipments that are often most conductive to learning.
- It complements and cooperates with other programs of the community. So, curriculum is responsive to the needs of the community.
- Each curriculum objective should constitute learning i.e.
  - (i) **Durable**—Will be useful to the student for a considerable period of his/her lifetime.
  - (ii) **Significant**—Will have a major effect upon how the student will function.
  - (iii) **Transferable**—Will be useful in meeting needs in other educational programmes or the student's personal life.

Each outcome assessment and evaluation should be accompanied by both the criteria by which the learning will be judged and the standards of quality which will apply.

Principles of Curriculum

The success of curriculum depends on certain principles which needs to be developed in mind, while framing a curriculum. These are as follows

1. **Principle of Child-Centredness** It means that what is to be given to children in the form of learning experiences at a particular age and grade should properly suit their age, abilities, capacities, interests, mental development and previous experiences. Therefore, in all circumstances it should fulfil the needs and requirements of the developing children.

2. **Principle of Comprehensiveness** Curriculum must have necessary details because merely a list of topics will not serve the purpose either of the teacher or the student. Material aids, techniques, life situations, related activities, possibilities of correlation, etc., should be listed in the curriculum, so, that these can serve as a guide to the teachers and authors of textbooks.

3. **Principle of Correlation** The curriculum should be such that all subjects are related to each other. Teaching all subjects separately would be unpsychological, so it must be kept in mind that the subject matter of various subjects has some affinity with each other so that they can help the child eventually.

4. **Principle of Utility** According to this principle, only those topics, subject materials and learning experiences should be included in the curriculum, which are found to possess any utility to the students.

5. **Principle of Forward Looking** The Principle of Forward Looking asks for an inclusion of those topics, contents and learning experiences that may prove helpful to the students in leading their future life in a proper way. Therefore, attempts should

always be made to include the topics and learning experiences.

6. **Principle of Environmental Centredness** The curriculum is developed keeping in view the physical and social environment of the students.

   Therefore, the selection of subject material and learning experiences should be based on or link with an events, the problems and situations prevalent in their physical and social environment.

Curriculum Development

Curriculum development refers to the actual implementation of the results of the decisions reached during curriculum planning. This means that when decisions have been made in respect to the nature, organisation and orientation of the curriculum, it becomes the place of curriculum development to build a curriculum based on the decisions.

According to **Nicholls** and **Nicholls**, "The planning of learning opportunities intended to bring about certain changes in pupils and the assessment of the extent to which these changes have taken place in what is meant by curriculum development".

So, curriculum development and planning has been visualised as a continuous and dynamic process.

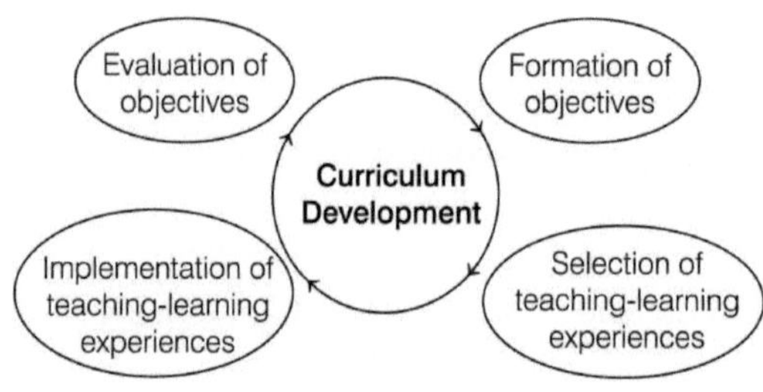

Strategies of Curriculum Development

There are few strategies that play a significant role in the curriculum development and these are discussed below

1. **Problem Identification** Firstly, while developing a curriculum, the problem areas are needed to be identified to meet the needs of the curriculum as it will help to improvise the content formation. It is an important strategy in curriculum development as it highlights the issues of relevance that needs modification for an effective curriculum.

2. **Needs Assessment of Learners** Curriculum development should be viewed as a process by which meeting student's needs lead to improvement of student's learning. It should include the desired outcomes or expectations of a high quality program, the role of an assessment, the current status of student's achievements and actual program content.

   An effective curriculum development process usually entails a structured needs assessment to gather information and to guide the curriculum development process.

3. **Goals and Objectives** Curriculum goals are general and broad statements that lead towards long-term outcomes. Specifically, goals are always for reaching the objectives and care usually based on the ideas that they lead students towards being better able to be productive members of the society.

4. **Educational Strategies & Implementation** An educational strategies must be clear as per the requirement of the curriculum. An innovative and productive approach will help the students to gather relevant information from the sources provided by their teacher.

Proper implementation of an educational strategies will fetch maximum output in the process of curriculum development.

5. **Feedback and Evaluation** The curriculum development cycle end then begins again with a careful evaluation of the effectiveness and impact of the program.

   The detailed review and analysis of quantitative and qualitative information of the programmes, impact and on people's perceptions of its strengths and weaknesses forms the foundation for the next round of curriculum development and improvement. Feedback helps the teacher to improve and modify the framework of curriculum as it provides an interpretation of performance.

Stages of Curriculum Development

There are four stages in the process of curriculum development that are discussed below

1. **Planning** The curriculum planning considers the vision, mission and goals. It also includes the philosophy of strong education belief of the school. All of these will eventually, be translated to classrooms desired learning outcomes for the learners.

   The planning stage lays the foundation for all of the curriculum development steps that are identifying the needs according to the curriculum and need to conduct assessment and analysis.

2. **Curriculum Designing** It is the way in which curriculum is conceptualised to include the selection and organisation of the content, the selection and organisation of learning experiences as well as the selection of an assessment procedure to measure achieved learning outcomes. A curriculum design will also include the resources to be utilised and the statement of the intended learning outcomes.

3. **Curriculum Implementing** It means putting into action the plan which is based on the curriculum design in the learning environment.

   The teacher is the facilitator of learning and together with the learners uses the curriculum as to design to what will transpire in the classroom with the end in view of achieving the intended learning outcomes. Implementing the curriculum is where action takes place.

4. **Evaluation** It determines the extent to which the desired outcomes have been achieved. This procedure is ongoing in finding out the progress of learning. Along the way, an evaluation will determine the factors that have supported the implementation.

   It will help in making improvements and taking corrective measures. The result of an evaluation is very important for curriculum planners and implementors.

Syllabus

A syllabus is a document containing the information about the different topics on the portion that needs to be covered for a particular subject or a course.

While forming a syllabus, the experts ensure that the fundamentals of a particular subject or course are added in a unique combination of theoretical and practical learning methods. A syllabus is provided to students and teachers at the beginning of an academic session.

A syllabus is considered as a guide to the incharge as well as to the students. It helps the students to know about the subject in detail, why it is a part of their course of study, what are the expectations from students, consequences of failure, etc. It contains general rules, policies, instructions, topics covered, assignments, projects, test dates and so on.

Difference between Syllabus and Curriculum

Syllabus and curriculum both are important terms used in reference to an educational programme but they have different meanings.

Curriculum	Syllabus
A curriculum is a combination of topics, subjects or activities that are to be included in an educational programme.	Whereas, the syllabus covers portions of topics in a particular subject.
Curriculum defines the intricate structure of how the syllabus, teaching periods and prescribed study materials would be.	Syllabus includes all the chapters and topics in detail along with the reference books, study guides and academic instructions.
The curriculum is provided for a whole year.	The syllabus is for a certain academic session like a semester and text books differ as per the syllabus for each session as well as the curriculum for each year.

Co-Curricular Activities

Curriculum, which works as a complementary to the main syllabus, is called co-curricular activity.

Co-curricular activities are very important parts of the curriculum, which play an effective role in the development of the personality of the students as well as in strengthening the classroom education.

From the point of view of all-round development of boys/girls, co-curricular activities are very important, meaningful and necessary.

According to the accepted principles of modern psychology, co-curricular activities are very important for the development of all-round development of children. It becomes necessary to organise in educational institutions. Therefore, the importance of co-curricular activities increases in the education sector.

On the basis of fields, co-curricular activities are mainly divided into two parts

1. **Outdoor co-curricular activities** These types of activities are usually, organised outside the school. Under this, the following activities are included-mass parade, yoga, gardening, plantation, exercise, group assembly, social service, conducting surveys, organising games and tours, excursions, etc.
2. **Indoor co-curricular activities** Indoor co-curricular activities are mainly conducted in the school auditorium; such as drama, music and dance, painting and dyeing, decoration, clay modeling, first-aid, sewing, rangoli competition and book-binding, arts and crafts, quiz competition and organising debate competition, etc.

Types of Co-Curricular Activities

1. **Physical Development Activities** They include activities like various sports, yoga, swimming, judo, driving, athletics, etc.
2. **Educational Development Activities** Under this, various clubs are included. Geography club, history club, science club and quiz, survey, project construction activities come under this.
3. **Literary Activities** It includes activities related to literary development like art of language, debate, seminar, workshop, poetry recitation, book publication, newspaper reading and activities related to libraries.
4. **Cultural Development Activities** Under this, music, dance, drama, folk music/ dance/drama, fancy dress, exhibition, painting and other group activities are included.
5. **National Integration Development Activities** Educational tour, language competition, organisation of National and International Day, etc.

Role of Co-Curricular Activities in the Development of Students

Through co-cirricular activities, the student is able to understand the practical knowledge experience. Practical education or knowledge understands the teaching and training of the classroom. Intellectual knowledge of the students is developed in the classroom. Good character building and spiritual development also take place through co-curricular activities.

Following are the roles of co-curricular activities in the development of students

- The expressive ability of the students is strengthened by participating in group discussion.
- Helps in developing the spirit of healthy and effective competition.
- Co-curricular activities are considered important in keeping children physically and mentally energetic and fit.
- It plays an important role in building skill development. It tells how any work can be done effectively.
- There is concern among youths about their career. Sometimes they get stressed, in such a situation, this conflict can be completely eliminated through co-curricular activities.

National Curriculum Framework, 2005

- The NCF, 2005 was created to review the National Curriculum Framework (NCF), 2000 in the context of the 1993, 'Education without Burden' report.
- The National Curriculum Framework, 2005 has been translated into all the languages listed in the Eighth Schedule of the Constitution.
- The main objective of the National Curriculum Framework, 2005 is to link the school life of the children with the life outside. This principle is in stark contrast to the legacy of bookish knowledge, with the effect of which our education system maintains the gap between school and home.

- The curriculum and textbooks based on the new National Curriculum are an attempt to follow this basic philosophy.
- National Curriculum Framework, 2005 is an innovative document in the field of education. This framework has been prepared by international level academicians, scientists and subject experts.
- NCF, 2005 emphasises on continuous and comprehensive evaluation for evaluation of children. Under this, it has been said that the teacher should develop the qualities of innovative thinking, reasoning ability, creative thinking and scientific investigation qualities in the children.

National Education Policy, 2020

The education policy in India is being changed from time to time.

At present, 34 years old education policy of 1986 was implementing in India, which was becoming ineffective with the changing environment that is why the Ministry of Human Resource Development presented India's New Education Policy, 2020, which was approved by the Cabinet. It can be understood in the following ways

- In the New Education Policy, till the fifth class, the mother tongue, local or regional language will be the medium of instruction, although it has also been said in this policy that no language will be imposed.
- The 10+2 structure of the school curriculum will be replaced by a new curriculum structure of $5+3+3+4$ for children in the age group of 3 to 8, 8 to 11, 11 to 14 and 14 to 18 years, respectively.
- In this, there is a provision to bring children of those 6 years who have been kept away till now under the school curriculum, which has been recognised globally as an important stage for the metal development of the child.

- E-syllabus will be developed in regional languages, under which virtual labs will be developed and a National Educational Technology Forum (NETF) will be established.
- Emphasis will be given on basic ability of reading, writing and addition and subtraction (numerical knowledge).
- NCERT will develop a National Curricular and Pedagogical Framework for Early Childhood Care and Education (NCPFECCE) for children up to the age of 8 years.
- No special distinction will be made between academic streams, curricular activities and vocational education in schools.
- Special provision has been made on the education of Socially and Economically Disadvantaged Groups (SEDGs).
- Music and art will be promoted by including these in the curriculum.

Role of NCTE in Curriculum Development

- Since 1973, the National Council for Teacher Education was an advisory body for the central and state governments, on all matters pertaining to teacher education, with its secretariat in the Department of Teacher Education of the National Council of Educational Research and Training (NCERT).
- It lays down norms for any specified category of courses or training in teacher education including course content and mode of curriculum.
- It makes recommendations to the central and state governments, universities, UGC and its recognised institutes in matters of preparing plans and programmes for teacher education.
- From time to time, NCTE brings about necessary changes in curriculum. It prepared National Curriculum Framework for Teacher Education (2009).

- This curriculum has given a systematic and comprehending framework for teacher education and also highlights the strategies to implement it.
- In this curriculum framework almost every aspect of teacher education got preference.
- The NCFTE (2009) paved the way for implementing of curricular areas by giving practical and reasonable strategies.
- Its main role is to achieve planned and coordinated development of teacher education system throughout the country which is important part of curriculum development process.
- It aims at training individuals for equipping them to teach pre-primary, primary, secondary and senior secondary stages in schools, non-formal and part-time education.
- It also promotes and conduct innovation research in various areas of teacher education.

It has revised the regulations in 2014 that includes

(i) Establishment of teacher education in composite institutions that consists of multi-disciplinary education programmes.

(ii) Each programme curriculum gives importance to yoga education, ICT, inclusive education, etc.

(iii) Open and distance learning has developed and improved the performance due to inbuilt quality assurance mechanisms.

Curriculum is an instructional and educative programme, by following which the pupils achieve their goals, ideals and aspirations of life. The curriculum should integrate cognitive, affective and psychomotor objectives and abilities.

Curriculum development have to satisfy the different foundations of curriculum and thereby, they could be adopted in multi-cultural classroom settings. Hence, great effort should be taken to frame such a curriculum before executing the process of teaching at all levels of education.

1 A _____ is a document containing the information about the different topics or the portion that needs to be covered for a particular subject or a course.
  (a) curriculum   (b) project
  (c) syllabus   (d) textbook

2 Why is syllabus necessary in school?
[MP Pre BEd 2016]
  (a) It helps in the proper functioning of the school
  (b) It makes the classroom education under control
  (c) A teacher can rule every work outside the class in a proper manner
  (d) All of the above are possible

3 Syllabus is a part of
  (a) curriculum   (b) classroom
  (c) activities   (d) society

4 Curriculum in education is a
  (a) plan for learning
  (b) plan for growth and development
  (c) control of knowledge
  (d) None of the above

5 An important factor of curriculum is to help to achieve the
  (a) education   (b) objectives
  (c) values   (d) job

6 Which of the following is the nature of curriculum?
  (a) Critical
  (b) Creative
  (c) Conservative
  (d) All of the above

7 Curriculum provides guidance for
  (a) schools   (b) teachers
  (c) students   (d) parents

8 Curriculum presents an instructional material, is stated by
  (a) Elizhalh Maccis
  (b) Jack Kerr
  (c) W Teller
  (d) Smith

9 Who said that "Curriculum is the sum of all the activities, experiences and learning opportunities for which an institution takes responsibility either deliberately or by default"?
  (a) John Dewey   (b) Coles
  (c) Tanner   (d) Smith

10 Curriculum comprises of two major dimensions i.e.
  (a) vision and control
  (b) structure and activities
  (c) vision and structure
  (d) All of the above

11 Curriculum in a fixed programme of courses is a _____ of curriculum.
  (a) old concept
  (b) contemporary concept
  (c) logical concept
  (d) All of the above

12 Modern concept of curriculum is helping in the evolution of
  (a) average personality
  (b) balanced personality
  (c) extrovert personality
  (d) reserved personality

13 Psychological foundation plays its role in development of curriculum in view of the
  (a) student's needs
  (b) student's interests
  (c) student's capabilities
  (d) All of the above

14 Major concern of curriculum is
  (a) change in an individual's behaviour
  (b) preparation for service
  (c) personal satisfaction
  (d) None of the above

15 The importance of curriculum in the system of education is just like a
  (a) preparation of students for service
  (b) Constitution in a country
  (c) provision of latest knowledge
  (d) None of the above

16 The curriculum is supposed to
  (a) be organised
  (b) achieve an objective
  (c) Both (a) and (b)
  (d) None of the above

17 Curriculum reflects the culture of
  (a) college   (b) home
  (c) area   (d) society

18 The core curriculum does not emphasise
  (a) democratic procedures
  (b) problem-solving
  (c) total experiences in the school
  (d) unit and lesson plans prepared by the teacher

19 Concept of curriculum flexibility was introduced to benefit
  [BHU BEd Entrance Exam 2018]
  (a) Disabled children
  (b) Madarsas and Maktabs
  (c) Scheduled castes and scheduled tribes
  (d) All of the above

20 An effective curriculum is based on the principle of
  (a) continuous monitoring
  (b) continuous evaluation
  (c) Both (a) and (b)
  (d) None of the above

21 A curriculum is the blueprint of an institution of that includes experiences for the
  (a) expert   (b) teacher
  (c) learner   (d) curriculum planner

22 The Principle of Forward Looking is necessary because
  (a) it will be helpful for the students
  (b) it will be helpful for teachers
  (c) it will solve the problems
  (d) All of the above

23 The curriculum development refers to the total process of curriculum
  (a) implementation   (b) evaluation
  (c) designing   (d) All of these

24 Balanced curriculum is also known as
  (a) integrated curriculum
  (b) experienced curriculum
  (c) activity centered curriculum
  (d) core curriculum

25 An effectiveness of curriculum is determined by
  (a) evaluation   (b) objective
  (c) method   (d) design

26 When, what, why and how, to teach is the main task of
  (a) Educational psychology
  (b) Educational philosophy
  (c) Economics
  (d) History

27 The forces that effect the development of curriculum are called
  (a) curriculum design
  (b) curriculum evaluation
  (c) elements of curriculum
  (d) foundation of curriculum

28 Philosophical foundation of the curriculum is concerned with
  (a) ideas   (b) history
  (c) economy   (d) contour

29 Student's needs and interests are important in
  (a) sociological foundation
  (b) psychological foundation
  (c) economical foundation
  (d) historical foundation

30 Psychological foundation of curriculum helps curriculum developers to understand the nature of
  (a) content   (b) learner
  (c) teacher   (d) ideas

31 The sources of information for Psychological foundation are
  (a) learning process
  (b) teaching method
  (c) student's characteristics
  (d) All of the above

32 The curriculum based on thinking of John Dewey is
  (a) learner centered curriculum
  (b) activity centered curriculum
  (c) subject centered curriculum
  (d) None of the above

33 The factor(s) effecting curriculum development is/are
  (a) sociological factor (b) economical factor
  (c) scientific factor   (d) All of these

34 Making value judgement about curriculum is
(a) curriculum development
(b) curriculum evaluation
(c) curriculum elements
(d) curriculum design

35 Curriculum effectiveness is determined by
(a) community cooperation
(b) teacher's competence
(c) student's interest
(d) quality of supervision

36 Curriculum improvement should be a .... process.
(a) initial
(b) last
(c) continuous
(d) internal

37 The implementer for curriculum is
(a) curriculum bureau
(b) curriculum wing
(c) textbook board
(d) educational institutions

38 Curriculum decision is affected by
(a) aims of an education
(b) the structure of knowledge
(c) the worth whiteners of knowledge
(d) All of the above

39 The most important factor which resists the curriculum change is
(a) aristocratic class of the society
(b) political leaders
(c) teachers
(d) parents

40 The process in which strengths and weaknesses of the curriculum are identified is called
(a) content selection
(b) content organisation
(c) teaching methodology
(d) evaluation

41 Curriculum construction in Indian education is mostly influenced by
(a) child's psychology
(b) teacher's personality
(c) family structure
(d) constitutional provisions

42 Which is the second stage of curriculum development?
(a) Planning
(b) Evaluation
(c) Curriculum implementing
(d) Curriculum designing

43 .... is the stage of curriculum development which determines the extent to which the desired outcomes are achieved.
(a) Planning
(b) Evaluation
(c) Designing
(d) Implementing

44 It is the strategy that highlights the issues of relevance for an effective curriculum.
(a) Feedback
(b) Goals and objectives
(c) Problem identification
(d) Educational strategies

45 An effective curriculum development process usually entails
(a) need based assessment
(b) feedback
(c) structured objectives
(d) None of the above

46 The strategy which fetch maximum output in the process of curriculum development is
(a) evaluation
(b) problem identification
(c) implementation
(d) None of the above

47 The strategy which helps the teacher to improve and modify the framework of curriculum is
(a) needs assessment
(b) feedback and evaluation
(c) implementation
(d) All of the above

48 It is a tool for improving performance.
(a) Evaluation
(b) Feedback
(c) Objectives
(d) Benchmarking

49 What are the determinates of 'objectives' in the development of curriculum?

   I. Socio-psychological needs of an individuals of the level concerned.

   II. Economical needs of the society.

   III. Thrust areas at the time of curriculum development.

   IV. National aims of secondary education.

Codes
(a) I, II and IV
(b) II, III and II
(c) I and II
(d) I, II and III

50 The stage(s) of curriculum development is/are

   I. planning

   II. designing

   III. implementing and evaluation

   IV. improvement and progress

Codes
(a) I, II and IV
(b) I, III and IV
(c) I, II and III
(d) Only IV

51 Which one of the following combinations gives a correct reason for including philosophy of education in Teacher Education Curriculum?

   I. Philosophy is an oldest discipline.

   II. Philosophy helps in understanding educational concepts in a holistic way.

   III. Philosophy and education are two sides of the same coin.

   IV. Philosophy helps in developing a better personality of prospective teachers.

   V. Philosophical analysis of educational concepts helps in developing a rational view point.

Codes
(a) I, II, III and V
(b) II, III and V
(c) II, III, IV and V
(d) I, II, III and IV

52 In which of the following approaches to curriculum design constructivist orientation will be manifest?
(a) Job analysis of learning tasks
(b) Evaluation approach to curriculum design
(c) Concept map as a tool for curricular choice
(d) Input emphasis on curriculum

53 Curriculum is regarded as the sum total of experiences acquired by the learner in a school. Which combination of the following set of experiences will be deemed congruent in this regard? **[2017]**

   I. Planned and known experiences.

   II. Unplanned and known experiences.

   III. Experience gained during co-curricular activities.

   IV. Lived experiences which promote creative outlook.

Codes
(a) I, II, III and IV
(b) I, II and III
(c) I, III and IV
(d) I and III

54 Which of the following do lay foundation for curriculum?
(a) Societal priorities, government and resources
(b) Philosophy, Sociology and Psychology
(c) Study material, training facilities and societal needs
(d) Psychological base of education

55 A curriculum maker is interested in designing the functional curriculum would need understanding of
(a) Educational philosophy
(b) Psychological principles
(c) Pedagogical procedures
(d) All of the above

56 Which one of the following is incorrect about curriculum? **[KVS TGT 2017]**
(a) Curriculum is prescriptive in nature
(b) Curriculum refers to the overall content which is to be taught in an educational institution
(c) Curriculum varies from teacher to teacher
(d) Curriculum has a wider scope

Direction (Q. No. 57 to 61) Given below are two statements, one labelled as Assertion (A) and other labelled as Reason (R). In the context of the given statements, select the correct answer from the codes given below.

Codes
(a) Both A and R are true
(b) Both A and R are false
(c) A is true, but R is false
(d) A is false, but R is true

57 Assertion (A) Traditional curriculum includes only the academic aspects.

Reason (R) Traditional curriculum touches the life of the students at all points.

58 Assertion (A) Curriculum is intimately related with an education in every aspect.

Reason (R) Education is a process and curriculum is a means to the process.

59 Assertion (A) Effective curriculum is a continuously evolving in nature.

Reason (R) It meet the needs of modern and dynamic community.

60 Assertion (A) Democratic curriculum is based on new learning in a collaborative way.

Reason (R) It is for the students to discover knowledge.

61 Assertion (A) Education promotes peace and harmony.

Reason (R) Democratic curriculum is practiced in the classrooms.

62 Games and sports at the elementary school level help students to
[KVS TGT 2017]
(a) learn cooperation, fairness and negotiation
(b) be more competitive and exact in their tasks
(c) ensure success at any cost
(d) learn basic rules of all sports

63 The unspoken or implicit academic, social and cultural messages that are communicated to students while they are in school constitute   (KVS TGT 2017)
(a) spiral curriculum
(b) explicit curriculum
(c) hidden curriculum
(d) integrated curriculum

64 Variety of activities and experiences must be included in the curriculum to
[IGNOU BEd Entrance Exam 2019]
(a) provide joy and freedom from boredom
(b) enable each and every child some activities to excel in
(c) enable children to develop all their capabilities equally

(d) it helps to learn difficult subjects better if there are supportive activities

65 Which is not the part of co-curricular activities in schools?   [Bihar BEd 2020]
(a) Debates
(b) Music and song competitions
(c) Class lecture
(d) Drama

66 Co-curricular activities must be held
[Bihar BEd 2018]
(a) during school timings
(b) outside school timings
(c) either during or after school timings
(d) should not be held at all

67 Which of the following statements is correct?   [Bihar BEd 2018]
(a) Curricular activity is formal while co-curricular is informal
(b) Curricular activity is informal while co-curricular is formal
(c) Both are formal
(d) Both are informal

68 According to the National Curriculum Framework, 2005, learning is ...and...... in its character.
[BHU BEd Entrance Exam 2018]
(a) passive, simple
(b) active, social
(c) passive, social
(d) active, simple

69 .... is the apex institution involved in the planned and coordinated development of teacher education system in the country.[BHU BEd Entrance Exam 2018]
(a) UGC
(b) NCTE
(c) NCERT
(d) None of the above

70 Which is the statutory body for regulation of Teacher Education in India?
[BHU BEd Entrance Exam 2020]
(a) RCTE   (b) SIEMAT
(c) NCTE   (d) IGNOU

71 NCTE has revised its regulations on techer education in
(a) 2009   (b) 2014
(c) 2015   (d) None of these

72 Consider the following statements about the role of NCTE.

Statement I Its main role is to achieve planned and coordinated development of teacher education system throughout the country.

Statement II It aims at training individual to teach at pre-primary, primary and secondary level.

Codes
(a) Only Statement I is true
(b) Only Statement II is true
(c) Both statements, I and II are true
(d) Neither Statement I nor Statement II is true

73 National Curriculum Framework for Education in India, 2005 was developed by
(a) NCERT
(b) NUEPA
(c) NCTE
(d) NPE

74 Which State Government has recently launched the 'Happiness Curriculum' focusing on holistic education by including, meditation, education and mental exercise?

[BHU BEd Entrance Exam 2020]
(a) Jammu and Kashmir
(b) Maharashtra
(c) Kerala
(d) Delhi

75 Match the following.

	List I		List II
A.	UGC	1.	Initiating innovations in teacher's education
B.	NCERT	2.	Provides fellowships and scholarships
C.	NCTE	3.	Educational research body

Codes

	A B C		A B C
(a)	2 3 1	(b)	3 2 1
(c)	1 2 3	(d)	None of these

Answers

1.	(c)	2.	(d)	3.	(a)	4.	(a)	5.	(b)	6.	(d)	7.	(c)	8.	(d)	9.	(b)	10.	(c)
11.	(a)	12.	(b)	13.	(d)	14.	(a)	15.	(c)	16.	(c)	17.	(d)	18.	(b)	19.	(d)	20.	(c)
21.	(c)	22.	(a)	23.	(d)	24.	(d)	25.	(a)	26.	(a)	27.	(d)	28.	(a)	29.	(b)	30.	(b)
31.	(d)	32.	(b)	33.	(d)	34.	(b)	35.	(c)	36.	(c)	37.	(d)	38.	(d)	39.	(c)	40.	(d)
41.	(d)	42.	(d)	43.	(b)	44.	(c)	45.	(a)	46.	(c)	47.	(b)	48.	(d)	49.	(c)	50.	(c)
51.	(b)	52.	(c)	53.	(b)	54.	(d)	55.	(d)	56.	(c)	57.	(a)	58.	(d)	59.	(d)	60.	(d)
61.	(a)	62.	(a)	63.	(c)	64.	(b)	65.	(c)	66.	(a)	67.	(a)	68.	(b)	69.	(b)	70.	(c)
71.	(b)	72.	(c)	73.	(c)	74.	(d)	75.	(a)										

Aptitude Towards Teaching Profession

A profession may perhaps be defined as "an occupation based upon specialised intellectual study and training, the purpose of which is to supply skilled service and to advise others for a definite fee or salary."

Payment of a fee or salary is not the only attribute of a profession. This is in fact, common to the non-professionals, daily wagers and casual employees too, who have no identifiable skills. Some degree of intellectual study and training is involved in some other occupations too, such as, nursing, computer typing, etc.

According to **Alexander Flexner**, there are many criteria which distinguish professions from mere occupations.

A profession is one that meets these following criteria

- It involves essential intellectual operations.
- It derives its raw materials from science and learning.
- It works with this material (science and learning) to a practical and definite end.
- It possesses an educationally communicable technique.
- It tends toward self-organisation.
- They are becoming increasingly altruistic in nature.
- A broad range of autonomy for both the individual practitioners and for the occupational group as a whole.

Teaching as a Profession

Teaching is about inspiring and motivating students to realise and exceed their potentials.

Teaching as a profession provides highly specialised intellectual services. It is based on long specialised, intellectual training representing a high degree of creative thought and contributing to the development of a wide range of research specialists. A teacher is one of the highly valued personality in a society. As such, teaching is considered to be the most sacred and distinctive profession.

With the change in demands, the profession of teaching has become demanding. Many factors have been at work for years in bringing the change in the attitude towards teaching.

Thus, now it is a learned profession. Global emphasis on literacy through programme like Education For All (EFA) and Right To Education (RTE) shows the world's concern for the teacher's role in the development of the society.

Teaching as a profession can be described as an occupation, intellectual services. It is a body of erudite knowledge, a set of attitude and a technique which is applied to the service of mankind through an educated group. It needs a long period of training and certification.

Teaching as a profession, also fulfills certain conditions which supports it as a profession, like teachers are organised at local, state and national levels. Teaching requires careful skills and understanding. Teachers are required by law to complete certain requirements for certification and entrance into the profession.

Characteristics of Teaching Profession

- It essentially involves an intellectual operation.
- It draws material from science.
- It transforms raw material for a practical and definite end.
- It possesses an educationally communicable technique.
- It tends towards self-organisation.
- It essentially performs a social service.
- It involves a lengthy period of study and training.
- It has a high degree of autonomy.
- It is based upon a systematic body of knowledge.
- It has a common Code of Ethics.
- It generates in-service growth.

Levels of Teaching

The activities of teaching and learning may be organised at various levels of abstraction; ranging from the use and application of simple mental powers to the most complex ones.

Through teaching, the teacher brings desirable changes in the learner. Both the concepts teaching and learning are interrelated to each other. Development of all round personality of the learner is the final goal of teaching and learning.

During teaching, interaction takes place between an experienced person (teacher) and an in-experienced person (student). There are three identifiable levels of teaching and learning activities. These are

1. Memory Level of Teaching (Herbert's Teaching Model)
2. Understanding Level of Teaching (Morrison's Teaching Model)
3. Reflective Level of Teaching (Hunt's Teaching Model)

Memory Level of Teaching

The first level of teaching is Memory Level of Teaching. It is also called thoughtless teaching. Herbert is the main proponent of Memory Level of Teaching. At Memory Level of Teaching, the focus is on memorisation. It is usually used in lower classes.

The instructional arrangement is such that the learner is helped in cramming the content presented to him. Here, the teaching-learning process is mainly a Stimulus-Response (S-R).

The famous educationist Woods Worth says, "Memory is the direct use of what is learned." In this level, emphasis is laid down on the presentation of the facts and information and its cramming.

Teaching and learning at memory level are basically about committing factual material to our memory. It has three major aspects

- Learning of the material.
- Retention of the material.
- Reproduction of the material as and when required.

1. Objectives

- Knowledge gained by the learner is basically factual that is acquired through memorisation and rote learning.
- It covers only the knowledge based objectives of Bloom's Taxonomy.
- Teaching is subject-centered in which simple memorable things are taught to students.

- The subject material is well organised and simple in nature.
- The knowledge delivered is definite structured and observable.

2. Structure

Herbert includes the following steps in Memory Level of Teaching

(i) **Preparation** Questions are asked to test the previous knowledge.

(ii) **Statement of Aim** To acquaint the name of the topic.

(iii) **Presentation** Stimulating the mental activity, the pupils are provided with opportunities for self-learning.

(iv) **Association** Mutual relationship is established among facts, events and experts by comparison.

(v) **Generalisation** Principles and laws are formulated for the future life situations.

(vi) **Application** New learnt knowledge is used in new situations.

3. Psychological Basis

According to **Jean Piaget**, "Memory level is meant for starters. The learners are at pre-operational level of cognitive development in the school. They cannot operate upon abstract concepts. As per their mental development, they can learn simple concepts without analysing their true meaning and nature."

Pavlov and **Skinner** advocated the Conditioning Theory that underlies the concept that correct response made by the individuals is strengthened reinforcement to retain the learned subject matter longer and to facilitate ease in further learning.

The concept of Pavlov's Classical Conditioning considers the mechanical process as applied at Memory Level of Teaching. Correct learning by the student is awarded and retained for future use.

4. Teaching Method

Teaching method of this level is subject centered which aim to make the students memorise the subject.

The teaching methods include drill, review, revision and asking questions. Drill refers to constant practice and repetitions to memorise a particular subject.

Review relates to learners forming new associations with the subject. Next step is revising the concepts and asking questions which is used to examine whether objectives are achieved or not. Teacher's role is active as subject content, teaching technique and methods are decided by the teacher. Learner's role is passive.

Teaching equipments include teaching aids like audio-visual aids, models, charts, maps, pictures, TV, radio, etc.

5. Evaluation System

The evaluation system mainly includes both essay and objective type questions. Oral tests are conducted to check the level of memorisation. The tests and tools need proper planning which could evaluate the students' ability to comprehend, grasp, analyse, synthesise and discriminate. Fill up, matching, short answer, MCQ, recall type and recognition are some examples of evaluation system.

6. Suggestions

- The teaching material should progress from simple to complex.
- The teaching material should be objective and useful.
- Teaching aids should be adequate and parts of the content should be integrated and well sequenced.
- There should be scope for continuous reinforcement during the course of instruction.
- Systematic and organised way of presentation of subject matter should be there.

Understanding Level of Teaching

The main proponent of Understanding Level of Teaching is Morrison. The teaching at the Understanding Level is of higher quality as compared to the teaching at Memory Level.

It is more useful and thoughtful as it focuses on the mastery of the subject. Teaching at this level is done to develop intellectual behaviour. Learners become more capable to think and present the facts in good manners. They also analyse the facts properly and draw inferences.

Motivation at the Understanding Level of Teaching is extrinsic as well as intrinsic in nature.

Teaching-learning at the Understanding Level emphasises seeing solitary facts in relation to general principles. It involves exploration, presentation, assimilation, organisation and recitation through oral presentation or in the form of written paper.

This type of teaching- learning can be carried out with the students in upper primary, middle and higher classes.

1. Objectives

It is according to revised Bloom Taxonomy, understanding level of teaching aims at the following objectives

(i) **Understanding Objectives** These are the understanding of instructional message by means of interpreting, exemplifying, classifying, comparing and inferring, etc.

(ii) **Application Objectives** These include the use of a proper procedure for executing and implementing the use of principles/rules in practical life situations.

2. Structure

Morrison has divided the Understanding Level of Teaching into five steps. These are

(i) **Presentation** Content is presented, diagnosed and recapitulated till students understand.

(ii) **Exploration** Testing previous knowledge, analysing the content.

(iii) **Assimilation** Generalisation, individual activities, working in laboratory and library, test of content.

(iv) **Organisation** Pupils are provided with the occasions for representation.

(v) **Recitation** Pupil presents the content orally.

3. Teaching Method

Teaching method of this level is subject centered as well as teacher centered. Teacher plans the proceedings of the classroom in advance and works accordingly. Teacher adopts a permissive role and allows more freedom so that learners can interpret the information in their own way.

Teacher motivates the learners in their learning process. Teacher uses different types of methods in teaching such as Lecture Method, Discussion Method, Inductive - Deductive Method, Exemplification (explain by using examples), etc. Teacher's role is active as classroom activities and teaching methods are decided by the teachers. These learners are more active in comparison to learners at Memory Level of Teaching.

4. Evaluation System

Planned tests are prepared to evaluate the student's ability to comprehend, grasp, synthesise, discriminate, generalise and the insight to apply the generalised principles further.

Besides asking questions for oral testing, written testing should be conducted. Comprehensive essays are also a tool for evaluation.

5. Suggestions

There should be effective classroom interaction, organised subject matter, use of teaching aids and proper classroom environment alongwith motivation by teachers.

Reflective Level of Teaching

Reflective Level of Teaching is also known as Introspective Level of Teaching.

Hunt is the main proponent of Reflective Level of Teaching. It is the highest and the most practical level of teaching.

This level basically involves the use of scientific methods to understand the problems. The Reflective Level of Teaching is highly thoughtful and useful. A learner can achieve this level only after Memory Level and Understanding Level.

Students at this level, develop curiosity, interest, inquiry and persistence which culminates in a scientifically determined conclusion or solution of a problem.

Teaching-learning at Reflective Level involves careful and critical examination of an idea or problem through the 'Problem-Solving Approach'. It is only possible at the high school level as older learners usually develop certain habits and abilities that were not strong in earlier years.

1. Objectives

- To develop insight into the learner to solve problems.
- To develop the ability of independent thinking and decision-making in the students.
- To develop rational and critical thinking in the students.

2. Structure

Hunt has divided the Reflective Level of Teaching into further five steps. These are

1. **Creating a Problematic Situation** Teacher creates a problematic situation before students, which students try to solve.
2. **Formulation of the Hypothesis** Students formulate different hypothesis as per the problem given to them.
3. **Verify Hypothesis** Students after formulating hypothesis verify this with the problem.
4. **Collection of Data** Different data are collected from different sources, like interview, internet articles, newspaper cuttings and so on.
5. **Testing of Hypothesis** The verified hypothesis then taken by students and tested with the given problem.

3. Teaching Method

The teaching method of this level is student centered. There is lot of interaction between the teacher and learners. Study material or classroom proceeding is neither organised nor pre-planned. The interaction is highly thoughtful and learners are allowed to bring up their own ideas to solve specific problem. Teacher plays a democratic role in this level of teaching.

4. Evaluation System

The evaluation system at the reflective level of teaching should test the higher order cognitive abilities like reasoning, creativity, original thinking, problem-solving, critical thinking, etc.

5. Suggestions

- Proper atmosphere should be provided.
- Encourage independent learning and expression of thoughts.
- Proper direction.
- Proper evaluation.

1 A profession may be defined as an occupation if
 (a) It is based upon specilised intellectual study
 (b) It is based upon specilised training
 (c) Its purpose is to supply skilled service
 (d) All of the above

2 Which attribute defines the profession?
 (a) Specialised knowledge
 (b) Accountability
 (c) Self-regulation
 (d) All of the above

3 Who gave the criteria which separates profession from occupation?
 (a) Liberman
 (b) Alexander Flexner
 (c) Adorn
 (d) Gestalt

4 Which of the following is the criterion of profession given by Flexner?
 (a) It involves essential intellectual operations
 (b) It derives its raw materials from science and learning
 (c) It works with this material (Science and Learning) to a practical and definite end
 (d) All of the above

5 Which attribute separates profession from vocation?
 (a) Profession grounded with sound knowledge
 (b) Profession ground with expertise
 (c) No Code of Conduct
 (d) Both (a) and (b)

6 A profession is one that meets some criteria. Which of the following can be termed as a criteria for it?
 I. It possesses an educationally communicable technique.
 II. It tends towards self-organisation.
 III. It is becoming increasing attruistic in nature.
 IV. It works with this material (Science and Learning) to a practical and definite end.

Codes
 (a) I and II
 (b) II and III
 (c) Only IV
 (d) All of these

7 Which of the following is not a chracteristic of a teaching profession?
 (a) It essentially performs a social service
 (b) It has a high degree of dependency
 (c) It has a common Code of Ethics
 (d) It generates in-service growth

8 Professionals have deep personal commitment to
 (a) improve their skills
 (b) build a strong peer group
 (c) behave professionally
 (d) develop a good behaviour

9 Professinals are competent. It means they are
 (a) honest
 (b) reliable
 (c) competitive
 (d) self-made

10 What is the vital element of professionalism?
 (a) Reliability
 (b) Self-regulation
 (c) Accountability
 (d) Sincerity

11 Teacher's professionalism means
 (a) the extent to which a teacher subscribes to a professional code
 (b) a teacher has to teach for the sake of getting salary
 (c) a teacher must have completed professional teacher training
 (d) All of the above

12 Which one of the following is true for a professional teacher?
 (a) Creates problems in school administration
 (b) Is friendly and predictable
 (c) Have good knowledge
 (d) Is lazy

13 Professional exert a substantial control over the
 (a) curriculum
 (b) admission
 (c) accreditation of professional training school
 (d) All of the above

14 Teaching as a profession is based on
 (a) long specialised training
 (b) intellectual training
 (c) high degree of creative thought
 (d) All of the above

15 Teaching as a profession is a
 (a) body of erudite knowledge
 (b) a set of attitude
 (c) a technique
 (d) All of the above

16 Professional development means
 (a) updating skills and knowledge
 (b) undergoing workshops and conferences
 (c) taking part in in-service traning
 (d) All of the above

17 How the professionals are compensated?
 (a) Meagre salary
 (b) High salary and benefits
 (c) Gifts
 (d) All of the above

18 What quality does a teacher should possess?
 (a) Understanding the students
 (b) Be just and courteous
 (c) Promotes a spirit of enquiring
 (d) All of the above

19 What is the role of a teacher in society?
 (a) Performing duties
 (b) Participating in community activities
 (c) Both (a) and (b)
 (d) None of the above

20 Professionally powerful …… is very important in our contemparany society.
 (a) Learning
 (b) Knowledge
 (c) Living
 (d) Teaching

21 Professionalism of teaching should have
 (a) Competence
 (b) Performance
 (c) Good conduct/behaviour
 (d) All of the above

22 Teaching is a ………… profession.
 (a) global
 (b) loving
 (c) lazy
 (d) monetary

23 What kind of barrier does a professional faces in the classroom?
 (a) Cultural barrier
 (b) Social-economic difference
 (c) Both (a) and (b)
 (d) None of the above

24 On which aspect, professionals conduct depends on
 (a) Aesthetic
 (b) Language
 (c) Behaviour
 (d) All of these

25 A professional teacher must have
 (a) communication skills
 (b) adventure training
 (c) personality
 (d) None of the above

26 Good education system needs a good quality
 (a) learner
 (b) curriculum
 (c) professional teacher
 (d) All of the above

27 Which of the following defines characteristics of teaching profession?
 (a) It essentially involves an intellectual operation
 (b) It draws material from science
 (c) It has a high degree of autonomy
 (d) All of the above

28 Which of the following is the final goal of teaching and learning?
 (a) Development of all round personality of the learner
 (b) Maintaining classroom environment
 (c) Having good communication skills
 (d) All of the above

29 Which one of the following does not pertain to objectives as an aspect of teaching some subject?   [KVS TGT 2017]
 (a) Objectives are end points of possible achievement
 (b) Objectives are immediate and attainable goals
 (c) Objectives provide frame of reference for selection of content
 (d) Objectives are broad and general

30 Effective teaching, by and large, is a function of   [CG BEd 2018]
 (a) teacher's schoarship
 (b) teacher's honesty
 (c) teachers making students learn and understand
 (d) teacher's liking for the job of teaching

31 A teacher can enhance effective learning in her elementary classroom by [CTET 2016]
(a) drill and practice
(b) encouraging competition amongst her students
(c) connecting the content to the lives of the students
(d) offering rewards for small steps in learning

32 Which of the following is the first level of teaching?
(a) Reflection level
(b) Memory level
(c) Understanding level
(d) All of the above

33 Who is the proponent of memory level of teaching?
(a) Herbert
(b) Morrison
(c) Hunt
(d) All of these

34 Who said that "Memory is the direct use of what is learned"?
(a) Woodsworth
(b) Morrison
(c) Herbert
(d) Hunt

35 Which of the following is the aspect of memory level of teaching?
(a) Learning of the material
(b) Retention of the material
(c) Reproduction of the material as and when required
(d) All of the above

36 Which level of teaching covers only the knowledge based objectives of Blooms Taxonomy?
(a) Memory level of teaching
(b) Understanding level of teaching
(c) Reflective level of teaching
(d) None of the above

37 Which of the following is the step of memory level of teaching?
(a) Association
(b) Preparation
(c) Generalisation
(d) All of the above

38 Teaching method of memory level of teaching is
(a) subject centered
(b) student centered
(c) teacher centered
(d) All of these

39 Who is the main proponent of understanding level of teaching?
(a) Morrison
(b) Hunt
(c) Woodsworth
(d) None of these

40 At which level of teaching motivation is extrinsic and intrinsic?
(a) Memory level
(b) Understanding level
(c) Reflective level
(d) None of the above

41 To enable students to make conceptual changes in their thinking, a teacher should [CG BEd 2018]
(a) offer rewards to children who change their thinking
(b) discourage children from thinking on their own and ask them to just listen to a teacher and follow that
(c) offer an explanation in lecture mode
(d) make clear and convincing explanations and have discussions with the students

42 In a diverse classroom, learners find it difficult to speak and write good English and often uses their mother tongue. It is because [CG BEd 2017]
(a) they do not have the ability to learn English
(b) they are low learners
(c) they are not motivated to learn
(d) they lack enough competence and the structures of the two languages are different

43 Purpose of evaluative phase of teaching is [UK BEd 2016]
(a) to know to what extent objectives are realised
(b) to know the shortcomings of the teacher
(c) to know the effectiveness of strategies
(d) All of the above

44 Who is the main proponent of reflective level of teaching?
(a) Hunt
(b) Morrison
(c) Woodsworth
(d) None of these

45 Which is the highest and most practical level of teaching?

(a) Reflective level   (b) Memory level
(c) Understanding level (d) All of these

46 Which level of teaching involves problem solving approach?

(a) Understanding level
(b) Memory level
(c) Reflective level
(d) None of the above

47 Which of the following is the step of reflective level of teaching?

(a) Creating a problematic situation
(b) Formulation of the hypothesis
(c) Verify hypothesis
(d) All of the above

48 To ensure effective learning in classroom, which one of the following is irrelevent? **[KVS TGT 2017]**

(a) The teacher should ensure that the students are able to learn at their own paces
(b) The teacher should ensure that information to be learned is presented in small steps
(c) There should be pin drop silence in the class so that the teacher may teach undisturbedly
(d) The students should be given immediate feedback concerning the accuracy of their learning

49 After teaching the concept of square to class V students, a teacher asked students the following two questions? **[KVS TGT 2017]**

I. What is the definition of a square?
II. Draw a square.

Identify the level of cognitive development, the two questions intend to measure.

(a) I Knowledge II Synthesis
(b) I Knowledge II Application
(c) I Understanding II Synthesis
(d) I Understanding II Application

50 Why did you adopt teaching profession? **[MP BEd 2016]**

(a) Your parents wanted it
(b) At the advice of your friend
(c) No member in your family is in this profession
(d) You have interest in it

51 In your class, a student always behaves indiscipline, then what kind of solution has been taken by you? **[UK BEd 2017]**

(a) Inquire about hereditary and enviroment of him/her then mentors in right direction
(b) Beat student daily whenever she/he leaves the indisciplinary activities
(c) Suggest the principal to rustricate him/her
(d) Take appointment from a psychologist for him/her

Answers

1.	(d)	2.	(d)	3.	(b)	4.	(d)	5.	(d)	6.	(d)	7.	(b)	8.	(a)	9.	(b)	10.	(c)
11.	(a)	12.	(c)	13.	(d)	14.	(d)	15.	(d)	16.	(d)	17.	(b)	18.	(d)	19.	(c)	20.	(d)
21.	(d)	22.	(a)	23.	(c)	24.	(d)	25.	(a)	26.	(c)	27.	(d)	28.	(a)	29.	(d)	30.	(c)
31.	(c)	32.	(b)	33.	(a)	34.	(a)	35.	(d)	36.	(a)	37.	(d)	38.	(a)	39.	(a)	40.	(b)
41.	(d)	42.	(d)	43.	(d)	44.	(a)	45.	(a)	46.	(c)	47.	(d)	48.	(c)	49.	(b)	50.	(d)
51.	(a)																		

Chapter 07

Qualities of a Good Teacher

In the present scenario, the teacher has moved far ahead from his/her traditional role of just being a subject transact placed during the colonial times. Today, he/she plays a far more important and significant role not only in a student's life but also in the development of society. Society itself has undergone a lot of transformations and changes.

As a consequence, expectations from the teacher have also changed. It is very important that teachers become aware of their new and multiple roles and get ready to take them up with zeal and enthusiasm.

Educational Qualification of Teacher

It is mandatory to have a minimum educational qualification for teaching in a teacher. It is also necessary for a teacher to be well-trained in his/her profession.

1. **Educational Qualification for Primary and Secondary Classes** A teacher must posses B.Ed. degree with graduation as the minimum educational qualification for teaching in primary and secondary classes, or B.T.C., or it is mandatory to have D.El.Ed.

2. **Educational Qualification for Higher Secondary Classes** To teach Higher Secondary classes, a person must have M.A. degree or have honours in a particular field/subject.

Qualities of a Good Teacher

Qualities of a good teacher can be seen through the following points

Subject–Matter Expert

- Possesses thorough knowledge of subject matter and demonstrates a contagious enthusiasm for it.
- Goes further than the standard textbook materials.
- Researches and develops important and original thoughts on the subject speciality.
- Thinks about discipline, analyse its nature and evaluates its quality.
- Follows intellectual developments in the discipline regularly and related fields.
- Takes strong interest in broader issues and is intellectually admirable.

Pedagogical Expert

- Sets appropriate learning goals and objectives and communicates them clearly.
- Demonstrates a positive attitude and trust in students and continually works to

overcome obstacles that might subvert learning.

- Evaluates and grades students' work fairly and promptly.
- Encourages students to think and empowers them to find their own creativity.
- Promotes a wide range of ideas and an open expression of diverse opinions while maintaining an atmosphere of integrity, civility and respect.
- Guides students successfully through exploration of the creative, critical thinking and problem-solving processes and helps students grapple with ideas and information they need to develop their own understanding.
- Promotes students' self-discovery.
- Pursues teaching and learning as scholarly activities.
- Exhibits a strong sense of commitment to the academic community in addition to personal success in the classroom.
- Provides on a regular basis constructive and objective feedback to students.
- Finds unique and creative ways to connect students to each other.

Excellent Communicator

- Demonstrates effective oral and written communication skills.
- Demonstrates good organisational abilities and planning skills.
- Helps students learn effective communication skills.
- Listens attentively and is available and approachable.
- Utilises teaching tools appropriately and effectively.
- Simplifies and clarifies complex subjects that result in provocative insights.
- Bridges language and cultural barriers.

Student-Centered Mentor

- Makes students' learning the highest priority.
- Experiments willingly to facilitate students' learning.
- Strives to stimulate each student to learn through a variety of methods and encourages and invites active student participation.
- Helps students connect different learning experiences and facilitates development of self-knowledge.
- Conveys to students that they must reach beyond facts to the understanding and application of concepts.
- Instills a desire in students for life-long learning.
- Inspires them to higher intellectual levels and does not give up on students.
- Connects with students easily and is understanding and personable.

Systematic and Continual Assessor

- Develops and uses appropriate student outcome assessments to continuously improve student learning experience in keeping with stated course objectives.
- Employs a systematic approach to assess teaching, keeps the class material fresh and new, makes appropriate changes where indicated and sets clear objectives that indicate the kind of thinking and acting expected from students.
- Creates an environment that invites constructive student feedback to the instructor.
- Adapts teaching style to accomplish the objectives of successful student learning. Recognises own limitations and shortcomings, confronts and learns from them.
- Advocates learning over testing.

Role and Abilities of Teacher

1. **Teacher as a Facilitator** While the student today has access to various sources of knowledge, the job of a teacher becomes more important since he/she has to lead the students towards locating resources.

   The teacher should be able to provide students different ways of viewing the world, communicating about it and successfully coping with questions and issues of daily living.

2. **Teacher as a Counsellor and Guidance Worker** When students come up to the teacher with their personal problems, teacher's role is that of a counsellor who is an empathetic and an active listener, non-judgemental and has a positive attitude.

   Teacher should always keep in mind that no bias should arise against or in favour of the student after listening to him/her.

3. **Teacher as a Mental Health Worker** A teacher is expected to play the role of a mental health worker and be a sensitive observer of human behaviour. The teacher should respond constructively when a student's emotions get in the way of learning.

4. **Teacher as a Role Model** Teachers have the inevitable edge over others to mould their students behaviour. No matter what a teacher does, he/she will be acting as a model for students.

   Teaching a subject enthusiastically is likely to have more impact than a bored instructor lecturing on the value of the subject. At times, modelling can also be used intentionally.

5. **Teacher as a Sensitising Agent** The teacher while taking his/her classes can also act as a sensitising agent where he/she inspires students to do various things in life and can also sensitise the students towards important issues related to politics, environment, world, etc.

6. **Teacher as a Trainer for Citizenship** A teacher's role expands beyond that of a sensitising agent and he/she can act as a trainer for citizenship with civil and social responsibility.

   The primary aim of schools is not only to help students to score good marks in examinations and get into good colleges but also to help students to grow as socially responsible citizens. As a trainer, teacher should be able to help students in making them aware of their fundamental rights and duty towards society.

7. **Teacher as an Agent for Social Change** Both the roles of the teacher as a sensitising agent and a trainer together mark his/her role as an agent for social change.

   The teacher's role as an agent for social change does not demand from the teacher to take out any rallies or to bring about any revolution, but slow and steady work with the students, sensitising them towards various social issues, inspiring them to take action and encouraging them to come out with various suggestions regarding the way change can be brought about will lead to major and long-lasting changes.

8. **Teacher as a Researcher** Teacher's role is now not only to transact knowledge but also to act as an action researcher.

   While passing the school corridors or while talking to students discovering that they have numerous problems, the teacher should not only discuss these problems but also carry out proper action research to find solutions and to apply the same to deal with the problems.

9. **Teacher as a Reflective Professional**
Reflective teachers try to understand why particular actions have certain effects in their classes; they anaylse the teaching from a number of different perspectives or theoretical orientations.

Their analysis is guided by a rich store of knowledge about students, classrooms, schools, learning, teaching and the subject matter being taught.

They enjoy teaching but are never completely satisfied with their current level of expertise and always try to improve. Reflective teachers are not content by simply trying to reflect, analyse and study.

1 A good teacher's priority in his school shall be his
(a) Principal
(b) Secretary of the Managing Committee
(c) Colleagues
(d) Students

2 An excellent communicator
(a) experiments willingly to affect student learning
(b) makes students learning the highest priority
(c) listens attentively and simplifies complex subjects that result in provocative insights
(d) promotes student self- discovery

3 Student-centered mentor
(a) makes student learning the highest priority
(b) experiments willingly to affect student learning
(c) strives to stimulate each student to learn
(d) All of the above

4 A pedagogical expert
(a) evaluates and grades student work fairly and promptly
(b) promotes student self-discovery
(c) pursues teaching and learning as scholarly activities
(d) All of the above

5 'Setting up of learning goals and objectives' is the characteristic of which attribute of an excellent teacher?
(a) Pedagogical expert
(b) Excellent communication
(c) Subject matter expert
(d) Students centred mentor

6 Which one of the following is the most important quality of a good teacher?
(a) Content mastery and reactive
(b) Content mastery and authoritative
(c) Content mastery
(d) Punctuality and sincerity

7 The primary duty of a teacher is to
(a) Imbibe value system in the students
(b) Improve the physical standard of the students
(c) Raise the intellectual standard of the students
(d) Help in all round development of the students

8 An effective teacher in a classroom, where students come from diverse backgrounds, would　　　　[CG BEd 2019]
(a) focus on their cultural knowledge to address individual differences among the group
(b) push students from deprived backgrounds to work hard, so that they can match up with their peers
(c) ignore cultural knowledge and treat all his students in a uniform manner
(d) create groups of students with those from the same economic background put together

9 An ideal teacher is one who
[BHU BEd 2020]
(a) has strong desire to learn continuously
(b) favourite of all colleagues
(c) confident of the Principal
(d) popular in students community

10 For which of the following characteristics students usually most dislike their teacher?   [BHU BEd 2020]
(a) Illegible blackboard writing
(b) Lack of knowledge of subject
(c) Bias behaviour
(d) Always late in class

11 Which statement is most suitable for successful teacher?   [BHU BEd 2020]
(a) Explains lesson clearly
(b) Uses textbook only
(c) Asks questions
(d) Inspires students

12 Which one should be followed by a good teacher in a class?   [Bihar BEd 2020]
(a) Teach fast learners
(b) Teach mediocre learners
(c) Teach slow learners
(d) Teach (a), (b) and (c) together

13 Which one is most important for a teacher?   [Bihar BEd 2020]
(a) Expertise in subject content
(b) Expertise in teaching skills
(c) Rapport with students
(d) Good health

14 Which of the following is a teacher related factor affecting learning?   [UP BEd 2020]
(a) Mastery over the subject matter
(b) Proper seating arrangement
(c) Availability of teaching-learning resources
(d) None of the above

15 A teacher should   [CTET 2019]
(a) communicate that she respects and values all cultures in the classroom
(b) maximise comparison amongst students
(c) promote students belonging to certain cultures
(d) ignore cultural differences and diversity amongst students

16 Teacher's main responsibility is   [UK BEd 2019]
(a) to create and teach a text plan
(b) conducting as many activities as possible
(c) maintaining strict discipline
(d) providing learning opportunities according to different learning style of students

17 Which of the following should be considered the most important feature in a teacher at the primary level?   [UK BEd 2019]
(a) Eagerness to teach
(b) Patience and perseverance
(c) Proficiency in knowledge of teaching methods and topics
(d) The efficiency of reading in a very standard language

18 Which of the following is the most important for teachers?   [UK BEd 2019]
(a) Maintaining good discipline
(b) To solve the difficulties of students
(c) Punctuality
(d) Have a good time

19 A teacher can become more effective if,   [Bihar BEd 2019]
(a) student score higher marks
(b) teacher uses good quality supporting study material
(c) he helps the learners achieve proficiency in studies
(d) he helps students in raising questions

20 The most important work of a teacher is   [Bihar BEd 2019]
(a) complete focus on development of students
(b) to provide remedial and whenever needed
(c) to provide effective education
(d) to maintain order and discipline in the class

21 As applicable to the classroom, the teacher's role in motivation is essentially subject of   [Bihar BEd 2019]
(a) awakening the needs in the students
(b) channelising the energies of aware and conscious students in creative direction
(c) inculcating new interests
(d) providing attractive incentives that are accessible to the students

22 The chief responsibility of the teacher is   [Bihar BEd 2019]
(a) planning educational experiences
(b) enhancing relations with parents
(c) using the novel techniques of teaching
(d) implementing the administrative policies

23 A teacher's work is to   [Bihar BEd 2019]
(a) help students in self-studies
(b) motivate students for studies
(c) enable friendly environment for studies
(d) tell the students their mistakes

24 A teacher shall keep his voice in ....
in a class.   **[Bihar BEd 2019]**
(a) high tone   (b) slower voice
(c) louder voice   (d) normal voice

25 Which one of the following best describes
a teacher's role?   **[CTET 2018]**
(a) Creating a relaxed space where children
learn through dialogue and inquiry
(b) Teachers most important role in the
classroom is to maintain discipline
(c) A teacher should adhere to the
prescribed textbook.
(d) Completing the syllabus on time and
leaving enough time for revision is
important

26 Role of a teacher in a class is to
                              [BHU BEd 2018]
(a) follow the timetable strictly and stick to
the course
(b) provide authentic learning situations and
facilitate independent thinking in students
(c) fill the students with his/her own knowledge
and prepare them for examinations
(d) transmit knowledge in a straight fashion
and prepare students for right answers

27 The mental health problems of today's
child are increasing. What can be a
possible reason for it?
(a) Teachers are spending less quality time
with parents of their students
(b) Students are spending less quality time
with their teachers
(c) Teachers are spending less quality time
with their students
(d) Parents are spending less quality time
with their children

28 In the present day context, the teacher's
role is not visualised as that of an
authority figure, rather he/she is seen as
a .... of learning who acts as a
guiding light for the student.
(a) tool   (b) facilitator
(c) institution   (d) path

29 When students come up to a teacher
with their personal problems, what role
should she/he take to be an empathetic
and active listener, non-judgemental and
exhibit a positive attitude?
(a) Parent   (b) Friend
(c) Counsellor   (d) Big-brother

30 When a teacher helps at all the four
levels, namely, preventive, promotional,
curative and conservative, he/she is
playing a role of a
(a) mental health worker
(b) counsellor
(c) parent
(d) role model

31 The demonstrations of experiments or
various activities done by the teachers in
class are examples of
(a) modelling
(b) practical lecture
(c) mental health worker
(d) direct modelling

32 When a teacher has to inspire many
students of the class to do various things
in life, he/she will have to work as a
(a) role model   (b) sensitising agent
(c) friend   (d) guide

33 Acting as a trainer, a teacher cannot
only help students to score good marks
in examinations and get into good
colleges but also help students
(a) get jobs and earn good money
(b) in their personal problems
(c) grow as socially responsible citizens
(d) become good teachers

34 Acting as an agent for social change a
teacher should
(i) Take out rallies
(ii) Bring about revolution
(iii) Inspire students to take action
(iv) Come out with various suggestions
regarding the way change can be brought
Codes
(a) Only (ii)   (b) (i) and (iv)
(c) (iii) and (iv)   (d) All of these

35 Often while passing the school corridors
or while talking to students, teachers
discover that students have numerous
problems, what should a teacher do to
help them?
(i) Discuss those problems
(ii) Carry out proper action research to
find solutions
(iii) Apply the research to deal with the
problems

Codes
(a) Only (i)   (b) (i) and (ii)
(c) (ii) and (iii) (d) All of these

36 What are the characteristics needed by a teacher to become a counsellor?
(a) Empathy   (b) Active listening
(c) Non-Judgemental (d) All of these

37 In today's world, when students have access to all the information through TV, internet, radio etc., the role of teacher becomes more of a
(a) mental health worker
(b) facilitator
(c) trainer
(d) social worker

38 The phrase 'Action speak louder than words' is apt for which role of teacher?
(a) Role of mental health worker
(b) Role of counsellor
(c) Role of sensitising agent
(d) Role model

39 A teacher discusses various issues related to politics, environment, health, etc., while teaching in class, she is playing the role of
(a) mental health worker
(b) sensitising agent
(c) counsellor
(d) role model

40 For a teacher to become an agent for social change, which of the following combination is needed?
(a) Sensitising agent and trainer
(b) Trainer and mental health worker
(c) Mental health worker and counsellor
(d) Trainer and role model

41 While acting as counsellor guidance worker, what among the following should be avoided by a teacher?
(a) Positive attitude
(b) Empathy
(c) Getting biased towards student after listening to him/her
(d) Acive listener

42 Which of the following is not a trait of reflective teacher?
(a) Enjoy teaching and is not satisfied with his/her current level expertise
(b) Always try to improve

(c) He/She research on his/her teaching effectiveness
(d) Does not like any suggestion from colleagues

43 What is not expected as a role of teacher?
(a) Role model   (b) Counsellor
(c) Authority figure (d) Sensitising agent

44 A successful teacher is one who is
(a) compassionate and disciplinarian
(b) quiet and reactive
(c) tolerant and dominating
(d) passive and active

45 Which of the following is the most important single factor in underlying the success of beginning a teacher?
          [DU BEd 2018]
(a) Scholarship
(b) Communicative ability
(c) Organisational ability
(d) Personality and its ability to relate to the class and to the pupils

46 A teacher   **[DU BEd 2018]**
(a) should have command over his subject
(b) should introduce the lesson before he starts teaching
(c) should have command over his language
(d) All of the above

47 Roli is unable to pronounce the words 'study' and 'society' clearly. As her teacher what will you do? **[CG BEd 2018]**
(a) Humiliate Roli by isolating her and asking her to repeat the words
(b) Asking the entire class to repeat the words and appreciating Roli when she repeats them correctly
(c) You will just ignore it
(d) You will ask the class to laugh at her

48 Most psychologists believe that development is due **[CG BEd 2018]**
(a) largely to nature
(b) largely to nurture
(c) to nature and nurture acting separately
(d) to an interaction of nature and nurture

49 Teacher's main responsibility is
          [CG BEd 2017]
(a) to create and teach a text plan
(b) conducting as many activities as possible
(c) maintaining strict discipline
(d) providing learning opportunities according to different learning styles of students

50 Which of the following should be considered the most important feature in a teacher at the administrative level?
[CG BEd 2017]
(a) Eagerness to teach
(b) Patience and perseverance
(c) Proficiency in knowledge of teaching methods and topics
(d) The efficiency of reading in a very standard language

51 The most important quality of an effective teacher is [IGNOU BEd 2017]
(a) deep knowledge about the subject taught
(b) a strict disciplinarian
(c) good rapport with the students
(d) a good motivator

52 To remove the gender inequality, a teacher plays a role of [UK BEd 2017]
(a) He/She does not encourage the stereotype ideas regarding gender inequality
(b) She/He engages boys in hardwork and girls in comparatively lower level
(c) She/He makes understand to boys that do not involve in household works
(d) She/He encourages boys for sports and girls for knitting and sewing

53 In teaching learning, teacher's work is [UK BEd 2017]
(a) to encourage student to learn
(b) read student
(c) to stop playing to student, encourage to study
(d) to encourage student only in reading book

54 In an elementary classroom, an effective teacher should aim at the students to be motivated [CTET 2016]
(a) to rote memorise so that they become good at recall
(b) by using punitive measures so that they respect the teacher
(c) to perform so that they get good marks in the end of the year examination
(d) to learn so that they become curious and love learning for its own sake

55 How is a teacher an independent variable? [UK BEd 2016]
(a) Teacher's behaviour is modified in order to modify the behaviour of pupils
(b) Teacher's behaviour can be studied in isolation in the class
(c) Teacher's behaviour can be measured
(d) All of the above

56 In what ways a teacher is similar to a doctor? [UK BEd 2016]
(a) Both of them diagnose the defects first then adopt remedial measures
(b) Both of them gives prescriptions
(c) Both of them study the effects of their prescription, i.e., a doctor studies the effects of drugs on the patients and a teacher evaluates his students to know the effectiveness of his teaching
(d) All of the above

57 Insightful learning is [CG BEd 2016]
(a) a goal based learning
(b) opposed to quantification of behaviour
(c) Both (a) and (b)
(d) None of the above

58 In order to become skillful in his job, a teacher [MP BEd 2016]
(a) should study new books on his subject
(b) should take part in the debates of the school
(c) should write on his subject
(d) All of the above

59 A teacher impresses his students [MP BEd 2016]
(a) by showing his authority and dominance
(b) by his regularity in teaching
(c) by misbehaving with his students
(d) by indulging in gossip with the students

Answers

1. (d)	2. (c)	3. (d)	4. (d)	5. (a)	6. (c)	7. (d)	8. (a)	9. (a)	10. (b)
11. (d)	12. (d)	13. (b)	14. (a)	15. (a)	16. (d)	17. (b)	18. (b)	19. (d)	20. (a)
21. (b)	22. (c)	23. (c)	24. (d)	25. (a)	26. (b)	27. (d)	28. (b)	29. (c)	30. (a)
31. (d)	32. (b)	33. (c)	34. (c)	35. (d)	36. (d)	37. (b)	38. (d)	39. (b)	40. (a)
41. (c)	42. (d)	43. (c)	44. (c)	45. (d)	46. (d)	47. (b)	48. (d)	49. (d)	50. (b)
51. (a)	52. (a)	53. (a)	54. (d)	55. (a)	56. (d)	57. (c)	58. (d)	59. (b)	

Aptitude Towards Teaching Work

Teaching is a process in which the learner achieves goals through this process by acquiring knowledge and skills, thus teaching develops human values.

Teaching aptitude is a natural process of teaching, in which a teacher tries to develop the student's behavior in accordance with the needs and views of the society.

Teaching aptitude includes different aspects in it. For example, teaching aptitude and attitude, aptitude towards curriculum, aptitude in school administration and supervision, aptitude and commitment to teaching profession, aptitude for problem of teaching and teaching support system, aptitude for teaching work, teacher qualification and in-depth study of properties, motivation and learning and communication and other inter-personal relationships, research, evaluation, etc.

Teaching Work

Whenever a system is created to motivate or conduct learning, the teaching work starts. Teaching is a very important link in the process of learning and education has to fulfill many responsibilities through various tasks. From the point of view of facilitating the study of teaching works, we can divide it into three parts

1. Functions related to classroom teaching
2. Functions related to teaching outside the classroom
3. Basic functions

Functions Related to Classroom Teaching

In the process of teaching, the teaching work that takes place inside the classroom is the most important. The teacher plays an important role in performing these tasks of teaching.

In a nutshell, the main functions related to classroom teaching are given below

- Organising the classroom.
- To analyse the textual content and functions.
- To solve the problems related to learning of students.
- To evaluate the educational qualifications of the students.
- To solve the problems related to aptitude, development and other educational problems.
- Determination and submission of courses for the achievement of learning objectives through assured methods.
- To formulate and select teaching plans and procedures.

- To understand students on the basis of their individual differences and to conduct their education accordingly.

Functions Related to Teaching Outside the Classroom

The teacher's work is not completed after the students are taught in the classroom. The process of teaching runs smoothly through mutual relations of society, school and family.

The process of teaching continues outside the classroom through sports, school trips, theatre, debating competitions, etc. So, there are important functions of teaching outside the classroom as well, which are as follows

- Organising the students for teaching related activities outside the classroom.
- Providing students with experience and independent practice opportunities to achieve mastery in various activities.
- To select and supervise diverse tasks outside the classroom according to individual differences of the students.
- To teach various activities and skills to the students as per the scheme of education.
- To undertake various activities for the all-round development of students and for the development of their personality.
- To evaluate students' activities outside the classroom.
- To provide necessary guidance to the students for improvement.

Basic Functions of Teaching

In addition to teaching functions outside and inside the classroom, there are some functions which are related to both types of teaching tasks. It is the responsibility of the teacher to coordinate these tasks and provide instruction to the students.

Teaching and learning both are such processes which are friendly and amicable and play a positive role in education.

This type of environment increases the feeling of safety and the path of education goes on smoothly. We find some new conclusions and theories from many research works done outside the classroom teaching.

We can understand the basic teaching functions through the following points

- Familiarise students with new research and theories.
- Directing students and trying to tie them up into a formula for classroom tasks and tasks outside the classroom.
- To provide safety to the students.
- Developing curriculum and training materials.
- To be familiar with new research and newly published material and literature.

Nature of Teaching Work

The general meaning of teaching is to impart knowledge of various subjects to children. Today, teaching has been made completely child-centric. It is very important to understand the nature of teaching in order to clarify the concept of teaching work, which is described as follows

1. **The Meaning of Teaching is Guidance**
   The work of teaching is not just to convey the information related to the text, rather teaching means to direct children's interests, habits, actions and tendencies in the right direction. **Raeburn** and **Risk** have stated that "Teaching should be defined as a demonstrator."

   From the perspective of guidance, the two main activities of teaching are to present the content of education and to guide the mental functioning of the children.

2. **Teaching Means the Organisation of Learning** Organisation of learning refers to the actions of teacher and students. All these actions involve all kinds of tasks, teaching methods and conditions.

   Thus, the organisation of learning refers to the unification of all the tools of the conditions of teaching work.

   Marshall believes that "Teaching is not the path of learning, but an organisation of learning".

3. **Teaching is a Three-fold Process** The three main points of teaching process are teachers, students and content. The process of teaching is only possible through mutual exchange of these three.

   According to **Raeburn**, "The more intimate the relationship between the teacher and the student, the more effective is the teaching".

   The teacher should take care of the following three things while teaching

   (i) The teacher should have full knowledge of the nature of the students.

   (ii) The teacher should also have full knowledge of himself.

   (iii) He should also have complete knowledge of the subject.

4. **Teaching Means to Provide Information** Teaching means to provide information to students. During the teaching process, the teacher gives the textual information to the students as well as other practical knowledge. Teachers who are proficient in story-telling method are able to convey these information to the students very effectively.

5. **Teaching Means to Teach** The work of teaching cannot be possible without being taught. Children cannot be imparted knowledge until they are ready to learn. The teacher's responsibility does not end only by giving information, but his responsibility is to prepare the children for learning.

   According to the **Warden**, "Teaching gives excitement, guidance and encouragement in learning".

6. **Harmony with the Environment** Society is dynamic. The physical, economic and social conditions of the society keep changing and in this environment the students have to live their life. Therefore, the objective of the teacher is not just to educate the students in the classroom, but to make them capable so that they develop the ability to harmonise with these situations of the society.

   In this regard, **Simson** believes that, "Teaching is the means by which society trains its children as quickly as possible in the process of adapting them to the chosen environment in which they want to live".

7. **Making the Child Active** An active child has an innate tendency and ability, which he expresses through his various tendencies and reactions. The teacher's job is to provide opportunities for the child's innate instincts to make him active.

   The teacher should educate the children in such a way that they can take full advantage of this activity. Through appropriate guidance, children can be engaged in purposeful and profitable activities suited to this tendency.

8. **Encouraging Children** Encouraging and inspiring children can be called an important function and meaning of teaching. Motivation and encouragement make the difficult task very easy.

   The teacher should find out the major interests and tendencies of the children and give them appropriate guidance, so that it is possible to form correct perceptions in the life of the children.

9. **To Train the Emotions of the Children** Teaching also means to train the emotions of the children. Psychologists fully agree that the majority of behavior of children is governed by their emotions. There should be a system to change and operate these emotions of the students in the teaching process. Many teaching related activities are helpful to control the emotions of children. It is possible to attract the emotions of children towards good things only through teaching. It can be concluded on the basis that the teacher has an important place in both the society and the education system.

The success of educational programs depends on the behaviour, methodology and abilities of the teacher. The teacher can awaken the new generation and their point of view by giving them information about social elements. Teaching is not just a result of the knowledge acquired in the relevant subject and the skill of teaching, because it is not just a mechanical process.

1 Which of the following is a process in which the learner achieves goals through this process by acquiring knowledge and skills?
   (a) Learning
   (b) Teaching
   (c) Communication
   (d) Subsequent education

2 Teaching aptitude is which type of process of teaching?
   (a) Natural   (b) Social
   (c) Spiritual   (d) Cognitive

3 Teaching aptitude includes which of the following aspects?
   (a) Teaching aptitude
   (b) Teaching attitude
   (c) Aptitude towards curriculum
   (d) All of the above

4 Which of the following takes place whenever a system is created to motivate or conduct learning?
   (a) Skill innovation
   (b) Educational innovation
   (c) Teaching works
   (d) Teaching attitude

5 Teachers are significant pillars of
   (a) societal culture
   (b) societal development
   (c) societal diplomacy
   (d) societal construct

6 Tender education helps in the development of teacher's
   (a) practicality   (b) accountability
   (c) proficiency   (d) motivation

7 Teaching skill helps the teacher to
   (a) plan and import instruction
   (b) conduct fullproof assessment
   (c) promote classroom management
   (d) All of the above

8 On the basis of facilitating the learning, teaching work is divided into how many types?
   (a) 5   (b) 4
   (c) 3   (d) 2

9 Who plays an important role in performing the teaching works?
   (a) Teacher
   (b) School administration
   (c) Students
   (d) Educational environment

10 Which of the following is the function related to the classroom?
  (a) Organising the classroom
  (b) To analyse the textual content and function
  (c) To solve the problems related to learning of the students
  (d) All of the above

11 Which of the following is true about functions related to the classroom?
  (a) It aims to evaluate educational qualifications of the students
  (b) It aims to formulate and select teaching plans and procedures
  (c) It aims to solve the problems related to aptitude, development and other educational problems
  (d) All of the above

12 Which process runs smoothly through mutual relations of society, school and family?
  (a) Learning process
  (b) Teaching process
  (c) Process of invovation
  (d) Process of skill

13 The process of teaching continues outside the classroom through
  (a) sports only　　　　(b) school trips only
  (c) theatre only　　　　(d) All of these

14 Which of the following is the function related to teaching outside the classroom?
  (a) Organising the students for teaching related activities outside the classroom
  (b) Providing students with experience and independent practice opportunities to achieve mastery in various activities
  (c) To select and supervise diverse tasks outside the classroom according to the individual differences of students
  (d) All of the above

15 Which of the following is true about functions related to teaching outside the classroom?
  (a) It aims to teach various activities and skills to the students as per the scheme of education
  (b) It aims to evaluate students' activities outside the classroom

  (c) It aims to provide necessary guidance to the students for improvement
  (d) All of the above

16 Which of the followng is such a process which is friendly, amicable and plays a positive role in education?
  (a) Teaching
  (b) Learning
  (c) Inductive method of teaching
  (d) Both (a) and (b)

17 Which of the following is the basic function of teaching works?
  (a) Familiarise students with new research and theories
  (b) Directing students and trying to tie them up into a formula for classroom tasks and tasks outside the classroom
  (c) To provide safety to the students
  (d) All of the above

18 Which of the following is true about basic functions of teaching works?
  (a) It aims to provide safety to students
  (b) It aims to develop curriculum and training materials
  (c) It aims to be familiar with new research and newly published material and literature
  (d) All of the above

19 The general meaning of teaching is to
  (a) impart knowledge of various subjects to children
  (b) to teach students perfectly
  (c) to develop different skills among students
  (d) All of the above

20 Today, teaching has been made completely
  (a) child-centric　　　　(b) subject-centric
  (c) teacher-centric　　　　(d) All of these

21 Which of the following is the meaning of teaching?
  (a) Teaching is guidance
  (b) Teaching is organisation of learning
  (c) Teaching is a a three-fold process
  (d) All of the above

22 Teaching means
  (a) to direct children's interests
  (b) to direct children's lakits
  (c) to direct children's actions
  (d) All of the above

23 Raeburn and Risk have stated that
(a) Teaching should be defined as a administrator
(b) Teaching should be defined as a performer
(c) Teaching should be defined as a demonstrator
(d) Teaching should be defined as a mediator

24 Main activity of teaching is
(a) to demonstrate the method of education
(b) to present the content of education
(c) to ensure the perfect learning
(d) to minimise the hurdleness in education

25 Organisation of learning refers to
(a) the actions of teacher and students
(b) the unification of all the tools of the conditions of teaching work
(c) Both (a) and (b)
(d) None of the above

26 The teacher should take care of which of the following things while teaching?
(a) The teacher should have full knowledge of the nature of the study
(b) The teacher should have full knowledge of himself
(c) The teacher should have complete knowledge of the subject
(d) All of the above

27 Teaching means to provide education to
(a) the students
(b) the colleagues
(c) the educators
(d) None of the above

28 The success of teaching will be considered only when
(a) the students accept the knowledge given by the teacher
(b) the students get good job
(c) the students become a successful person
(d) the students lead a peaceful life

29 According to Warden, teaching gives ...... in learning.
(a) excitement
(b) guidance
(c) encouragement
(d) All of these

30 The objective of the teacher is not just to educate the student but
(a) to make them a good citizen
(b) to make them a learned person
(c) to make them capable to develop the ability to harmonise with these situations of the society
(d) None of the above

31 The teacher's job is to
(a) provide opportunities for the child's innate instinct to make him active
(b) educate the children in such a way that they can take full advantage of activities
(c) provide guidance that children can be engaged in purposeful and profitable activities suited to their tendency
(d) All of the above

32 Major educationists such as Froebel and Monstessori have laid special emphasis on
(a) play way method in education
(b) learning in education
(c) activities in education
(d) teaching in education

Answers

1. (b)	2. (a)	3. (d)	4. (c)	5. (b)	6. (c)	7. (d)	8. (c)	9. (a)	10. (d)
11. (d)	12. (b)	13. (d)	14. (d)	15. (d)	16. (d)	17. (d)	18. (d)	19. (d)	20. (a)
21. (d)	22. (d)	23. (a)	24. (b)	25. (c)	26. (d)	27. (a)	28. (a)	29. (d)	30. (c)
31. (c)	32. (d)								

Teaching Aids and Support Materials

Teaching aids and support materials are very essential which make teaching-learning process easy and interesting. These are valuable resources and instrumental devices that help the teacher in carrying out the teaching-learning process.

These include textbooks, institutional magazines, journals, periodicals, etc. So, it is important to select such an effective teaching aid which could be useful in transmitting knowledge among the learners.

Need of Teaching Aids

- Teaching aids help in retaining concepts more permanently for those students who have the tendency to forget frequently.
- Teaching aids can motivate the students for learning and encourage them to develop deep insights of the matter.
- Students can easily learn and grasp the topic and the concept with the help of teaching aids.
- Teaching aids increase the understanding level of students by creating the proper image in the mind of students. Teaching aids help to increase the learning faster and accurate.
- It has been seen that visual effects create learning of permanent nature rather than audio effects. Teaching aids help the students learning through direct experience.

Significance of Teaching Aids

Clarification Through teaching aids the teachers clarify the subject matter more easily. Students can easily understand and generate a clear picture of the concept.

Classroom Live and Active Teaching aids play an important role to make the classroom live and active.

Learning from Direct Experience Students take the direct experience of teaching aids. They do not need to presume the things incorrectly, they can just learn by seeing the things.

Discouragement of Cramming Teaching aids can facilitate the proper understanding to the students which discourage the act of cramming.

Increase the Vocabulary Teaching aids help to increase the vocabulary of the students more effectively and efficiently. These help the students to learn the use of different new words.

Generate Motivation Teaching aids motivate the students to understand the study material. For instance, a concept-based movie will attract more audience than a speech on the similar topic.

Saves Time and Money Teaching aids are helpful to save time, money and energy of teachers as well as students. For instance, learn while playing exactly works for the kinder. So many play schools run on this concept.

Classification of Teaching Aids

Teaching aids can be classified in the following ways

Visual Aids

The traditional aids which involve the sense of vision are called visual aids. Types of visual aids are as follows

1. **Blackboard** In the absence of other teaching related tools, conversation and blackboard have an important place in teaching work. With the help of blackboard the teacher develops the comprehension ability in the students through symbols and words. Blackboard is the most useful aid material in traditional teaching system.

2. **Bulletin Board** It is a surface intended for the posting of public messages, for example, to advertise items wanted or for sale, announce events, or provide information in the classroom.

3. **Real Objects** These are very important in the teaching of students on the basis of perception of objects, the students get apparent experience. Objects like rocks, soils, minerals, etc., can be shown in the class.

4. **Newspapers** A teacher can use a newspaper for finding parts of speech, teaching about life skills, or to keep students up-to-date by current news events.

5. **Graphs** These are a wonderful teaching aids and can be used for any subject. Teachers can make their own graphs and use them for comparing population growth, numbers, ratios of objects, or even use them for charting students' growth.

6. **Maps** A map is something to use when a teacher is describing where a city, state, country or continent are located. Maps are great for social studies and science and give students a great understanding of spatial relations.

7. **Charts** A chart is a symbolised-visualised teaching support system with pictures of relationships and changes which are used to tabulate a large mass of information or show to progression.

   Charts can help to communicate different and dull subject matter in an interesting and effective way. They are also helpful in summarising information and presenting abstract ideas in visual form.

8. **Magnetic Board** It can be a sheet of template and simply a type of chalk board, the surface of which is coated with porcelain like substance.

   The base of the board is steel and pictures and objects can be pasted or mounted with small magnets and can easily be moved about.

   Here, objects can be moved across the board easily to show the movement.

9. **Three Dimensional Model** Real things may not be available all the time and in the desired form. Three Dimensional Model helps to overcome this problem. A model is a recognisable representation of real things in three dimensional view such as height, width and depth. This makes understanding better and easy.

   They are long lasting and inexpensive, so it is used in high class teaching institutes.

10. **Power Point Presentation** It is a computer programme that allows the presenter to create and show slide to support his presentation. Here, one can combine text, graphics and content to create professional presentation.

    Through Power Point Presentation, one can easily explain the context by showing a particular slide. It can be used for teaching various concepts. Many teachers take support of PPT and through this they can deliver their concepts well to students.

Audio Aids

The aids which involve the sense of hearing are called audio aids. These are the modern teaching aids. Types of modern teaching support systems are as follows

1. **Radio** Teachers have explored the use of radio in the classroom almost since radio technology entered into the mainstream of society. Radio offers teachers a large amount of authentic sound documents to use in the classroom.
   Examples are Gyan-Vani (educational FM Radio Channel of India).

2. **Digital Audio Player** A digital audio player is sometimes referred to as MP3 player and has the primary function of storing, organising and playing audio files.

   Some digital audio players are also referred to as portable media players as they have image viewing and video playing support. An ideal example is iPod, a fourth generation audio instructional facility. Through this, teachers can store their teachings and later students can listen this repeatedly to learn more effectively.

Audio-Visual Aids

The aids which involve the sense of hearing as well as the sense of vision are known as audio-visual aids. They are most effective and useful than other teaching aids as they use more than one sense simultaneously. These are ICT based teaching support systems.

Types of ICT based teaching support systems are as follows

1. **Television** It is used to communicate information, ideas, skills and attitudes. It enhances and reduces the dependency on verbal teaching and teachers. It provides mass education opportunities.

2. **Computer/Laptop** These are the good examples of ICT based teaching support system. Computer/Laptop can be defined as any electronic device that allows students to access the internet to research, create and complete the work. These are greatly used for teaching purposes nowadays.
   Well-constructed programmes have the capacity to realistically present material which would not be available by other teaching methods.

3. **Films Strips and Films** Knowledge about various functions, discoveries and other information related to subject can be imparted with the help of film strips and films.
   In the film strips and films each subject is given in systematic sequence and in detail and it gives clear knowledge of the subject.

4. **Multimedia** Multimedia classroom provides students a chance for interacting with diverse texts that give them a solid background in tasks and content of mainstream courses. It includes sources like media, audio, video, films, etc.

5. **Pen Tab** It is a digital drawing tablet. It is a computer input device that enables the user to draw images, animations and graphics with special pen like stylus similar to the way person draws images with the use of wooden or plastic pencil.
   It is also known as graphic tablet. It is useful in displaying the matter while one speaks the words which are written on the monitor. Today, many teachers and professors are using this technique as it gives a feeling of online class.

1 Teaching aids can help teachers to make
   (a) teaching less burdensome
   (b) teaching interesting
   (c) content easy and concrete
   (d) lesson seem fancy

2 Which of the following is true about teaching aids?
   (a) These can motivate the students for learning and encourage them to develop deep insights of the matter
   (b) Students can easily learn and grasp the topic and the concept with the help of teaching aids
   (c) These help to increase the learning faster and accurate
   (d) All of the above

3 An effective teaching aid is one which
   (a) is visible to all the students
   (b) is easy to prepare and use
   (c) is colourful and good looking
   (d) activates all senses of students

4 Which of the following best describes the significance of teaching aids?
   (a) These make classroom live and active
   (b) Students take the direct experience of teaching aids
   (c) These help to discourage act of cramming
   (d) All of the above

5 Which of the following is not true?
   (a) Teaching aids decrease vocabulary
   (b) Teaching aids generate motivation among students
   (c) Teaching aids save time and money
   (d) Teaching aids discourage cramming

6 Which of the following is/are included in teaching aids?
   (a) Textbooks   (b) Magazines
   (c) Periodicals   (d) All of these

7 Which of the following is the most useful aid material in traditional teaching system?
   (a) Blackboard   (b) Radio
   (c) Computer   (d) Pentab

8 For a teacher, which of the following methods would be correct for writing on the blackboard?
   (a) Not writing not important points as clearly as possible

   (b) Writing important points as clearly as possible
   (c) Writing fast and as clearly as possible
   (d) None of the above

9 Which of the following aids is based to advertise items wanted or for sale or announce events or provide information in the classroom?
   (a) Blackboard   (b) PPT
   (c) Bulletin Board   (d) Graphs

10 Real objects include
   (a) Pieces of rocks   (b) sample of soils
   (c) sample of minerals (d) All of these

11 A teacher can use newspaper for
   (a) Finding parts of speech
   (b) Teaching about life skills
   (c) Keeping students up-to-date by current news and events
   (d) All of the above

12 Graphs can be used for
   (a) Comparing population growth
   (b) Locating ratios of objects
   (c) Charting student's growth
   (d) All of the above

13 Maps are useful for which subjects?
   (a) Psychology   (b) Science
   (c) Social Science   (d) Both (b) and (c)

14 The use of teaching aids is justified if there is
   (a) effective engagement of students in learning
   (b) optimised learning outcomes
   (c) attracting student's attention
   (d) minimised indiscipline problems

15 .... is a symbolised-visualised teaching aid with pictures of relationships and changes which are used to tabulate a large mass of information or show to progression.
   (a) Maps   (b) Newspapers
   (c) Chart   (d) PPT

16 With the help of which teaching aid, pictures and objects can be moved about?
   (a) Blackboard   (b) Graphs
   (c) Charts   (d) Magnetic board

17 A PPT file contains
  (a) images   (b) sentences
  (c) sounds   (d) All of these

18 You are planning to teach human anatomy. The most suitable teaching aid would be to
  (a) show them MS Power Point Presentations and videos depicting location and functions of part of the human body
  (b) show the learner's model of the human body
  (c) read from the text and simultaneously explaining verbally
  (d) Put up a chart on human anatomy

19 Which of the following is an example of radio channel?
  (a) Prasar Bharti
  (b) Krishi Darshan
  (c) Gyan-Vani
  (d) Topper learning

20 A teacher uses audio-visual aids and physical activities in her teaching because these
  (a) provide relief to the teacher
  (b) facilitate effective assessment
  (c) utilise maximum number of senses to enhance learning
  (d) provide a diversion to learners

21 Which teaching aids have the ability to engage the students in subjective activities and enhance their cognitive skills?
  (a) Traditional teaching aids
  (b) Modern teaching aids
  (c) ICT based teaching aids
  (d) None of the above

22 Which of the following defines the use of television?
  (a) It enhances and reduces the dependency on verbal teaching and teachers
  (b) It is used to communicate information, ideas, skills and attitudes
  (c) It provides mass education opportunities
  (d) All of the above

23 Any electronic device that allows students to access the internet to research, create and complete the work is known as
  (a) Television   (b) Computer
  (c) Film strips   (d) PPT

24 In which teaching aid each subject is given in systematic sequence and in detail?
  (a) Television   (b) Computer
  (c) Film strips   (d) Pen tab

25 In which teaching aid images, animations and graphics are drawn with a special pen like styles
  (a) Computer   (b) Film strips
  (c) Pen tab   (d) PPT

26 Which one of the following is irrelevent when a teacher desires to adopt ICT based teaching-learning approach for students? **[KVS TGT 2017]**
  (a) There should be internet connection available so that students can explore
  (b) There must be compatibility between content and technology
  (c) The students must be able to use available ICT devices
  (d) The knowledge of students gained through ICT devices must be assured in examinations.

27 The most important factor in effective teaching process is **[BHU BEd 2017]**
  (a) Payment of time displayed by teachers and students
  (b) Teacher subject matter
  (c) Teacher-students dialogues
  (d) Completion of course on time

28 Effectiveness of teaching has to be judged in terms of **[UK BEd 2018]**
  (a) course coverage
  (b) student's interest
  (c) learning outcomes of students
  (d) use of teaching aids in the classroom

Answers

1.	(b)	2.	(d)	3.	(d)	4.	(d)	5.	(a)	6.	(d)	7.	(a)	8.	(b)	9.	(c)	10.	(d)
11.	(d)	12.	(d)	13.	(d)	14.	(a)	15.	(c)	16.	(d)	17.	(d)	18.	(a)	19.	(c)	20.	(c)
21.	(c)	22.	(d)	23.	(b)	24.	(c)	25.	(c)	26.	(d)	27.	(d)	28.	(c)				

Chapter 10

Teaching Methods and Innovation

Methods of teaching are directly related to the presentation of the lesson. Which method a teacher should use depends on the nature of the subject matter and the ability of the learners. There are a variety of teaching methods which can be used by the teacher for teaching theory and skills in the classroom setting. These are broadly classified as

1. Teacher centred teaching methods
2. Learner centred teaching methods

Teacher Centred Teaching Methods

Lecture Method

Lecture method is one of the most commonly used and oldest methods of teaching. It is a method of teaching whereby the teacher attempts to explain facts, principles and relationships to help students to understand the concepts.

In this method, the teacher is an active participant and students are passive listeners.

The teacher talks more or less continuously in the class. The class listens, writes and notes facts and the ideas for remembering and to think them over later. Usually, the students do not converse with the teacher during lecture by the teacher. It is a one way method. A few questions may be asked by the students to clarify a point but no discussion is usually held.

Merits

- It is economical; a single teacher can teach a large number of students at a time which is not possible by using other methods.
- It saves much time and the syllabus can be very easily covered within a limited time.
- It simplifies the work of the teacher. The teacher has to put much less efforts to prepare his/her lessons and can develop the presentation according to his/her plan.
- She/he needs not worry for demonstrating a procedure.
- It is useful for imparting factual information and drawing attention to its vital elements. It gives a feeling of security to the teacher.
- Interruptions and distractions are avoided.

Demerits

- Provides very little opportunity for student activity, unless the teacher takes special care to make the class interesting.
- Does not facilitate learning or how to solve problem.
- Offers limited opportunities for checking learning progress, whether the students are attending and understanding all that the teacher is explaining.
- The interests, abilities and intelligence of students are not taken care of.
- Does not consider individual pace of learning.

- The rate of imparting information by the teacher may be too fast for the learner to get necessary connection of thought.

Biographical Method

In this method of teaching, some biographies are used to analyse the author's personal life.

In this method, teachers' role become significant and learners play their inductive role in learning process.

Merits

- It is used to tackle pedagogical difficulties associated with the increasing marketisation of higher education and the depoliticised attitudes of the students.
- It is suitable at higher level of teaching where students are capable to reach at an inference on their own.

Demerits

- Students can be damaged by engaging openly and publicly with curricula that asks them to draw on their own biographies.
- Students sometimes get diverted into learning criminological theories and end up being criminal later.

TV or Video Presentation

It is an improved presentation of radio or audio presentation and it can virtually bring the whole world inside the classroom. Screening of video presentation is followed by discussion or task.

Merits

- Specifically useful for adult learners.
- Easily accessible for learners in remote areas.
- Specifically useful for subjects, such as geography and astronomy.
- Many important personalities and experts are brought to the classroom through video presentations.

Demerits

- Less possibility for two-way communication.
- There can be difficulty in adjusting the complicate schedules to telecast the presentation video.

Team Teaching Method

Team Teaching involves a group of instructors working purposefully, regularly and cooperatively to help a group of students.

In this method of teaching, teachers set goals for course, design a syllabus, prepare individual lesson plans, teach students and evaluate the results.

The team teaching method allows for more interaction between teachers and students. Teachers evaluate students on their achievement of the learning goals and students evaluate teachers on their teaching proficiency.

The team teacher's main contribution is that the pupils can have maximum opportunities of facing maximum specialists.

Working in teams spreads responsibility, encourages creativity, deepens friendships and builds community among teachers. Hence, the pupils can gain the advantage of specific knowledge of different teachers.

Merits

- It provides stimulus to the ideas of the pupils and teachers.
- It develops strong will and responsibility of participation among the pupils and teachers.
- It is very economical in terms of time and energy.

Demerits

- In this method many teachers are required.
- It is not useful for all subjects.
- It requires much time for planning and scheduling.

Learner Centred Teaching Methods

In learner centred methods of teaching, teachers and students play an equally active role in the learning process. Following are the learner's centred methods of teaching

Laboratory Method

The laboratory method is a planned learning activity dealing with original or raw data in the solution of a problem. It is a procedure involving first hand experiences with materials or facts derived from investigations or experimentation.

The primary aim of laboratory method is to give first-hand experience to the students.

Merits

- It is used to designate a teaching procedure in physical sciences that use experimentation with apparatus.
- It builds scientific attitude and sense of achievement among learners.

Demerits

- It is not suitable for all the subjects because all knowledge cannot be verified through experiments.
- It is effective only in a small group.

Project Method

Project method is one of the modern methods of teaching in which the student's point of view is given importance in designing the curricula and content of studies. This method was devised by Dr. William H. Kilpatrick. This method is based on the Pragmatic Educational Philosophy of John Dewey, the noted American Philosopher-cum-Educationist.

It is based on the principle of 'learning by doing'. In this strategy, pupils perform constructive activities in natural condition, realistic and experiential. Project method of teaching encourages the spirit of scientific enquiry as it involves validation of hypothesis based on evidence gathered from field through investigation.

Merits

- It takes the student beyond the walls of the classroom and makes learning realistic and experimental.
- It encourages the spirit of scientific enquiry as it involves validation of hypothesis based on evidence gathered from field through investigation.
- It allows the students a great degree of freedom to choose from the options given to them, hence it provides a psychological boost.

Demerits

- It is time consuming and can be extended endlessly.
- It requires meticulous planning and execution otherwise it can give unreliable results.
- There can be many uncontrolled social or natural factors which may affect the outcome of the project.
- In the absence of effective and alert supervision, a student may take unreliable data.

Assignment Method

This method is an instructional technique which comprises of guided information, self-learning, writing skills and report preparation among the learners.

It is important to note that the assignment must be lesson concerned and related with the textbook and curriculum.

The assignment must be explained with the availability of resources. The tough and difficult portions of the assignment need to be explained well.

Merits

- It provides information analysis and research attitude to the learners.
- It develops the learning experiences from various sources.
- It inculcates the self-learning attitude among the students.

Demerits

- There are always chances of plagiarism and increased chances of copy-paste.
- The slow learners need much more attention from the teacher, again it gives more burden to the teacher.
- The time limit given threatens the students which makes the sub-standard work.

Discussion Method

Discussion method of teaching is a group activity involving the teacher and the student to define the problem and seek its solution.

This method is also described as a constructive process involving listening, thinking as well as the speaking ability of the students.

Merits

- It allows learners to take responsibility of their own learning, thus making them more mature and independent learners.
- It facilitates student reflection on what they learnt.
- It provides freedom of decision-making and forming judgements.

Demerits

- It is highly time-consuming.
- It may lead to invalid and illogical interference.
- It encourages the dominance of a few members from the group of learners.

Brainstorming Method

It is a group creativity technique by which efforts are made to find conclusion for a specific problem by gathering a list of ideas spontaneously contributed by its members.

The term was popularised by Alex Faickney Osborn in the 1953 book 'Applied Imagination'.

According to him, people are able to think more freely and they suggest many spontaneous new ideas as possible. All the ideas are noted down and are not criticised and after brainstorming session the ideas are evaluated.

Merits

- It popularises the group method of finding ideas.
- It applies to solve the goal of the group.
- It provides platform for everyone to speak and to create ideas.
- It is very economical.

Demerits

- It may lead to constant arguing due to virtues.
- Team members who have displayed creativity are more likely to succeed.
- It can be over-applied easily.
- It is not a very systematic way of studying a subject.

Seminar Method

It is a method in which a group of people come together for discussion and learn specific techniques and topics.

Usually, there are several keynote speakers within each seminar and these speakers are usually experts in their own fields or topics.

Merits

- A wealth of knowledge, usually presented by many speakers at a time, at one place.
- In this method, individuals can meet to others with same interests/problems or concerns.
- It is a great way for those who do not like to read, or attend classes, to improve their knowledge of a specific subject.

Demerits

- There are chances that the speakers share the incorrect knowledge.
- It is time consuming as well as costly.
- There are chances that attendees will expect too much from a seminar and may be disappointed.

Question-Answer Teaching Method

Question answer teaching strategy is an old strategy also known as "Socratic Method of Teaching". It was developed by the famous philosopher Socrates.

According to **Parke**, "The question is the key to all educative activities above the habit-skill level".

Its strategy is focused on achieving the cognitive objectives and bringing knowledge to the conscious level.

Merits

- While asking questions, the teacher keeps in mind the abilities, needs and interest of the learner.
- It involves learners' participation towards the subject- matter and teaching acts.
- It helps in achieving cognitive objectives and bringing knowledge at conscious level.
- With the help of this method, classroom verbal interaction is encouraged between teacher and students. It is a useful strategy at all the levels of education.

Demerits

- It is difficult to prepare good questions and arrange them logically. The whole content-matter cannot be taught by this strategy.
- The teacher wants structured answers from the learners. There is no freedom for imaginative answers.

Demonstration Method

Demonstration is a method of teaching by exhibition and explanation. It implies presentation of organised series of events or equipments to a group of students for their observation. Through this method a teacher can explain salient features, utility, efficiency of each article, each step of a procedure, experiment and so on.

Merits

- Activates several senses and provides better learning opportunity.
- Provides opportunities for developing observational skills.
- Commands interest by use of concrete illustration.
- Helps to correlate theory with practical.
- Serves as strong motivational force. The student has the opportunity to gain knowledge and apply it immediately.

Demerits

- Not useful if students are inattentive.
- Teacher may be tempted to waste time in exploration.
- Students may blindly follow the laboratory manual or the procedure sheets.
- Discussion may not be encouraged.

Role Play Method

Role play is defined as the spontaneous acting of roles in the context of clearly defined social situations by two or more persons for subsequent discussions by the whole class.

The role play is the medium to express one's opinion and feelings about certain social situation, what people can think, feel and why do they behave and what can be done to handle the situations through presentation and discussion in the group.

This method, thus can generate data about human behaviour and human relations which are not available by traditional methods.

Merits

- It is energising.
- It helps the suppressed and illiterates to express their feelings.
- It is simple and low cost.
- It focuses on problems which are very real in nature.
- It does not need material or advance preparation.

Demerits

- There is a possibility of it becoming entertainment which interferes learning.
- Participants can get too involved in their roles and later loose objectivity during analysis.
- Acting can become an end in itself and participants correct or distort the roles.
- That the observers need to observe must be explained clearly or else the discussion, which occurs later on the basis of this observation will be inadequate.

Innovation in Education

The literal meaning of 'innovation' is 'new conduct' or 'behavior'. Innovation is that which brings change and innovation. The new ideas, concepts, experiments, etc., which are developed in the education and training of the instructor, all come under the category of innovation.

Innovation is not just change, it is an idea for which discovery and practice are made to achieve a particular objective. Innovations and their use give effected conclusions after meeting the test and experiment. Therefore, it can also be called science.

Various scholars have given the following definitions of innovation

According to **Rogers**, "That thought, method and known objectives have been called innovation that which the individual considers to be the purpose."

According to **Prof. Uday Pareek and TV Rao**, "Innovation refers to the new idea or method which a person or system has found useful for the fulfillment of some purpose."

Need of Innovation in Teaching Method

Teacher is the part of the society, which is a factor of change through education. Both the school and the teacher take influence from their environment.

There is a close relationship between teacher training and school education, both of which affect each other. Effective teacher training ensures the quality of school education. The need for innovation in teaching education can be seen in the following contexts

- To make teaching change with the times.
- For qualitative and quantitative development in education.
- To make education technological.
- For the development of expression ability and teaching skills.
- To enable the student-teachers to impart direct knowledge.
- To make student-teachers active.
- To inculcate healthy attitude in the student teachers.
- To establish coordination between teacher education institutions and schools.
- To bring innovation in teaching methods.
- To fulfill social aspirations and expectations.
- For the dissemination of scientific and technical knowledge.
- For the purpose of education, for the development of minimum content in its curriculum.

Importance of Innovation in Teaching Method

- Through innovation, teachers are able to give joyful and interesting education to the children by removing from them the cumbersome, boring and uninteresting teaching.
- It helps the teacher to adop a constructive, responsible, concrete and practical approach towards his work.
- Through innovation, the teacher can develop new competencies by breaking the traditional educational inertia.
- Through innovation, teachers themselves become creative and studious.

- Innovation leads to educational revival of the teacher.
- Student teacher can make necessary preparation and effective implementation for carrying out practical tasks in teaching.
- Make the best use of existing resources of the school and community through innovation.
- The student-teacher will be able to understand the concept of continuous and comprehensive evaluation.
- Organisation of post-teaching activities is possible only through innovation.
- Through innovation, student-teachers can learn the process of child-centred approach and activity based teaching-learning.

1. There are variety of teaching methods which can be used by the teacher for teaching theory and skills in the classroom setting. These are broadly classified as
(a) Teacher-centred teaching methods
(b) Student-centred teaching methods
(c) Learning-centred teaching methods
(d) Both (a) and (b)

2 Which of the following is considered as the oldest teaching method?
(a) Lecture method
(b) Demonstration method
(c) Seminar method
(d) Micro-teching method

3 The lecture method is useful when a teacher is dealing with
(a) small group   (b) junior group
(c) large group   (d) training group

4 Which of the following should a teacher adopt in a lecture?
(a) Elongated tone
(b) Precise and low tone
(c) Moderate tone
(d) Precise and high tone

5 The lecture method is an effective way to
(a) introduce a new skill
(b) assess understanding of learners
(c) stimulate participation of learners
(d) introduce new information / concepts

6 Lecture as a teaching method can be more effective if a teacher
(a) enriches the content of lectures with appropriate examples from other discipline
(b) teaches extempore
(c) reads from his/her notes
(d) uses prepared pointers and organises discussions around the same

7 While delivering a lecture if there is some disturbance in the class then a teacher should
(a) keep quiet for a while and then go on
(b) punish those causing the disturbance
(c) not bother about what is happening in the class
(d) All of the above

8 What is/are the advantage(s) of Lecture Method?
(a) It is economical
(b) It saves time and syllabus
(c) Gives feeling of security to the teacher
(d) All of the above

9 We can make lecture strategy a success by   **[CG BEd 2016]**
(a) presenting the content in a logical sequence with force
(b) making the language of the content easy
(c) adding visual aids to the lecture
(d) All of the above

10 Students are passive in   **[IGNOU BEd 2017]**
(a) project method   (b) discovery method
(c) lecture method   (d) inquiry method

11 We can make lecture strategy a success by   **[UK BEd 2016]**
(a) presenting the content in a logical sequence with force
(b) making the language of the content easy
(c) adding visual aids to the lecture
(d) All of the above

12 While delivering lecture in the class a teacher   **[CG B Ed 2016]**
(a) must give illustrations to clarify the difficult points
(b) take the help of notes
(c) deliver long lectures
(d) All of the above

13 A teacher cannot avoid which of the following strategies at any cost?   **[CG BEd 2016]**
(a) Lecture   (b) Exposition
(c) Textbook   (d) Both (a) and (b)

14 Teacher plays only the role of a guide and helper in   **[UK BEd 2016]**
(a) discussion method
(b) analysis and synthesis methods
(c) inductive and deductive methods
(d) All of the above

15 Team teaching has the potential to develop
(a) cooperation
(b) competitive spirit
(c) highlighting the gaps in each other's teaching
(d) the habit of supplementing the teaching of each other

16 Team teaching   **[IGNOU BEd 2019]**
(a) involves teams of teachers to optimise resources, interest and expertise
(b) is a way out to manage with the shortage of teachers
(c) encourage healthy competition among teams of teachers in a school
(d) involves small teams of students as per their ability

17 Which of the following methods has a primary aim to give first-hand experience to students?
(a) Team-teaching method
(b) Laboratory method
(c) Demonstration method
(d) Seminar method

18 In order to promote direct learning, which of the following methods would be best suited?
(a) Project method
(b) Team teaching method
(c) Discussion method
(d) Lecture method

19 Which method was devised by Dr. William H. Kilpatrick?
(a) Role Play method
(b) Seminar method
(c) Demonstration method
(d) Project method

20 Which method is based on the Pragmatic Educational Philosophy of John Dewey ?
(a) Lecture method
(b) Demonstration method
(c) Project method
(d) Seminar method

21 Which of the following points is not a step involved in a project method?
(a) Recording
(b) Planning
(c) Estimation
(d) Choosing and purposing

22 Which of the following is the characteristic of project method?

(a) Purposeful, natural and life like activity to attain goals
(b) Whole hearted activity which results in concrete and positive results
(c) Problem centred activity
(d) All of the above

23 The task in which the children get experience, while enjoying themselves is known as **[IGNOU BEd 2019]**

(a) consumer type task
(b) producer type task
(c) problem type task
(d) drill and practice task

24 Project teaching method is associated with **[IGNOU BEd 2019]**

(a) Froebel
(b) John Dewey
(c) Armstrong
(d) McDougal

25 As a teacher, who firmly believes in Social Constructivist Theory of Lev Vygotsky, which of the following methods would you prefer for assessing your students? **[CTET 2016]**

(a) Standardised tests
(b) Fact-based recall questions
(c) Objective multiple-choice type questions
(d) Collaborative projects

26 Emphasises activity based on teaching **[CG BEd 2017]**

(a) disciplined class
(b) to complete the activity in a fixed time period
(c) active participation by all students
(d) to take the exam after the end of the activity

27 Use of methods where learner's own initiative and efforts are involved is an example of **[CTET 2019]**

(a) traditional method
(b) inter-personal intelligence
(c) deductive method
(d) learner centred method

28 Which of the following is the advantage of assignment method?

(a) It provides information analysis and research attitude to the learners
(b) It provides the learning experiences from various sources
(c) It inculcates the self-learning attitude among the students
(d) All of the above

29 A teacher can achieve maximum involvement of the students in developing the lesson through

(a) lecture method
(b) use of teaching aids
(c) discussion method
(d) demonstration method

30 Discussion in class will be more effective if the topic of discussion is

(a) not introduced
(b) stated before the start of the discussion
(c) written on the board without introducing it
(d) informed to the students in advance

31 Which of the following is not a demerit of discussion method?

(a) It requires more time and effort of both teachers and students
(b) It may involve unnecessary arguments
(c) It may create emotional stress
(d) Simulating thinking process

32 Which of the following methods stimulates students' thinking process to analyse and integrate facts and help in developing their abilities in presentation of their ideas and facts clearly and fluently?

(a) Lecture method
(b) Seminar method
(c) Discussion method
(d) Demonstration method

33 Which one of the following is not a merit of the Discussion method ?

(a) Analysis and integration of facts, ideas and concepts
(b) Stimulating thinking process
(c) Discovering talented students
(d) It is suitable for all the topics

34 In which form of discussion a teacher acts as the Chairman?
(a) Classroom discussion
(b) Formal group discussion
(c) Both (a) and (b)
(d) None of the above

35 Which of the following is the most effective method to encourage conceptual development in students? [CTET 2016]
(a) Replace the student's incorrect ideas with correct ones by asking them to memorise
(b) Give students multiple examples and encourage them to use reasoning
(c) Use punishment till students have made the required conceptual changes
(d) New concepts need to be understood on their own without any reference to the old ones

36 The purpose of which method is to provide opportunity to students to actively participate in finding answers to questions or solutions to problems using scientific approach of doing analysis and synthesis of facts observed?
(a) Conference method
(b) Seminar method
(c) Demonstration method
(d) None of the above

37 Effectiveness of Seminar depends upon
(a) Preparation of the topic
(b) Selection of the topic
(c) Participation of students
(d) Both (a) and (b)

38 Which of the following is not an advantage of seminar method?
(a) It gives training in self-learning
(b) It provides independent thinking
(c) It promotes team spirit and cooperative attitude
(d) All of the above

39 Which of the following is not a disadvantage of seminar method?
(a) It consumes considerable time in presentation
(b) It consumes considerable time in planning
(c) There are chances that the speakers share incorrect knowledge
(d) All of the above

40 If a seminar is being conducted in your city concerning education, what will you do?
(a) I will take part in it without the permission of the principal
(b) I shall seek the permission of the principal
(c) I shall take leave from the school
(d) I shall take no interest in it

41 Good teaching is best reflected by
(a) attendance of students
(b) number of distinctions
(c) pin drop silence in the class
(d) meaningful questions asked by students

42 Questioning in teaching is most useful in
(a) ensuring active participation of learners in the class
(b) rote memorisation of facts by the learners
(c) disciplining the learners
(d) preparing learners for examination

43 To evaluate student's performance a good question is best technique, but questioning should have a good characteristic of question. What is good characteristic of question one ask?
(a) Totally depend upon goal
(b) Question should be from questionnaire field
(c) Limitation of answer must be defined
(d) All of the above

44 Should student be allowed to ask questions in the class? [MP BEd 2016]
(a) No
(b) Yes
(c) Sometimes
(d) As per the wish of the teacher

45 When factual information from the responded is needed which tool is used? [UK BEd 2016]
(a) Questionnaire
(b) Interview
(c) Both (a) and (b)
(d) None of the above

46 Open end questionnaire consists of those questions which require [UK CG BEd 2016]
(a) long and narrative responses
(b) free responses on the part of the respondents
(c) factual information
(d) None of the above

47 Questions are asked in the class.
                    [UK BEd 2016]
(a) to introduce a lesson
(b) to develop a lesson
(c) to arouse curiosity of pupils
(d) All of the above

48 Assumption of questioning strategy is
that   [UK BEd 2016]
(a) knowledge can be drawn out from within
    the individual by asking questions
(b) questions can arouse curiosity of pupils
(c) they are the means to develop interaction
    between the teacher and pupils
(d) All of the above

49 Which of the following points should be
kept in view in order to make questioning
strategy a success?   [UK BEd 2016]
(a) Every question must be related to the
    next one
(b) Pupils should be given full freedom to
    ask questions in the class
(c) No such questions should be asked whose
    answers start with yes or no
(d) All of the above

50 What instructions should a teacher give
to the students to seek the answer to the
questions?   [MP BEd 2016]
(a) Seek the answer to the questions
(b) Ask the answers to the questions from
    the teachers
(c) Tell the answer yourself
(d) Find out the answer from your superior
    colleagues

51 Mailed questionnaire is used when
                    [CG BEd 2016]
(a) sample is scattered to a wide area
(b) cost is problem for the investigator
(c) respondent is well educated
(d) All of the above

52 In informal interviews   [CG BEd 2016]
(a) number and sequence of questions are
    not determined
(b) method of scoring is fixed
(c) everything depends on the situation
(d) All of the above

53 Demonstration strategy is not useful for
                    [CG BEd 2016]
(a) teacher training colleges
(b) science students
(c) achieving psychomotor objectives
(d) teaching arts and crafts

54 Which one of the following is the best
method of teaching?
(a) Discussion   (b) Demonstration
(c) Lecture   (d) Narration

55 If the focus of learning is to increase
skills, the most suitable method of
teaching would be
(a) learning by doing (b) demonstration
(c) discussion   (d) All of these

56 Demonstration refers to a teaching
method in which learners
(a) do the process on their own
(b) work in groups and complete the process
(c) read from the text and internalise the
    steps of the process
(d) are provided with an opportunity to
    observe for themselves the object or
    processes that they wish to learn

57 Which of the following methods of
teaching is defined as a method of
teaching by exhibition and explanation?
(a) Seminar method
(b) Lecture method
(c) Demonstration method
(d) None of the above

58 Which of the following is not a limitation
of demonstration method?
(a) Not useful if students are inattentive
(b) Teacher may be tempted to waste time
    in exploration
(c) Discussion may not be encouraged
(d) Provide opportunity to develop
    observation skills

59 Demonstration effect means
                    [IGNOU BEd 2017]
(a) effect of advertisement
(b) imitating effect of consumption
(c) effect of entertainment
(d) effect of an experiment

60 In demonstration strategy, pupils drill
the acquired knowledge by [UK BEd 2016]
(a) asking questions from the teacher
(b) repeating the demonstration in the class
(c) conducting experiments in the laboratory
(d) doing homework

61 Which method of teaching can generate
data about human behaviour and human
relations which are not available by
traditional methods?
(a) Seminar method
(b) Discussion method
(c) Role play method
(d) Demonstration method

62 What is the key point that need to be
kept in mind while teaching through role
play method?
(a) Role play should be brief
(b) Encourage students to take notes while
watching
(c) Both (a) and (b)
(d) None of the above

63 A class V teacher directs students to a
role play to introduce the concept of
interdependence and harmony in
relationships. Which of the following
instruments would help him/her
determine the quality of role play by
students?   [KVS BEd 2017]
(a) Socio-metry
(b) Face-to-face interview
(c) Questionnaire
(d) Rating scale

64 In order to make story telling strategy a
success what should a teacher do?
[CG BEd 2016]
(a) Story should be made interesting by
communication skills and gestures
(b) Naturals sequence in the story should be
maintained
(c) Characters of the story should properly
elaborated and compared to the present
life situations
(d) All of the above

65 In order to make story telling strategy a
success what should a teacher do?
[UK BEd 2016]
(a) Story should be made interesting by
communication skills and gestures
(b) Natural sequence in the story should be
maintained
(c) Characters of the story should properly
elaborated and compared to the present
life situations
(d) All of the above

66 A field trip is arranged for
[IGNOU BEd 2017]
(a) making an excursion
(b) see other people doing things
(c) note the meaning of action
(d) All of the above

67 It can safely be assumed that a student
understands a principle when he/she can
[IGNOU BEd 2017]
(a) give more examples of it
(b) use it in solving problems to which it
applies
(c) recognise it again when he/she
encounters it again
(d) recall the principles as and when asked

68 Brainstorming Model of Teaching is used
to improve which of the following?
[IGNOU BEd 2019]
(a) Understanding
(b) Application
(c) Creativity
(d) Problem-solving

69 If the students are not taking interest in
the lesson, the teacher should
[IGNOU BEd 2019]
(a) change the method of teaching
(b) use audio-video aids to make the lesson
interesting
(c) leave the class
(d) begin a new work/task in the classroom

70 Imitative learning technique is
considered as   [BHU BEd 2017]
(a) Skill
(b) Theatrical method or technique
(c) Game method
(d) None of the above

71 Activity based teaching emphasises on
[BHU BEd 2017]
(a) disciplined class
(b) to complete the activity in a fixed time period
(c) active participation by all students
(d) to take the exam after the end of the activity

72. Which of the following is emphasised in teaching strategy? [CG BEd 2016]
(a) Application of psychology
(b) Application of natural science
(c) Application of technology
(d) All of the above

73 Purpose of teaching method is the effective presentation of the subject matter while the purpose of teaching strategy is [CG BEd 2016]
(a) creating conducive learning environment
(b) realisation of objectives
(c) increasing the interaction of the teacher and pupils
(d) All of the above

74 Eminent learning technique is considered
[CG BEd 2017]
(a) skill
(b) theatrical perimeter
(c) game method
(d) None of the above

75 Which of the following strategies of teaching-learning is obstacle in developing creativity? [UK MP BEd 2019]
(a) Help students to think in flexible ways
(b) Encourage students to take risk
(c) Overcontrol students during teaching-learning
(d) Guide students to be persistent and delay gratification

76 What is the difference between teaching methods and teaching strategies?
[UK BEd 2019]
(a) Text material   (b) Objectives
(c) Format   (d) Acts

77 Which of the following activities would best correlate science with language learning? [KVS BEd 2017]
(a) Asking students to write an essay on some scientific topic
(b) Arranging field visits for an exhaustive exploration of the environment and asking students to write the report there of
(c) Asking students to remember technical terms perfectly
(d) Organising a refresher course on science for language teachers

78 Regular change in teaching strategies in the class is required [UK BEd 2016]
(a) to reduce the burden level of pupils
(b) to match content and objective with strategy
(c) to match it with ability level of pupils
(d) All of the above

79 Which of the following is the major advantage of tutorial strategy?
[UK BEd 2016]
(a) Remedial teaching can be provided to weak pupils
(b) We can be considerate enough to deal with each and every individual
(c) Self-expression on the part of learners is maximum here
(d) All of the above

80 Purpose of teaching method is the effective presentation of the subject matter while the purpose of teaching strategy is
[UK BEd 2016]
(a) creating conducive learning environment
(b) realisation of objectives
(c) increasing the interaction of the teacher and pupils
(d) All of the above

81 Some of the students are below average. As a Principal of the school, your response to such students will be [MP B Ed 2016]
(a) equal behaviour with all the students in the school
(b) to disallow admission to them in the next class
(c) generous attitude towards them
(d) not pay any special attention to them

82 How should a student, who does not respond to all the efforts for improvement, be treated? [MP BEd 2016]

(a) He should be rusticated from the school
(b) Psychologists and social work experts should be consulted
(c) Arrangement should be made for his special education
(d) His activities should be overlooked

83 How will you develop the quality of discipline among the students?

[MP BEd 2016]

(a) By offering them responsibilities
(b) By getting knowledge about rules of conduct
(c) By punishing them
(d) By getting the rules obeyed

84 What will the teacher do when a student asks him an irrelevant question?

[MP BEd 2016]

(a) He will scold him and ask him to sit down
(b) He will make it clear
(c) He will send him out of the class
(d) He will advise him to wait for the answer

85 Too much liberty given to the student creates

[MP BEd 2016]

(a) ideal atmosphere for teaching
(b) much noise in the classroom
(c) indiscipline in the classroom
(d) no problem in the classroom

86 What will you, as a teacher, say to the students if they come late on a rainy day?

[MP BEd 2016]

(a) You would not say anything
(b) You would find out the reason of their being late
(c) You would punish them for getting late
(d) You would make them take an oath not to come late in future

87 How will you inculcate the sense of co-operation among students?

[MP BEd 2016]

(a) By telling them the importance of sports
(b) By explaining them that games promote mutual co-operation and mental balance
(c) By telling that games waste our time
(d) None of the above

Answers

1. (d)	2. (a)	3. (c)	4. (d)	5. (d)	6. (a)	7. (a)	8. (d)	9. (d)	10. (c)
11. (d)	12. (a)	13. (d)	14. (d)	15. (d)	16. (a)	17. (b)	18. (a)	19. (d)	20. (c)
21. (c)	22. (d)	23. (d)	24. (b)	25. (d)	26. (c)	27. (d)	28. (d)	29. (c)	30. (d)
31. (d)	32. (c)	33. (d)	34. (b)	35. (b)	36. (b)	37. (d)	38. (d)	39. (d)	40. (b)
41. (d)	42. (a)	43. (d)	44. (b)	45. (c)	46. (b)	47. (d)	48. (a)	49. (d)	50. (d)
51. (d)	52. (a)	53. (d)	54. (b)	55. (b)	56. (d)	57. (c)	58. (d)	59. (d)	60. (b)
61. (c)	62. (c)	63. (d)	64. (d)	65. (d)	66. (d)	67. (b)	68. (c)	69. (a)	70. (b)
71. (c)	72. (d)	73. (d)	74. (b)	75. (c)	76. (b)	77. (b)	78. (c)	79. (d)	80. (d)
81. (c)	82. (b)	83. (a)	84. (b)	85. (c)	86. (b)	87. (b)			

Chapter 11

Teaching and Teaching Support System

Concept of Teaching

Teaching is a methodology in which various activities are involved. The word 'teaching' is derived from the word 'to teach' which means 'to instruct'.

Teaching means a process in which one individual gain knowledge or learn something from a more knowledgeable peroson.

Teaching is skillful application of knowledge, experience and scientific principles with an objective to set up an environment to facilitate learning.

Teaching is a series of events through which a teacher attempts to bring desired change in behaviour of the students. This brings about a change in the feeling, thinking and action of the students. It helps them to adapt to their environment.

Definitions of Teaching

According to **HC Morrison**, "Teaching is an intimate contact between a more mature personality and a less mature one which is designed to further the education of the latter."

According to **Clarke**, "Teaching refers to activities that are designed and performed to produce change in students' behaviour."

According to **NL Gage**, "Teaching is a form of interpersonal influence aimed at changing the behaviour potential of another person."

According to **Albert Einstein**, "Teaching is a supreme art to awaken joy in creative expressioin and knowledge."

According to **APJ Abdul Kalam**, "Teahcing is a noble profession that shapes the character, caliber and future of an individual. If people remember me as a good teacher that will be a biggest honour for me."

Objectives of Teaching

The main aim of teaching is to generate learning among the learners.

The objectives of teaching have been explained by the scholars through different classifications, which are as follow

Bloom's Taxonomy/Bloom's Classification

Bloom Taxonomy, a new vision of teaching was developed by **Benjamin Bloom** in 1956. Bloom's taxonomy is the set of three hierarchical models used to classify educational learning objectives into level of complexity and specificity.

The three lists cover the learning objectives in **cognitive**, **affective** and **psychomotor** domains.

1. The Cognitive Domain

The cognitive domain is a knowledge-based domain. It is broken into following six levels of objectives

(i) **Knowledge** It involves recognising or remembering facts, terms, basic concepts, or answers without necessarily understanding what they mean.

(ii) **Comprehension** It involves demonstrating understanding of facts and ideas by organising, comparing, translating, interpreting, giving descriptions and stating the main ideas.

(iii) **Application** It involves using acquired knowledge, applying facts, techniques and rules.

(iv) **Analysis** It involves examining and breaking information into component parts, and determining how these parts relate to one another and finding evidences to support generalisations.

(v) **Synthesis** It involves building a structure or pattern from diverse elements.

(vi) **Evaluation** It involves presenting and defending opinions, by making judgements about information, the validity, or quality of work based on a set of criteria.

2. The Affective Domain

It is emotion based domain and moves through the lowest order processes to the highest. It is broken into following five levels

(i) **Receiving** It is about the student's memory and recognition as well.

(ii) **Responding** It involves participation of students in learning process.

(iii) **Valuing** It involves the value knowledge that are acquired by students.

(iv) **Organising** It involves the different values, information and ideas, that students accommodate on what has been learned.

(v) **Characterising** It involves to build abstract knowledge.

3. The Psychomotor Domain

It is an action-based domain that focuses on change or development in behaviour or skill. Skills in the psychomotor domain describe the ability to physically manipulate a tool or instrument like a hand and hammer.

The psychomotor domain is broken into following five levels

(i) **Observing** It involves active mental attending of a physical event.

(ii) **Imitating** It involves attempted copying of a physical behaviour.

(iii) **Practicing** It involves trying a specific physical activity over and over.

(iv) **Adapting** It involves fine tuning, making minor adjustments in the physical activity in order to perfect it.

(v) **Naturalisation** It involves individual ability to adapt, modify or design the new techniques, methods or procedures according to the requirement of a situation.

Thus, learning takes place through three different channels i.e., cognitive, psychomotor and affective, it takes place as one process.

Gagne and Briggs Model

This model is also called Gagne's Nine Conditions of Learning or Gagne's Taxonomy of Learning. According to this model, the educational learning objectives fall under following categories

(i) **Verbal Information** It refers to the ability to state knowledge that an individual acquires.

(ii) **Intellectual Skills** It refers to the ability to solve problem using rules. It includes concept learning, rule learning and problem solving.

(iii) **Cognitive Skills** It refers to the ability to solve problem by creating rules. It also includes methods and techniques for one's own learning, remembering and thinking skills.

(iv) **Motor Skills** It refers to motions that are carried out with the help of the brain, nervous system and muscles.

(v) **Attitudes** They are referred to an internal state of an individual.

Characteristics of Teaching

- **Dynamic, Social and Humane** Teaching is not a fundamental concept because it is greatly influenced by social and human factors which are dynamic in themselves.
- **Teaching is a Science** Teaching is a systematic activity. It is done with a definite aim and involves the use of scientific strategies and techniques. Different strategies are tested for their effectiveness and all observations along with scores of the students in tests are recorded. Therefore, teaching is a science.
- **Teaching is an Art** Teaching involves the creativity of the teachers in explaining concepts to different type of learners. Teachers need to form strategies, adjust to various situations and understand the personality of each student. Therefore, teaching can also be considered as an art.
- **Diverse Application** In application, teaching is of diverse nature. It may have various forms as formal, informal, directional, instructional, formational, training, conditioning, indoctrination, talking, showing, doing, remedial, etc.
- **A System of Actions** Teaching is a system of actions varied in form and related with content and pupil behaviour under the prevailing physical and social conditions.
- **A Professional Activity** Teaching is a professional activity involving teacher and student with a view to the development of students' personality.

Professionalism helps teachers in being regular and making harmony with their students along with achievent of goals.

- **An Interactive Process** Teaching is highly dominated by the communication skill. Teaching is an interactive process carried with purpose and objectives.
- **Subjected to Analysis and Assessment** Teaching can be analysed and assessed based on the given task and also provide a feedback for further improvement.
- **A Specialised Task** Teaching is a specialised task and may be taken as a set of skills for realisation of certain objectives.
- **A Collection of Various Modes** Teaching is a collection of various modes of itself. It is a broader term. Terms like conditioning, training, instruction, indoctrination denote a kind of teaching.
  These terms are a part of teaching but not a synonym of teaching. These are modes of teaching which contributes towards teaching.
- **A Continuous Process** Teaching is not a static but an evolving, continuous and lifelong process. The concept of continuous learning has become important because it places priority on acquiring, adapting and learning from change.

Teaching Problems

The field of education is very wide and many problems arise from administrative to classroom teaching and efforts are also made to redress them from time to time. We can understand the problems related to teaching in the following ways

1. **Faulty Curriculum** Curriculum in India is not up to the mark. It lacks utility and is not related to life and is purely theoretical. In the last few years the courses have been made much more cumbersome. For all these reasons, students fail their examinations.

2. **Faulty Teaching Method** The methods of teaching adopted in Indian schools are very

problematic and un-scientific. In these corrupt practices, the physical and mental levels of the students are not taken care of and the students become indifferent to education as a result of individual differences.

3. **Teacher's Attitude Towards Students** If the attitude of teacher is aggressive, then students are afraid of him. If the teacher is more polite, they do not care about the teacher and show apathy in his/her actions.

4. **Home Work** A large amount of home work is given by the teachers and the home work given is either obscure to the children or it has not been practiced in the classroom.

   This does not lead to students doing their work. Due to lengthy home work and due to time constraints, students are not able to complete the assigned task of every teacher.

5. **Lack of Teachers** Lack of teachers is found in many schools. The shortage of teacher is also found in state schools. The problem of lack of teachers in state schools is even more serious. Due to lack of teachers, students are unable to study properly. Thus, the children with special needs have to face failure and also do not take interest in education.

6. **Dull Study** In most schools and especially at primary level, teaching work is done in a monotonous, traditional and non-psychological manner. It makes the students uninterested in their studies in the school.

7. **Lack of Personal Interest** Teachers do not take interest in teaching work. They consider it only as a duty. Teachers have relationships with their students in such a way that the students are not able to openly tell them their problems and thus, the difficulties faced in the teaching work are not resolved.

Measures to Solve the Problem of Teaching

It is necessary for the teacher to make his teaching effective and to make the students aware of the study and to develop such feelings that they have the curiosity to learn every time.

In other words, the effectiveness of teaching includes the principles of teaching, the purpose of teaching and patterns of teaching. On the basis of these, the measures to solve the problems of teaching are as follows

1. **Raise Interest in Children** It is the child's vested interest in any task that motivates him to take the task forward. That is why the first duty of the teacher is that he should inculcate interest in the child in order to inculcate the habit of study.

2. **To Relate Content to Life** The old experiences of the child should be related to the new knowledge, so that the knowledge of the children becomes permanent and he may develop the habit of study.

3. **Enlighten the Children** The result given for studying the subject matter should be made known to the students in advance.

   If the students know that by studying such thing they will get good marks in the examination, then they will carefully study that subject matter. Knowledge of the result makes the students active learners thereby creating interest in them.

4. **Knowledge of Purpose** Practice should be purposeful. The study cannot be successful in the absence of purpose. Each type of study has a purpose. If the teacher cannot explain the purpose of the study to the children, then they cannot get success in their work.

5. **Employing Content** The basis of success of every task is pre-planning. Therefore, the teacher should be able to get used to the

study, make the subject fully planned before the study.

6. **Appointment of Adequate Number of Teachers** There should be an adequate number of teachers of each subject in the school, so that the students do not face any difficulty in the teaching work.

7. **Decrease in the Home Work** The homework of the students should be of the same concept, which is well understood in the class and the teacher knows that it is fully understood by all the students. The amount of homework should also be taken care of. Homework should be so that students get enough time for other activities as well.

8. **Teacher-Student Relationship** Teacher-student relations should be pleasant. The personality of the teacher should be such that the student can express his problems in front of the teacher. The teacher should also take personal interest and solve the problems of students related to teaching.

Teaching Support System

Such resources which increase the intensity of the teaching and learning process are known as the Teaching Support System. Aptitude towards teaching support system are as follows

Traditional Teaching System

Education was imparted in Gurukul in ancient times. The teacher used to teach students only in their ashram.

They also used to give tasks to their disciples, which were done very politely by each student. We find an example of this in the Ramayana and Mahabharata, but the biggest drawback of the teaching system of this period was that the teaching work was done only for the descendants of the kings. In the common man-psyche, the knowledge of teaching method was negligible.

The greatest feature of ancient education was related to moral education. Ethics was what used to make a person immanent. In this, truth, honesty, kindness, religion and moral knowledge, etc. were also taught.

Modern Teaching System

In the era of modern education, there has been a lot of change in the life of the people. Modern education emphasises on all types of physical, mental, social and emotional development of the child.

Today modern teaching system is prevalent in schools, colleges, etc. All educational resources like computer, laptops, mobile phones, tablets, etc. are available at home. Also, emphasis is given on the intensity of the learning process through the Internet.

In such education, the child is encouraged to receive education on the basis of activities. Now-a-days new schemes are being formulated for education. So that illiteracy can be eliminated from the country.

ICT Based Teaching Support System

Information and Communication Technology (ICT) is a broad field that encompasses all types of technologies for the communication of information. It broadcasts information from applications of radio, television, cell phones, computers, etc.

It is an important tool for expanding educational opportunities and significant development in the field of education and for enhancing the quality of education. This can increase the quality of studies in remote places.

It facilitates the use of analysis of social media metrics for student performance, placement, website analytics and brand audits.

It is helpful in facilitating distance education along with course delivery by satellite and other means. Through this, teaching in e-learning and distance education programs is becoming interesting and easier.

Through this, teaching helps to reach the learner through internet and World Wide Web.

It helps in monitoring and coordinating the day-to-day administrative activities of the educational institution in a simple and transparent manner. It helps in providing information about registration, enrollment, course allocation, attendance monitoring, etc. in higher educational institutions.

Components of ICT

These are the various components of Information and Communication Technology (ICT)

1. **Computer Hardware Technology** This technology covers microcomputers, servers, large mainframes, computers as well as input, output and storage devices.

2. **Computer Software Technology** Under this operating systems, web browsers, database management systems, servers and commercial software come.

3. **Telecommunication and Network Technology** This technology involves telecommunications and cryptography based on wire or wireless to connect to the processor and the Internet through telecommunications.

Role and Importance of ICT in Higher Education

Information and Communication Technologies or ICTs have gained great importance in the present world. With a wide range of applications in various fields such as entertainment, medicine etc, it is not surprising that it has an enormous impact on the world of education. As a fundamental tool of education for students and teachers, ICTs have various benefits for students.

- **All Time Access** With ICTs, learning goes beyond the traditional classroom. Students can learn at any time of the day from any place. This ensures that the students are upto- date with their learning of the day.

- **No Bar for Strength** ICTs allow a large group of students to join a class in comparison to a traditional classroom. As students work collectively and discuss their learning as well as problems, their collaborative skills and communication skills improve.

- **Promotes Effective Learning** The use of varied resources such as videos, websites, graphics and games make learning more interesting as well as effective. This promotes active participation and knowledge retention of students in the class.

- **Individualised and Up-to-date Learning** With the help of the various tools of ICT, students are able to create, track and manage their own learning at their own pace. Further, the technology automatically keeps all the materials up-to-date for the students and teachers.

- **Cost Effective** ICTs also make learning cost-effective. The cost of the traditional classrooms, books and all other learning material and stationary reduces. Now, students and teachers just require a device with ICT technology to learn and teach.

- **Ensures More Practice** ICTs offer students as well as teachers a wide range of practice papers and other resources that test learning. Students can give a paper as many times as he/she wants. It helps the students understand their strong as well as weak points so that they can work on improving them.

- **Individual Evaluation** The use of technology in education aids a teacher in evaluating each student on the basis of his/her knowledge. As a result, the teacher can prepare individualised learning programs for each student to promote their learning.

- **Good Performance in Competitive Exams** The presence of ICT devices as the mode of exams allows a quiet, serious and a positive environment for the students. As a result, students can focus more and perform better.

Applications of ICT in Education

In today's modern world we experience many different technologies that make teaching-learning easy even when not directly connected to school-classrooms. Examples of these technologies are video conferencing applications like Zoom, Skype, Google Meet, GoTo Meeting, Webex, Google Duo and so on. These apps help to conduct online classes, video lectures and conferences without any physical movement.

Through e-learning, ICT can be used in education system. This has been discussed below

E-learning

E-learning is an innovative and essential part of modern education. It is the acquisition of knowledge which takes place through electronic technologies and media.

Some examples of e-learning are as follows

SWAYAM

SWAYAM stands for Study Webs Active-Learning for Young Aspiring Minds. It is a Massive Open Online Course (MOOC). This programme was launched by Government of India in 2017 which is designed to achieve the three cardinal principles of Education Policy i.e., access, equity and quality to all especially to the most disadvantaged groups.

Courses delivered through SWAYAM are available free of cost to school learners (from 9th to 12th class), under-graduate, post graduate and other professional courses.

Swayamprabha

It is a group of 32 DTH channels of high-quality programmes on 24×7 basis using the GSAT-15 educational satellite. The study material is provided by IGNOU, NCERT, NIOS, UGC, NPTEL, IITS, CEC, and the web portal is maintained by the INFLIBNET Centre.

The 32 DTH channels are set to cover Higher Education, School Education (9-12 Level), Curriculum-based Courses and assist students of Classes 11th and 12th to prepare for competitive exams.

MOOC

MOOC stands for Massive Open Online Course. It is a web-based platform.

It was set up in 2008 and became more active in 2012 as a popular learning tool. It provides opportunities to its learners such as video lectures, downloading notes, contributing their own and sharing their point of view by communicating with peers, professors and Teaching Assistants (TAs).

E-Pathshala

E-Pathshala was launched in November, 2015 which is a portal/app developed by the CIET, NCERT. The platform offers many educational resources, including digital textbooks of NCERT for all classes, audio- visual resources by NCERT, periodicals, supplementary books, question banks, teacher training modules and a variety of other print and non-print materials. These materials can be downloaded by the user for offline use with no limits on downloads.

Bharat Padhe Online

It is a campaign for crowdsourcing of ideas for improving the online education system in India which was launched by HRD Ministry in April, 2020. It is a one week programme.

It aims to invite all the best minds of the country to share their suggestions or solutions directly with the HRD Ministry in order to overcome the problems of online education along with promoting the available digital education platforms.

1 The word 'teaching' means
(a) to guide
(b) to instruct
(c) to teach
(d) Both (b) and (c)

2 Teaching means
(a) a skillful application of knowledge
(b) a skillful application of scientfic principles
(c) a process in which one individual gain knowledge from a more knowledgeable person
(d) All of the above

3 "Teaching is a supreme art to awaken joy in creative expression and knowledge." It is given by whom?
(a) Clarke
(b) HC morrison
(c) NL Gage
(d) Albert Einstein

4 Who said that "if people remember me as a good teacher that will be a biggest honour for me"?
(a) NL Gage
(b) Clarke
(c) APJ Abdul Kalam
(d) HC Morrison

5 Who said that "teaching refers to activities that are designed and performed to produce change in student's behaviour"?
(a) Alber Einsten
(b) NL Gage
(c) Clarke
(d) APJ Abdul Kalam

6 The main objective of teaching should be able to
(a) improve learning skills of students
(b) bring desired changes in student's attitude
(c) develop conceptual, intellectual and subject specific skills
(d) All of the above

7 Which is not a characteristic related to the concept of teaching?
(a) Teaching is an haphazard activity
(b) Teaching is an educational communication
(c) Teaching is a process in which learners, teachers and curriculum are organised in a systematic way to attained specific goals
(d) All of the above

8 Which of the following is not true?
(a) Teachers are born
(b) Teachers can be trained only
(c) Teaching is just an art
(d) All of the above

9 The important aim of teaching is
(a) to develop personality of students
(b) to give information
(c) to develop inquiring minds
(d) to help students pass their examinations

10 Teaching will be effective if teachers
(a) have much experience in teaching the subject
(b) use many instructional materials
(c) are the master of their subjects
(d) start from what students know already

11 The most important objective of teaching is to
(a) cover the prescribed syllabus
(b) create a relaxed teaching and learning environment
(c) take classes regularly
(d) facilitate students when it comes to the construction of knowledge and understanding

12 Which is considered a sign of motivated teaching?
(a) Pin drop silence in the classroom
(b) Maximum attendance of the students
(c) Students asking questions
(d) Students taking notes

13 What is more desirable in a classroom?
(a) A teacher delivering a lecture on the basis of course content and standard books
(b) A teacher answering questions raised by students
(c) A teacher delivering a lecture on the basis of the text and his own research
(d) A teacher maintaining strict discipline and taking attendance regularly

14 The basic requirement to teach efficiently is
(a) mastery over technology
(b) mastery over the topic
(c) mastery over different strategies of teaching
(d) All of the above

15 If students do not understand what is taught in the classroom the teacher should feel
(a) that he is wasting time
(b) terribly bored
(c) to explain it in a different way
(d) pity for the students

16 A teacher will become an effective communicator if
(a) he asks question in between teaching
(b) he uses instructional aids
(c) he helps students get meaning out of what he teaches
(d) he helps students get correct answer to the questions on the topic

17 Those teachers are popular among students who
(a) award good grades
(b) take classes on extra tuition fee
(c) help them solve their problems
(d) develop intimacy with them

18 In which year Benjamin Bloom developed his Bloom's taxonomy?
(a) 1901   (b) 1920
(c) 1930   (d) 1956

19 Which of the following domains was given by Benjamin Bloom?
(a) Cognitive   (b) Affective
(c) Psychomotor   (d) All of these

20 Knowledge, comprehension and evaluation are levels of which domain?
(a) Psychomotor domain
(b) Cognitive domain
(c) Affective domain
(d) None of the above

21 The cognitive domain includes
(a) application   (b) analysis
(c) synthesis   (d) All of these

22 Which of the following is emotion based domain given by Bloom?
(a) Cognitive domain
(b) Affective domain
(c) Psychomotor domain
(d) None of the above

23 The affective domain consists of
(a) receiving   (b) responding
(c) organising   (d) All of these

24 The psychomotor domain consists of
(a) Observing   (b) Imitating
(c) Practicing   (d) All of these

25 Which of the following is the problem related to teaching?
(a) Faulty curriculum
(b) Faulty teaching method
(c) Lack of teachers in school
(d) All of the above

26 Curriculum in Indian schools are
(a) lack utility
(b) not related to life
(c) purely theoretical
(d) All of the above

27 The teaching method adopted in Indian schools are
(a) up to the mark   (b) problematic
(c) unscientific   (d) Both (b) and (c)

28 Which of the following is the result of faulty teaching method?
(a) Physical level of students is not taken care of
(b) Mental level of students is not taken care of
(c) Students become indifferent to education
(d) All of the above

29 The attitude of teachers should be
(a) aggressive
(b) more polite
(c) neutral
(d) not considered much

30 What is the feature of a large amount of home assignments given to students in Indian schools?
(a) Obscure to students
(b) It does not practiced in classroom
(c) Up to the level of students
(d) Both (a) and (b)

31 Why do students not able to complete the assigned task of every teacher?
(a) Due to lengthy have assignments
(b) Due to time constraints
(c) Due to careless attitude of students
(d) All of the above

32 In which type of schools the problem of lack of teachers is more serious?
(a) National level schools
(b) Convent schools
(c) State level schools
(d) None of the above

33 In most Indian schools teaching work is done in a
(a) monotonous manner
(b) traditional
(c) non-psychological manner
(d) All of the above

34 A teacher is said to be fluent in asking questions if he can ask
(a) meaning questions
(b) as many questions as possible
(c) maximum number of questions in a fixed time
(d) many meaningful questions in a fixed time

35 When some students are deliberately attempting to disturb the discipline of the class by making mischief, what will be your role as a teacher?
(a) Expelling those students
(b) Isolate those students
(c) Reform the group with your authority
(d) Giving them an opportunity for introspection and improve their behaviour

36 For maintaining an effective discipline in the class, the teacher should
(a) allow students to do what they like
(b) deal with the students strictly
(c) give the students some problems to solve
(d) deal with them politely and firmly

37 Those teachers are popular among students who
(a) develop intimacy with them
(b) help them solve their problem
(c) award good grades
(d) take classes an extra tuition fee

38 On the first day of his/her class, if a teacher is asked by the students to introduce himself he should
(a) ask them to meet after the class
(b) tell them about himself in brief
(c) ignore the demand and start teaching
(d) scold the students for this unwanted demand

39 Which is very important for home work?
(a) It should be well taught in the class
(b) It should be well understood by all the students
(c) The amount of home work should not be too much
(d) All of the above

40 To make learning effective a goal must be meaningful in terms of
(a) objective of the curriculum
(b) intellectual ideas
(c) students of others
(d) the needs and purpose of students

41 Which of the following signifies the traditional teaching system?
(a) Gurukul
(b) Madarsa
(c) High-tech building
(d) None of the above

42 Which of the following was the biggest drawback of teaching system of ancient period?
(a) Teaching work was done only for common people
(b) Teaching work was done only for descendants of kings
(c) Teaching work was done for none of the communities
(d) None of the above

43 The greatest feature of ancient education was related to
(a) spiritual education
(b) moral education
(c) technical education
(d) political education

44 In ancient education system which of the following was taught?
(a) Truth   (b) Honesty
(c) Religion   (d) All of these

45 Modern education emphasises on
  (a) mental development of students
  (b) physical development of students
  (c) social development of students
  (d) All of the above

46 ICT stands for
  (a) Inter Connected Terminals
  (b) Intra Common Terminology
  (c) International Communication Technology
  (d) Information and Communication Technology

47 Which of the following is the appropriate definition of Information Technology?
  (a) Information technology refers to the use of hardware and software for processing information
  (b) Information technology refers to the use of hardware and software for distribution of useful information
  (c) Information technology refers to use of principle of physical sciences and social sciences for processing of information of many kinds
  (d) Information technology refers to the use of hardware and software for storage retrieval, processing and distributing information of many kinds

48 Which of the following is the component of ICT?
  (a) Computer hardware technology
  (b) Computer software technology
  (c) Telecommunication and network technology
  (d) All of the above

49 Which of the following can be useful in teaching learning process?
  (a) ICT
  (b) Computer only
  (c) Textbooks
  (d) All of the above

50 Which of the following comes under computer software technology?
  (a) Web browsers   (b) Servers
  (c) Storage devices   (d) Micro-computers

51 In which year SWAYAM programme was launched by the Government of India?
  (a) 2010   (b) 2011
  (c) 2013   (d) 2017

52 Courses delivered through SWAYAM are available free of cost to
  (a) school learners   (b) under-graduate
  (c) post-graduate   (d) All of these

53 In Swayamprabha the study material is provided by
  (a) IGNOU   (b) NCERT
  (c) NIOS   (d) All of these

54 E-Pathshala was launched in which year?
  (a) 2010   (b) 2012
  (c) 2015   (d) 2018

Answers

1. (d)	2. (d)	3. (d)	4. (c)	5. (c)	6. (d)	7. (a)	8. (d)	9. (c)	10. (d)
11. (d)	12. (c)	13. (b)	14. (d)	15. (c)	16. (c)	17. (c)	18. (d)	19. (d)	20. (b)
21. (d)	22. (b)	23. (d)	24. (d)	25. (d)	26. (d)	27. (d)	28. (d)	29. (c)	30. (d)
31. (d)	32. (c)	33. (d)	34. (d)	35. (d)	36. (d)	37. (b)	38. (b)	39. (d)	40. (d)
41. (a)	42. (b)	43. (b)	44. (d)	45. (d)	46. (d)	47. (d)	48. (d)	49. (d)	50. (a)
51. (d)	52. (d)	53. (d)	54. (c)						

Child Development and Socialisation

The term 'development' refers to the various qualitative and quantitative changes taking place simultaneously with the changes to growth. Therefore, development may be defined as a progressive series of mannered and coherent changes. The word development indicates the changes related to growth and the moves towards maturity.

In other words, development can be described as growth in physical, mental and emotional state of an individual.

In the process of development, new abilities and characteristics get manifested and there is a progressive change in the behaviour of an individual.

Concept of Child Development

Child development involves the scientific study of the patterns of growth, change and stability that occurs from conception through adolescence.

In the concept of child development, a child is very unique as there are no two children that are completely same. Even though, if a twin have same physical features they are different in terms of development, characteristic, personality, behaviour, etc.

In this concept childhood is a very important stage as it is the time when the child builds up his foundation for his life later on. At the same time, his cognitive development also takes place, where his memory, understanding, experience and knowledge gets accumulated.

Development is said to be a qualitative process that happens as progressive series in human beings from the day being conceived to baby, toddler children, teenager, adult and getting older and older until death.

Importance of Child Development

As a parent, teacher or a caregiver, it is very important to understand a child's behaviour in order to help him adapt to various situations in life.

Child development is important for various reasons

- To understand the child better and to understand development of a child.
- To know and understand the problems faced by a child that has a psychological origin and to establish an effective communication with the child.
- To gain confidence of the child and the parents, so that the environment in which the child is growing, can be understood.

- To help teachers recognise how to deliver the contents to students in a way that identifies individual learning differences.
- Through understanding child development, one can provide right direction, so as to develop proper skills in the child.
- Child development tells about the specific behaviour of the children and its particular causes when they help to deal with the conditions accordingly.
- Child psychology is the study of child's personality traits. This helps in understanding what the child is likely to be in future and helps the child throughout his life.

Principles of Child Development

There is a set of principles that characterises the process of growth and development. These principles describe typical development process as a predictable and orders process.

Following are the principles of child development

1. **Development Follows a Pattern or a Sequence** Child has a different rate of development. However, development of all human beings follows a similar pattern, similar sequence or direction. Sequential pattern of development can be seen in two directions.

   (i) **Cephalocaudal Sequence** According to this principle, child first gains control of the head, then the arms and then legs. Infant gains control of head and face movement within the first two months after birth.

   In the next few months, the child is able to lift himself by using his arms. By 6 to 12 months of age, infant starts to gain his leg control and also able to crawl, stand or walk.

   (ii) **Proximodistal sequence** Unlike the cephalocaudal sequence, the direction of development in proximodistal sequence is from the centre of the body to the extremities.

2. **Development Involves Change** Human being is never static. From the moment of conception to the time of death, the person undergoes changes.

   The major changes include changes in size and proportions, acquisition of new mental, motor behavioural skills. For e.g. a child shows language development and better ability to reason and remember.

3. **Development Proceeds from General to Specific** In the phases of pre-natal development and post-natal life, a child's responses are from general to specific.

   General activity proceeds to specific activity means the infant is able to grasp an object with the whole hand just after the birth before using only the thumb and forefinger.

   The infant's motor movements are very generalise undirectional and reflexive, like waving arms or kicking before being able to reach or creep towards an object.

4. **Development is Correlated or Integrated** All types of development i.e., physical, mental, social and emotional, are related to each other. For e.g. a child, who is physically healthy is likely to have superior sociability and emotional stability. The child develops as a unified whole.

   Each area of development is dependent on the other and thus, influences the other developments.

5. **Development is a Continuous Process** Development does not occur in spurts, it continues from the moment of conception until the individual reaches maturity.

   It takes place at a slow regular pace rather than by leap and bounds. Although, development is a continuous process, yet the tempo of growth is not even during infancy and early years, growth moves swiftly and later slackens.

6. **Development of Individuality** Interaction between heredity and environment influences lead to individual differences in the social and mental development of a child. These differences are caused by the genes one inherits and the environmental conditions like food, medical facilities, psychological conditions and learning opportunities.

7. **Development Occurs at Different Rates for Different Parts of the Body** The development of different physical and mental traits is continuous but all parts of the body do no grow at the same time rate.

   In some parts of body, growth may be rapid while in others, growth will be slow. For e.g. brain attains its full maturity around the age of 6 to 8 years; feet, hands and nose reach their maximum size in early adolescence, whereas heart, liver and digestive system grow during adolescence also.

8. **Development Proceeds Stage by Stage** The development of the child occurs in different stage. Each stage has certain unique characteristics. For e.g. during infancy stage, speech gradually develops from babbling, monosyllabic sounds to complete sentence formation.

9. **Early Development is More Important than Later Development** Early childhood experiences have more impact on the development of a child. It includes nutritional, emotional, social and cultural experience.

10. **Development is Predictable** It is possible for us to predict at an early age the range within which the mature development of the child is likely to fall. However, mental development cannot be predicted with the same degree of accuracy.

11. **Development do not Proceed at the Same Pace for all** (Theory of Maturation)

This theory was formed by Gesell. According to this theory, children go through similar stages of growth, although each child may move through these stages at their own rate. For e.g. all children learn to walk around the same age but some may learn faster than the others.

Stages of Human Development

The process of development continues even after the individual has attained physical maturity (means growth). The individual is continuously changing as he/she interacts with the environment.

The stages of development have been classified below

1. Infancy Stage

- This is the first stage of growth after pre-natal and it comprises 'new born to 2 years old.'
- According to the **Erik Erikson's Theory**, "The infant depends on the parents, especially the mother. The major developmental task in infancy is to learn whether or not other people, especially primary caregivers, regularly satisfy basic needs".
- The growth is mostly seen as increase in size, shape and weight. The cells become larger in size, the cervical and lumber curvatures of the spine show up as the baby starts to straighten the head and tries to sit and stand.

2. Childhood Stage

The childhood stage can be simplified into two stages i.e. early childhood and late childhood.

(i) Early Childhood Stage or Toy Age (2 to 6 years)

- The early childhood is a time of tremendous growth across all areas of development. At this stage, child likes to do work independently and can take care of his/her own body and interact effectively with others. It is a sensitive period of language development.

- In the initial stage, the child is a toddler and learns to walk like an adult. Despite the age of 4 years child has mastered many skills such as sitting, walking, using toilet, using spoon, scribbling and sufficient hand-eye coordination to catch and throw and also communicate with others and solve problems.

- By the age of six, most children demonstrate the fine-motor skills. A child learns to identify members of family and gets involved in his surroundings.

(ii) Late Childhood Stage (6 to 12 years)

- In this, a child refines his skills acquired during the early childhood period and learns new skills as well. At this stage, child gains height and also physical entities such as mass, number and area etc.
  Sigmund Freud's psychoanalytic theory labelled this stage of life as the latency stage, a time when sexual and aggressive urges are repressed.

- During this stage, children learn the values of their societies. Thus, the primary developmental task of late childhood could be called integration, both in terms of development within the individual and of the individual within the social context.

- The social skills learned through peer and family relationships and children's increasing ability to participate in meaningful interpersonal communication, provide a necessary foundation for the challenges of adolescence.

- Best friends are important at this stage and the skills gained in these relationships may provide the building blocks for healthy adult relationships.

3. Adolescence Stage (12 to 18 years)

- This stage is considered as the period of development and adjustment during the transitional period between childhood and adulthood.

- Adolescence is defined as a culturally constructed period that generally begins as individuals reach sexual maturity and ends when the individual has established an identity as an adult within his/her social context.

- In other words, the primary development task of adolescence is considered as the identity formation.

- Adolescence is an important period for cognitive development as well as it marks a transition in the way in which individuals think and reason about problems and ideas.

- Adolescents are trying on new roles, new ways of thinking and behaving and they are exploring different ideas and values. Erikson addressed this in his framework of life-span development.

- With so many intense experiences, adolescence is also an important time in emotional development. Mood swings are a characteristic of adolescence.

Dimensions of Development

Psychologists have divided development into the following parts from the point of view of convenience of study.

1. **Physical Development** Changes of the internal organs of the body are not visible externally, but they continue to develop properly inside the body. Initially, the baby is dependent on others for all his work, gradually as a result of the process of development; he becomes capable of fulfilling his needs.

   It is also necessary for teachers to have adequate information about the growth and development of the child, as interests, desires, attitudes and in a way his overall behaviour depends only on physical growth and development.

2. **Mental Development** Cognitive or Mental Development refers to the growth and development of all those mental abilities and capabilities of the child, as a result of which he is able to make adequate use of his mental powers in solving various types of problems.

   The ability to imagine, remember, think, observe, problem-solving, make decisions, etc., develop as a result of cognitive development. At the time of birth, the child lacks this type of ability, gradually with increasing age; the pace of mental development also increases in him.

   If a child is mentally weak, then for his treatment it is important to know what is the reason for his weakness. It can also help in designing appropriate textbooks keeping in mind the mental growth and development of children at different stages and age levels.

3. **Social Development** The literal meaning of social development is learning different aspects by living within the society. The development of character building, good behaviour (virtue) and practical education related to life takes place within the society itself. The first school for the development of children is considered to be the family, then the society.

   Through social development, feelings of cultural, religious and community development etc. generate in the children. Self-respect and ideology are born in the mind of the children.

   The child chooses his ideal people through the society and takes inspiration from them to become something. The best development of a person can be possible only in an educated society.

4. **Emotional Development** Emotion means a state that affects the behaviour of a person. For examples fear, anger, hatred, surprise, affection, happiness, etc.

As the child grows in age, these emotions also continue to develop. Emotional development is an important aspect of human growth and development. Emotional behaviour of a child affects not only his physical growth and development, but also his intellectual, social and moral development. Emotional development plays an important role in the balanced development of the child.

Factors Influencing Child Development

Child development is an ongoing process from birth until reaching adulthood and typically follows a pattern and a sequence, which means that each step takes place at certain age and in a usual order that is similar in most cases. There are two broad factors that influencing the development of children. They are as follows

Internal Factor

Internal factors influencing child development include heredity, physical factors, intelligence and emotional factors.

1. **Heredity Factor** The height, weight or body-build of a child largely depends on the genetical factor (Heredity). It means that the genetic materials operate throughout entire period of growth. Heredity influences the growth rate of early matures or late matures. The genetic factors probably play the leading part the differences between male and female patterns of growth.

2. **Physical Factor** Physical factors can influence different aspects of child development in different ways. Sometimes, physical influences on child development are easy to control.

   Good nutrition helps child's development in more adequate manner because it affects the bones, muscles and internal organs. Consistent physical activities can do more for minimising the risk for obesity and enhances muscle growth.

3. **Intelligence** It has been seen that intelligence affects the physical development. Children who are intelligent grow fast physically and children with low intelligence achieve their development tasks at a slow speed.

   Intelligence affects the thought process, creative thinking and retention of information thereby affecting the academic achievement of a child.

4. **Emotional Factors** The emotional factors affect the child's social, mental, physical and moral level of development. It also affects the language development. Balanced emotional development in a child helps to reciprocate feelings that are appropriate for one's age.

   Children having more easy going nature tend to have an easier time learning to regulate their emotions as well as other people's emotions more positively.

External Factors

The external factors influencing child development include family, physical environment and socio-economic conditions.

1. **Family** It plays a very important role in shaping up a child. An affectionate bond between the parents and child helps in proper development.

   A bigger family tends to give moral values and education as well as support to the child. While a small family makes the child independent. Children going through stressful family environment and broken families experience learning disabilities. Their emotional and social development is also affected negatively.

2. **Physical Environment** The environment in which a child grows up, affects his mental, emotional and physical development. Physical environment such

as pollution, noise level, overerowding, housing and neighbourhood quality are significant in children's development.

Pollution affects the health of the children. Parents in crowded homes are less responsive to the needs of the children.

Housing quality and the neighbourhoods in which a child grows up shapes the behaviour of a child.

3. **Socio-Economic Conditions** This is the social and economic condition in which the child grows up. A well-to- do family is able to send their children to private schools, inculcate hobbies and go to vacation where the children gather new experiences.

   This further increases the cognitive, physical and social skills. Children coming from less fortunate backgrounds, ill-health, depression, stress or lack of motivation lead to improper physical, cognitive and social development.

Socialisation

'Socialisation' is a term used by scholars to refer to the lifelong process of inheriting and passing on norms, customs, values and ideologies by providing an individual with the skills and habits necessary for participating within its own society.

Some of the most important socialisation occurs in infanthood and childhood. The child performs its unique and effective role in society when it is appropriately socialised.

Socialisation stands for the development of the human brain, body, attitude, behaviour and so forth.

The term 'Socialisation' refers to the process of interaction through which the growing individual learns the habits, attitudes, values and beliefs of the social group into which he has been born.

From the point of view of society, socialisation is the way through which society transmits its culture from generation to generation and maintains itself. From the point of view of the individual, socialisation is the process by which the individual learn social behaviour and develops himself/herself.

Definitions of Socialisation

According to **JJ Macionis**, "The lifelong process by which an individual becomes a proper member of society and develops human characteristics".

According to **PB Horton** and **CL Hunt**, "It is a learning process in which groups interact and learn social norms, also developing themselves".

According to **WF Ogburn**, "It is the process of learning the norms of the group and society".

According to **RM McIver**, "It is the process through which social beings develop relationships and association with each other".

According to **ES Bogardus**, "A process of learning to live and work together is called socialisation".

Features of Socialisation

Features of socialisation may be discussed as below

1. **Inculcates basic discipline** Socialisation inculcates basic discipline. A person learns to control his impulses. He may show a disciplined behaviour to gain social approval.

2. **Helps to control human behaviour** It helps to control human behaviour. An individual from birth to death undergoes training and his behaviour is controlled by numerous ways. In order to maintain the social order, there are definite procedures or mechanism in society.

   These procedures become part of the man's life and man gets adjusted to the society. Through socialisation, society intends to control the behaviour of its members unconsciously.

3. **Socialisation is rapid** Socialisation takes place rapidly if the agencies of socialisation are more unanimous in their ideas and skills. When there is conflict between the ideas, examples and skills transmitted in home and those transmitted by school or peer, socialisation of the individual tends to be slower and ineffective.

4. **Socialisation takes place formally and informally** Formal socialisation takes place through direct instruction and education in schools and colleges. Family is, however, the primary and the most influential source of education. Children learn their language, customs, norms and values in the family.

5. **Socialisation is a continuous process** Socialisation is a life-long process. As socialisation does not cease when a child becomes an adult, internalisation of culture continues from generation to generation. Society perpetuates itself through the internalisation of culture.

   Its members transmit culture to the next generation and society continues to exist.

Importance of Socialisation

- The process of socialisation is important for both individuals and society.

- Every society is faced with the necessity of making a responsible member out of each child born into it.

- Socialisation means transmission of culture, the process by which human learns the rules and practices of social groups to which he belongs.

- It is through it that a society maintains its social system, transmits its culture from generation to generation.

- Socialisation plays a unique role in personality development of the individual.

- The child has no self. The self emerges through the process of socialisation. The self, the core of personality, develops out of the child's interaction with others.
- In societies, inculcating the abstract skills of literacy through formal education is a central task of socialisation.
- Another element in socialisation is the acquisition of the appropriate social roles that the individual is expected to play.
- Role performance is very important in the process of socialisation. As males, females, husbands, wives, sons, daughters, parents, children, students teachers and so on, accepted social roles must be learned if the individual is to play a functional and predictable part in social interaction.
- In this way man becomes a person through the social influences which he shares with others and through his own ability to respond and weave his responses into a unified body of habits, attitudes and traits.

Types of Socialisation

Socialisation can be divided into two types. These are as follow

1. **Primary Socialisation** This is important for a child because it sets the groundwork for all future socialisation. It occurs when a child learns the attitudes, values and actions appropriate for a member of a particular culture. It is influenced most by the immediate family and friends.
2. **Secondary Socialisation** This refers to the process of learning the appropriate behaviour as a member of a smaller group within the larger society which is reinforced by socialising agents of society other than the immediate family.

   Secondary socialisation is usually associated with teenagers and adults. It takes place outside home. For instance, schools and colleges require very different behaviour from the home, and children must act according to the rules of school when they are there.

Factors Influencing Socialisation

1. **Social Interaction** Interacting socially in the family, neighbourhood and schools, as well as with friends, classmates and the community is an organised psychological process characterised by

   (i) **Imitation of Others** This means copying someone else's behaviour in our own style which develops a unique aspect of our personality.

   (ii) **Suggestion by Others** Suggestions may be conveyed through language, pictures or some similar medium to the child. They influence the child's behaviour with others as well as its own private and individual behaviour.

   (iii) **Sympathy** This helps the child to empathise with other and helps it to initiate conversation.

2. **Identification** In its early age, most of the child's actions are random, natural and unconscious. As the child grows, it realises the nature of things which satisfy its needs. Such things become the object of its identification like the mother, a toy or a picture book. Through identification the child becomes sociable.

3. **Language** It is the means of cultural transmission and social interaction. At first, the child utters some random syllabus which have no meaning, but gradually it comes to learn its mother-tongue.

   Erik Erickson mentioned eight stages of life (including adulthood), in each of which the individual faces a specific crisis challenge and moves from one stage to the next when the crisis is resolved.

Agents of Socialisation

Socialisation of an individual occurs through its interaction with various agents during its lifetime and these include family, peer group, school and mass media among others.

1. **Family** This is the primary agent of socialisation for most people, especially in the first five years of their lives. The family provides the child with its first social contact with the world and through it, the correct patterns of behaviour are internalised and learnt.

   Learning occurs informally and the right/wrong behaviour is approved/rejected through reward and punishment.

2. **School** When a child reaches school age, it starts to widen its socialisation cycle. The learning is more formal in school. Talents are evaluated on the basis of standards and requirements.

   The school helps a child to adapt to the social order, functioning to prepare the child for a stable adult life. The school imparts certain technical and intellectual skills as well as the cultural heritage of society so that the individual is able to integrate into society.

3. **The Peer Group** Peer group members are usually children of the same age and have similar status.

   For instance, a child who enters standard one in school and finds itself in a class of children of the same age, might become friendly with only some of them. Yet the whole class constitutes its peer group.

   However, as a child grows up, it starts to choose its own peer group based on common interests, activities, similar income level and status. The peer group affects the individual in such issues like appearance, lifestyles, fashion, social activities and dating, drugs, attitude to sex and technology.

4. **The Mass Media** Mass media transmits information in an impersonal manner which is all the time conducted in a one-way flow. Mass media also harms its audience and receivers by concentrating and stressing on certain topics. The media can create, manage and control impressions of what should be seen as real, important and as per norms.

5. **Religion** Religion plays a very important role in socialisation. Religion instills the fear of hell in the individual so that he should refrain from bad and undesirable activities.

   Religion not only makes people religious but socalises them into the secular order.

6. **Occupation** In the occupational world, the individual finds himself with new shared interests and goals. He makes adjustments with the position he holds and also learns to make adjustment with other workers who may occupy equal, higher or lower position.

   While working, the individual enters into relations of cooperation, involving specialisation of tasks and at the same time learns the nature of class divisions.

   Work for him is a source of income but at the same time, it gives identity and status within society as a whole.

7. **Political Parties** Political parties attempt to seize political power and maintain it. They try to win the support of the members of the society on the basis of a socio-economic policy and programme.

   In the process, they disseminate political values, norms and socialise the citizen. The political parties socialise the citizen for stability and change of political system.

Exercise

1 Development occurs in human being
(a) upto the end of adolescence period
(b) upto the end of childhood
(c) upto the starting of adulthood
(d) throughout the life

2 The meaning of development is
(a) progressive series of changes
(b) progressive series of changes as a result of motivation
(c) progressive series of changes as a result of motivation and experience
(d) series of changes as a result of maturation and experience

3 On the basis of child development, which statement is appropriate?
(a) All the children are homogeneous
(b) Some children are homogeneous
(c) Some children are unique
(d) Every child is unique

4 In child development
(a) emphasis is on process
(b) emphasis is on the role of environment and experience
(c) it is study from conception to adolescence
(d) All of the above

5 Human development is   [CTET Sept 2014]
(a) quantitative
(b) qualitative
(c) unmeasurable to a certain extent
(d) Both (a) and (b)

6 Which of the following is a significant fact about development?   [CG BEd 2019]
(a) It does not follow a predictable pattern
(b) it is a product of the interaction of hereditary and environment
(c) All individuals have similar rates of development
(d) Development proceeds from specific to general

7 "Development is a progressive change in human being or creature that direct towards a define goal", the Statement is said by   [UK BEd 2017]
(a) Harlock   (b) Jean Piaget
(c) James Drever   (d) Freud

8 Which of the following characteristic of development is an incorrect one?
(a) There are individual differences in development
(b) Development is the result of coincidences
(c) It is a continuous process
(d) It is predictable

9 Why is it important for a teacher to know all the aspects of child development?
(a) To understand and solve the problems of students
(b) To apply appropriate teaching methodology
(c) To develop proper learning environment for the students
(d) All of the above

10 Which of the following is a principle of development?
(a) It is a discontinuous process
(b) All processes of development are not inter-connected
(c) It does not proceed at the same pace for all
(d) Development is always linear

11 Naresh and Mukesh have same age group. They show difference in social and mental development. It is due to the following principle of development.
(a) Principle of modifiability
(b) Principle of definite and predictable pattern
(c) Principle of individuality
(d) Principle of uniform pattern

12 "Development is a never ending process". This idea is associated with [CTET Jun 2011]
(a) principle of interrelation
(b) principle of continuity
(c) principle of integration
(d) principle of interaction

13 It is said that 'Development is never ending process'. Which of the following defines it?   [CG BEd 2018]
(a) Principle of interaction
(b) Principle of continuity
(c) Principle of interrelation
(d) Principle of integration

14 The pace of development varies from one individual to another, but it follows ...... pattern. **[CTET Feb 2016]**
(a) a toe-to-head
(b) a haphazard
(c) an unpredictable
(d) a sequential and orderly

15 Which one of the following is correct about development? **[CTET Feb 2016]**
(a) Development begins and ends at birth
(b) Socio-cultural context plays an important role in development
(c) Development is unidimensional
(d) Development is discrete

16 Which one of the following is the true statement corresponding to Cephalocaudal Principle of child's development?
(a) Development is from head to foot
(b) Development is from foot to head
(c) Development is from middle to periphery
(d) None of the above

17 Which of the following is not a principle of development? **[CTET Dec 2019]**
(a) Development is lifelong
(b) Development is modifiable
(c) Development is influenced by both heredity and environment
(d) Development is universal and cultural contents do not influence it

18 Which one of the following is true regarding human development? **[UK BEd 2017]**
(a) General toward general
(b) General toward specific
(c) Specific toward general
(d) Specific toward specific

19 Which of the following is not a principle of development? **[KVS TGT 2017]**
(a) Development does not proceed at the same pace for all children
(b) Development is always linear
(c) Development is a continuous process
(d) All processes of development are interconnected

20 The period of infancy is from
  [CTET Sep 2015]
(a) birth to 2 years (b) birth to 3 years
(c) 2 to 3 years (d) birth to 1 years

21 In which of the following periods does physical growth and development occur at a rapid pace? **[CTET 2019]**
(a) Infancy and early childhood
(b) Early childhood and middle childhood
(c) Middle childhood and adolescence
(d) Adolescence and adulthood

22 Being a teacher what should you learn to understand the nature of children?
  [CG BEd 2018]
(a) Social Science (b) Physics
(c) Child Psychology (d) Geography

23 A period of make belief is **[CG BEd 2016]**
(a) infancy
(b) later childhood
(c) assimilation
(d) adulthood

24 Which of the following is not the characteristics of intellectual development of early childhood? **[UK BEd 2016]**
(a) Increased span of attention
(b) Exploration of environment
(c) Ability to verbalise all known concepts
(d) Ability to distinguish past, present and future

28 Why is it important for the teachers to know about the various stages of child development?

A. To produce a comfortable environment for teaching and learning process.
B. To know and understand the problems faced by a child.
C. To establish an effective communication with the child.
(a) Only A (b) Only B
(c) Both A and C (d) All of these

26 The feeling of shame and pride develops in this stage.
(a) Infancy (b) Childhood
(c) Adolescence (d) Adulthood

27 The children of 6-11 years become proportionately thinner because they
(a) do a lot of exercise
(b) gain height during this period
(c) eat junk food
(d) watch a lot of television

28 Reasoning, curiosity and observation are developed at the age of ....
(a) 7 years   (b) 11 years
(c) 9 years   (d) 6 years

29 Which one out of the following provides information about the roles and behaviours which are acceptable in a group, during early childhood period? **[CTET Feb 2015]**
(a) Siblings and teachers
(b) Teachers and peers
(c) Peers and parents
(d) Parents and siblings

30 Which of the following age groups falls under later childhood category? **[CTET Feb 2015]**
(a) 11 to 18 years   (b) 18 to 24 years
(c) Birth to 6 years   (d) 6 to 11 years

31 Early childhood is .... period focus language development. **[CTET Feb 2016]**
(a) a not-so-significant
(b) an unimportant
(c) a sensitive
(d) a neutral

32 Which of the following is a sensitive period pertaining to language development?
(a) Middle childhood period
(b) Adulthood
(c) Early childhood period
(d) Pre-natal period

33 The most critical period of acquisition and development of language is **[CTET 2019]**
(a) pre-natal period   (b) early childhood
(c) middle childhood   (d) adolescence

34 Which of the following is not a characteristic of childhood? **[DU BEd 2020]**
(a) Extreme gregariousness
(b) Lack of curiosity
(c) Stability in growth
(d) Participation in group and games

35 Which of the following is a sensitive period pertaining to language development? **[IGNOU 2019]**
(a) Middle-childhood period
(b) Adulthood
(c) Early childhood period
(d) Pre-natal period

36 Which among the following also known as the toy age? **[UK BEd 2018]**
(a) Infancy
(b) Early childhood
(c) Middle childhood
(d) Adolescence

37 During 6 to 10 years children start taking interest in **[CG BEd 2017]**
(a) religion   (b) human body
(c) sex   (d) school

38 A child's logical and problem ability grows upto the age of **[UK BEd 2017]**
(a) 15 years   (b) 12 years
(c) 7 years   (d) 8 years

39 In middle childhood, speech is more ...... rather than .... **[CTET Sep 2015]**
(a) socialised, egocentric
(b) animistic, socialised
(c) mature, immature
(d) egocentric, socialised

40 Adolescents get pleasure
(a) in the company of their friends
(b) by examining their body structure and physique
(c) in the company of opposite sex
(d) All of the above

41 In which of the following stages do children become active members of their peer group? **[CTET Jun 2011]**
(a) Adolescence   (b) Adulthood
(c) Early childhood   (d) Childhood

42 Adolescents may experience **[CTET Nov 2012]**
(a) feeling of fear about sins committed in childhood
(b) feeling of self-actualisation
(c) feeling of satiation about life
(d) anxiety and concern about themselves

43 Which is the incorrect way to support the language development? **[CTET Jul 2013]**
(a) Letting the child talk uninterruptedly on a topic
(b) Disapproving the use of their own language
(c) Supporting initiation taken by children
(d) Providing opportunities for using language

44 The period that initiates the transition to adulthood is   [CTET 2019]
(a) End childhood
(b) Adolescence
(c) Middle childhood
(d) Pre-operational period

45 Which years are globally recognised as the most critical years for life long development of a child?   [CG BEd 2018]
(a) 1-3 years   (b) 1-6 years
(c) 6-8 years   (d) 12-16 years

46 Which of the following is an important anger arousing situation during adolescence?
(a) Not getting the needs fulfilled
(b) Biased attitude against them
(c) Unfair and insulting attitude towards them
(d) All of the above

47 Boys are heavier than girls at all age levels except period   [UK BEd 2016]
(a) from 11-14 years   (b) from 4-5 years
(c) from 14-16 years   (d) None of these

48 The best place for a child's cognitive development is   [CG BEd 2017]
(a) playground
(b) auditorium
(c) home
(d) school and class environment

49 Child's basic instincts come from .... and development take place in ....
                    [UK BEd 2017]
(a) environment, heredity
(b) heredity, environment
(c) family, school
(d) society, family

50 Factors influencing the emotional development are
(a) physical health   (b) mental abilities
(c) fatigue   (d) All of these

51 Which of the following is an internal factor of child development?
(a) Intelligence
(b) Physical ability
(c) Heredity factor
(d) All of the above

52 Which of the following is external factor of development?
(a) Economic condition (b) Social condition
(c) Life experiences   (d) All of these

53 Human development is divided into domains such as   [CTET Jan 2012]
(a) physical, spiritual, cognitive and social
(b) physical, cognitive, emotional and social
(c) emotional, cognitive, spiritual and social-psychological
(d) psychological, cognitive, emotional and physical

54 The domains of development such as physical, cognitive, social and emotional are developed in which one of the following processes?   [CG BEd 2019]
(a) Distinctly
(b) Partially
(c) Randomly
(d) Integrated and holistically

55 Which of the following is not a component of human development?   [CG BEd 2018]
(a) Continuity
(b) Sequentiality
(c) Differentiality
(d) None of the above

56 To make understand the theory of child development, a teacher takes help from
                    [UK BEd 2017]
(a) to recognised the economic background
(b) why should teach-justify it?
(c) to address the different style of learning of the students
(d) to recognised social status

57 A child sees a crow flying past the window and says, "A bird." What does this suggest about the child's thinking?
                    [CTET 2016]
A. The child has previously stored memories.
B. The child has developed the concept of a 'bird'.
C. The child has developed some tools of language to communicate her experience.
(a) B and C   (b) A, B and C
(c) Only B   (d) A and B

58 In the context of education, socialisation means
(a) always following social norms
(b) creating one's own social norms
(c)) respecting elders in society
(d) adapting and adjusting to social environment

59 Socialisation is   **[CTET Jul 2013]**
(a) change in social norms
(b) rapport between teacher and taught
(c) process of modernisation of society
(d) adaptation of social norms

60 Socialisation includes social integration, culture transmission and
(a) providing emotional support
(b) discouragement of rebellion
(c) development of the individual's personality
(d) fitting individual into society forcefully

61 Which one is true about socialisation?
(a) Socialisation takes place rapidly if the agencies of socialisation have more common goals and ideas.
(b) Conflicting goals and ideas of socialisation agencies slower down the socialisation process of individuals.
(c) Formal socialisation takes place through direct instruction.
(d) All of the above

62 The general process of acquiring culture is referred to as
(a) acculturation   (b) socialisation
(c) moral development (d) None of these

63 Which of the following things is normally learned during the socialisation process?
(a) The roles we are to play in life
(b) The culture's norms
(c) The language of the people around us
(d) All of the above

64 Which of the following statements is true?
(a) Socialisation plays no part in personality development of individuals
(b) Large scale complex societies that are not culturally homogenous usually have unanimous agreement about what should be the shared norms
(c) Successful socialisation can result in uniformity within a society
(d) Both (a) and (b)

65 Individuals who have not been socialised in the same way as the majority of people are often considered by their society to be
(a) mentally ill
(b) abnormal or odd
(c) deviant
(d) All of the above

66 When does socialisation begin?
(a) At the time when an individual is conceived or within the first few weeks following conception
(b) At birth or shortly thereafter.
(c) On entering nursery school or kindergarten
(d) When children reach puberty and are able to understand the reasons for society's rules

67 Which of the following is true about socialisation?
(a) Early childhood is the period of the most intense and the most crucial socialisation
(b) Socialisation continues until we are adults and then usually stops because we have learned our culture by that time
(c) All cultures use the same techniques to socialise their children
(d) None of the above

68 In the context of education, socialisation means   **[UK BEd 2018]**
(a) always following social norms
(b) creating one's own social norms
(c) respecting elders in society
(d) adapting and adjusting to social environment

69 Process of socialisation does not include   **[BHU BEd 2018]**
(a) acquiring values and beliefs
(b) genetic transmission
(c) learning the customs and norms of a culture
(d) acquisition of skills

70 Which of the following signifies the importance of socialisation?
(a) Socialisation means transfer of culture
(b) It plays a unique role in personality development of the individual
(c) The self emerges throught the process of socialisation
(d) All of the above

71 In which of the following stages do children become active members of their peer group? **[CTET Jun 2011]**
(a) Adolescence
(b) Adulthood
(c) Early childhood
(d) Childhood

72 Children's attitudes towards persons of ethnic groups different from them are most strongly influenced by the attitudes of
(a) their parents
(b) their peers
(c) the mass media
(d) their siblings

73 Which one of the following is the primary agent of socialisation? **[CTET Sep 2015]**
(a) Computer (b) Heredity
(c) Political parties (d) Family

74 Family plays .... role in socialisation of the child. **[CTET Feb 2016]**
(a) a not-so-important
(b) an exciting
(c) a primary
(d) a secondary

75 Which of the following is the most influential agent of socialisation? **[CG BEd 2018]**
(a) Family (b) Peers
(c) Media (d) Teacher

76 Which of the following parenting styles is most effective for development of children's social competence? **[CG BEd 2019]**
(a) Authoritarian
(b) Neglectful
(c) Authoritative
(d) Indulgent

77 Which of the following is a passive agency of socialisation? **[CTET Sep 2014]**
(a) Health club
(b) Family
(c) Eco club
(d) Public library

78 Which of the following are secondary agents of socialisation? **[CTET Sep 2016]**
(a) School and neighbourhood
(b) School and immediate family member
(c) Family and relatives
(d) Family and neighbourhood

79 Play has a significant role in development of young children for the following reasons, except **[CTET 2018]**
(a) they acquire new skills and learn when to use them
(b) they gain mastery over their body
(c) it stimulates their senses
(d) it is just a pleasant way to spend time

80 In the context of socialisation, schools often have a hidden curriculum which consists of **[IGNOU BEd 2019]**
(a) negotiating and resisting socialisation of students through their families
(b) teaching and assessment of values and attitudes
(c) forcible learning, thinking and behaving in particular ways by imitating peers and teachers
(d) the informal cues about social roles presented in schools through interaction and materials

81 School is an institution of socialisation of children, where **[IGNOU BEd 2019]**
(a) school routines occupy the central position
(b) school activities occupy the central position
(c) school teachers occupy the central position
(d) school children occupy the central position

82 Which of the following are examples of secondary socialising agency? **[CTET 2019]**
(a) Family and neighbourhood
(b) Family and media
(c) School and media
(d) Media and neighbourhood

83 Which of the following are secondary agents of socialisation? **[CTET 2016]**
(a) School and neighbourhood
(b) School and immediate family members
(c) Family and relatives
(d) Family and neighbourhood

84 In the progressive model of education as implemented by CBSE, socialisation of children is done in such a way, so as to expect them to
(a) give up time-consuming social habits and learn how to score good grades
(b) be an active participant in the group work and learn social skills
(c) prepare themselves to conform to the rules and regulations of society without questioning
(d) accept what they are offered by the school irrespective of their social background

85 Which type of nature will you have in your class to increase the process of socialisation?
(a) Strict
(b) Loving and sympathetic
(c) Normal
(d) None of the above

86 According to Erikson, in which of the following stages in life is an individual able to start assisting in the socialisation of others?
(a) Stage of industry vs inferiority
(b) Stage of indentity vs role
(c) Stage of intimacy vs isolation
(d) Stage of generativity vs stagnation

87 Which would be the best first theme to start with in a nursery class?
(a) My family   [CTET Nov 2012]
(b) My best friend
(c) My neighbourhood
(d) My school

88 A teenager who decides not to steal because she believes it is wrong even though no one is looking would be guided by
(a) internal socialisation
(b) external socialisation
(c) secondary socialisation
(d) adult socialisation

89 Which of the following is the most effective way to help children develop social values?   [KVS-TGT-2017]
(a) Reciting good moral stories
(b) Disciplining them in mores and values that the society recognises
(c) Presenting one's own behaviour as a model for them
(d) Telling them about great people

90 'Gender' is a/an   [CTET 2016]
(a) physiological construct
(b) innate quality
(c) social construct
(d) biological entity

Answers

1. (d)	2. (c)	3. (d)	4. (d)	5. (d)	6. (b)	7. (c)	8. (b)	9. (d)	10. (c)
11. (c)	12. (b)	13. (b)	14. (d)	15. (b)	16. (a)	17. (d)	18. (b)	19. (b)	20. (a)
21. (a)	22. (c)	23. (a)	24. (c)	25. (d)	26. (b)	27. (b)	28. (c)	29. (d)	30. (d)
31. (c)	32. (c)	33. (b)	34. (b)	35. (c)	36. (b)	37. (d)	38. (b)	39. (a)	40. (d)
41. (a)	42. (d)	43. (b)	44. (b)	45. (d)	46. (d)	47. (a)	48. (d)	49. (b)	50. (d)
51. (d)	52. (d)	53. (d)	54. (d)	55. (d)	56. (c)	57. (b)	58. (d)	59. (d)	60. (c)
61. (d)	62. (b)	63. (d)	64. (c)	65. (d)	66. (b)	67. (a)	68. (d)	69. (b)	70. (d)
71. (a)	72. (a)	73. (d)	74. (c)	75. (a)	76. (c)	77. (d)	78. (a)	79. (d)	80. (d)
81. (d)	82. (c)	83. (a)	84. (b)	85. (b)	86. (c)	87. (a)	88. (a)	89. (c)	90. (c)

Chapter 13

Learning and Motivation

Learning

Learning, in psychology is the process by which a relatively lasting change in potential behaviour occurs because of practice or experience. Learning is also a process of acquiring modifications in existing knowledge, skills, habits, or tendencies through experience, practice, or exercise. Learning is a continuous process which starts right from the time of birth of an individual and continues till death.

We all are engaged in the learning endeavours in order to develop our adaptive capabilities as per the requirements of the changing environment. For a learning to occur, two things are important

1. The presence of a stimulus in the environment.
2. Innate dispositions like emotional and instinctual dispositions.

A person keeps on learning across all the stages of life, by constructing or reconstructing experiences under the influence of emotional and instinctual dispositions.

Definitions of Learning

According to **Gates** and **others**, "Learning is the modification of behaviour through experience".

According to **Skinner**, "Learning is the process of progressive behaviour adaptation".

According to **Munn**, "To learn is to modify behaviour and experience".

According to **ML Bigge**, "Learning may be considered as change in insights, behaviour, perception, motivation or a combination of these".

Nature of Learning

1. **Learning is Adaptation or Adjustment** All persons continuously interact with their environment. We often make adjustment and adapt to our social environment. Through a process of continuous learning, the individual prepares himself for necessary adjustment or adaptation.

2. **Learning is Improvement** Learning is often considered as a process of improvement with practice or training. We learn many things, which helps us to improve our performance.

3. **Learning is Organising Experience** Learning is not mere addition of knowledge. It is the re-organisation of experience.

4. **Learning Brings Behavioural Changes** Whatever the direction of the changes may be learning brings progressive changes in the behaviour of an individual. That is why he is able to adjust to changing situations.

5. **Learning is Active** Learning does not take place without a purpose and self activity. In any teaching learning process, the activity of the learner counts more than the activity of a teacher.

6. **Learning is Goal Directed** When the aim and purpose of learning is clear, an individual learns immediately. It is the purpose or goal, which determines what the learner sees in the learning situations and how he acts. If there is no purpose or goal, learning can hardly be seen.

7. **Learning is Universal and Continuous** All living creatures learn. Every moment the individual engages himself to learn more and more. Right from the birth of a child till the death, learning continues.

Characteristics of Learning

- Learning is a continuous modification of behaviour which continues throughout life.
- Learning is pervasive. It teaches all aspects of human life.
- Learning involves the whole person, socially, emotionally and intellectually.
- Learning is often a change in the organisation of behaviour.
- Learning is development. Time is one of its dimensions.
- Learning is responsive to incentives. In most cases, positive incentives such as rewards are most effective than negative incentives such as punishments.
- Learning is always concerned with goals. These goals can be expressed in terms of observable behaviour.
- Interest and learning are positively related. The individual learns best those things, which he is interested to learn. Most boys find learning to play football easier than learning to add fractions.
- Learning depends on maturation and motivation.

Factors Influencing to Learning

There are different factors which influence learning process

1. Personal Factors

The process of learning is influenced by a variety of factors. Thorough knowledge of these factors will prove to be very helpful for teachers and parents in understanding and guiding their children's learning.

(i) **Sensation and Perception** Apart from the general health of the students, sensation and perception are the psychological factors which help in learning. Sensation is at the core of perception. There are five sense organs i.e., skin, ears, tongue, eyes and nose. These sense organs are the gateways of knowledge and help in perception of various stimuli in the environment.

(ii) **Fatigue and Boredom** The difference between the two is that fatigue is mental or physical tiredness which decreases the efficiency and competency to work. Boredom, on the other hand is a lack of desire or an aversion to work. Such an aversion makes one feel fatigued without being actually fatigued. Studying seldom causes fatigue. It is mainly boredom which, besides causing the impresssion of fatigue, decreases student's efficiency in learning.

(iii) **Age and Maturation** Learning is directly dependent upon age and maturation. No learning can take place unless individual is matured enough to learn. Some children can learn better at earlier age while others take more time to learn the same content.

(iv) **Emotional Conditions** Desirable emotional conditions enhance the quality and speed of learning. Happiness, joy and satisfaction are always favourable for any type of learning. Adverse emotional conditions, on the other hand, hinder learning. Many studies have established the fact that emotional strain, stress, tensions, disturbances, etc. are extremely harmful.

(v) **Needs** A need is the lack of something. If need is fulfilled, it would facilitate child's usual behaviour. If lack of something is experienced by a child, the child then tries to perform that activity which culminates in the satisfaction of the need.

(vi) **Interests** As the child grows older his interests diversify and stabilise. You, a school teacher, should have thorough knowledge of children's interests. Once the student's interest is aroused in an activity you should expand more effort on it. No learning can be achieved without proper expenditure of effort on it.

(vii) **Intelligence** Intelligence is expressed by an IQ score on an intelligence test, is positively related to learning. Generally, students with higher IQ learn rapidly.

(viii) **Aptitude** A student who possesses appropriate aptitude for a particular subject of study or skill will learn better and retain it for a longer time. On the other hand, he will require relatively longer time to study a subject for which he lacks natural aptitude. He is liable to forget it soon.

(ix) **Attitude** The learning process is also influenced considerable by the attitude of the student. If he is alert, attentive and interested in the material to be learnt he is bound to have a favourable attitude towards it.

2. Environmental Factors

Environmental factors influence a child right from its birth. Environment of a child refers to his surroundings such as home, school, locality, neighbourhood, etc. At these places, the child interacts with his family members, teachers, classmates or peers and neighbours, and establishes relationship with them. The relationship with the members of the society and the surroundings may affect the development of the child and also the way he learns. Some of the environmental factors are discussed as follows

(i) **Surroundings Natural, Social and Cultural** Environment as the title of the sub-section indicates, we shall discuss here natural, social and cultural environment, the child interacts with and gets influenced.

(a) **Natural surrounding** covers the climatic and atmospheric condition. These conditions affect learning directly. It has been found that high temperature and humidity reduces mental efficiency. For a limited time, humidity and high temperature can be tolerated but prolonged humidity and high temperature become unbearable and decrease mental efficiency.

(b) **Social surrounding** includes especially the environment of home, school and locality. Physical conditions at home such as large family, small family, insufficient ventilation, improper lighting, uncomfortable temperature, noisy home environment due to the use of radio, television, etc. Noisy neighbourhood, constant visits by friends or relatives etc. influence the intellectual learning of the student.

(c) **Cultural demands** and social expectations also influence learning. The spirit of culture is reflected in its social and educational institutions. Children's learning, therefore, is greatly determined by the demands and expectations of their culture.

(ii) **Relationship with Teachers, Parents and Peers** The teacher is an important constituent in the instructional process. She/He plays an important role in shaping the behaviour of students. The way he teaches and manages the students has an effect on their learning.

Relationship with parents plays a vital role in the learning process of the student. If the child-parents relationship is based on mutual respect and faith, it can provide the child a congenial atmosphere which in turn can facilitate his/her learning. A distorted and unhealthy environment, on the other hand, adversely affects the learning of the student.

A healthy peer group relationship also plays an important role in learning. Student-student relationship in the classroom, school, society etc. create a particular type of emotional environment. The environment solely depends upon their relationships.

(iii) **Media Influence on Learning** Media has been considered an important component of transmitting information. Media can be divided into two broad categories print and non-print media. Print media refers to texts or printed materials. It is economical and has traditionally been used for pedagogical purposes.

Motivation

Motivation is the process that initiates, guides and maintains goal-oriented behaviours. Motivation as the name suggests, is what 'moves us'. It is what causes an individual to act, whether it is getting a glass of water to reduce thirst or reading a book to gain knowledge.

Motivation involves the biological, emotional, social and cognitive forces that activate behaviour. In everyday usage, the term 'motivation' is frequently used to describe why a person does something. It is the driving force behind human actions.

Motivation does not just refer to the factors that activate behaviours, it also involves the factors that direct and maintain these goal-directed actions (through such motives are rarely directly observable).

As a result, we often have to infer the reason why people do the things that they do based on observable behaviour.

Definitions of Motivation

According to **Skinner**, "Motivation is the super highway to learning".

According to **Good**, "Motivation is the process of arousing, sustaining and regulating activity".

Types of Motivation

There are two types of motivation or arousals. They can either be internally or externally driven. The desire for food or sex arises from within us (intrinsic), while the yearning to obtain recognition or approval is influenced by the conditions in our environment (extrinsic).

In view of the above explanation, motivation is divided into intrinsic and extrinsic, which are as follows

1. Intrinsic (Internal) Motivation

It is an internal force or motive or genetically predetermined disposition to behave in a particular way when an individual faces a particular situation.

This type of motivation includes feelings of self-confidence and competence in an individual.

A student who is intrinsically motivated may carry out a task because of the enjoyment he/she derives from such a task. In another way, a dog that sees a bone and runs for it did that because of the satisfaction it derives from eating bone. This type of behaviour does not require any prior learning.

2. Extrinsic (External) Motivation

It is the external or environmental factor, which sets the individual's behaviour into motion. The incentive/reinforce drives an individual's behaviour towards a goal.

A student, who is extrinsically motivated, will execute an action in order to obtain some reward or avoid some sanctions. For example, a student who studied hard for the examination because of the desire to obtain better grade.

Extrinsic rewards should be used with caution because they have the potential for decreasing intrinsic motivation.

Therefore, students' motivation automatically has to do with the students' desire to participate in the learning process. It also concerns the reasons or goals that underlie their involvement or non-involvement in academic activities.

Characteristics of Motivation

- Motivation is an internal feeling which generates within an individual. Motivation factors are always unconscious but they are to be aroused by managerial actions.
- Motivation is based on needs such as fundamental needs (food, clothes, shelter, etc.) and ego-satisfaction needs (self-development and self-actualisation). These needs vary with individuals and with the same individual over time.
- Motivation causes goal-directed behaviour. Feeling of needs by the person causes him to behave in such a way that he tries to satisfy himself. Goal and motives cannot be separated.
- Motivation implies à drive toward an outcome while satisfaction involves outcomes already experienced. Satisfaction is the contentment experienced when a want is satisfied.
- Motivation is an unending process. Wants are innumerable and cannot be satisfied at one time. If one basic need is adequately satisfied for a given individual, it loses power as a motivator, but other needs continue to emerge.

Factors influencing Learner's Motivation

1. **The Activities in the Teaching Learning Process** This factor is important because a great part of the learner's interest in the subject will depend on the types of activities developed in class.
2. **The Final Results** Good results are understood as a reward for the learner, whereas bad results are similar to a punishment. In this case, motivation is the consequence of these results. Students with good final results are going to be more motivated than students with bad results.
3. **Internal Motivation** This is connected to the student's inner drive about the subject as a consequence of previous experience and the use of the subject to their daily lives.
4. **Extrinsic Motivation** The influence of external stimuli such as rewards or punishments.

Fundamentals of Motivation

Motivating students is a complicated business no matter what age they may be. When students want to complete their work and want to succeed, things will go well in your classroom, they will learn and you will have a rewarding day at school. Here are ten very brief ideas that are useful in teaching practices

1. **Purpose of Learning** Teachers and students should work together to establish long-term goals so that the work is relevant to students' lives and driven by a purpose. There is rarely a student who want to work just for the sake of working.

2. **Need of Skills and Knowledge** All the students require necessary knowledge to complete their work and achieve their goals. Help students to achieve short-term goals to develop the competencies they need to be successful. Keeping binders in order, learning to listen carefully, paying attention, etc. These are just some of the skills that students need to make learning accessible.

3. **Specified Direction** When students know exactly what they must do to complete assignments, they will approach their work with confidence and interest. Giving good directions is an art form. Keep them simple, brief and logical.

4. **Teaching with Fun** Teachers who offer enjoyable learning activities find that students are less likely to be off task. (Teachers also want to have fun when they work).

5. **Activity based on Skills** Students find open-ended questions and critical thinking more engaging than activities involving just recall of facts. Rote drills do have a place in any learning environment, but few kids are really inspired by them. Work that requires higher-level thinking skills will move the students in the right direction.

6. **Curiosity** When students want to learn more about a topic, they will tackle challenging assignments in order to satisfy their curiosity.

Even something as simple as asking a provocative question to get students thinking in a new way can spark curiosity.

7. **Regular Encouragement** Teachers who offer sincere praise and encouragement establish a positive, nurturing classroom atmosphere. When students know that they are on the right track, they will want to continue.

8. **Regular Rewards Policy** Rewards help in increasing the student's focus and time in doing his task. When a teacher uses both the motivation rewards separately, each of these motivates the students. But when the teacher uses these rewards simultaneously, the effect of these is much greater.

9. **Collaboration** When students work together, motivation and achievement both soar.

10. **Involvement of Students in Work** The effectiveness of a task is based on the positive behaviour of a teacher towards his students.

Why should students work for a grouchy teacher? If your students know that they matter to you, then they will be much more inclined to stay on task than if they believe that you are not invested in their success.

Exercise

1 Learning can be enriched if
 (a) situations from the real world are brought into the class in which students interact with each other and the teacher facilitates them
 (b) more and more teaching aids are used in the class
 (c) teachers use different types of lectures and explanation
 (d) due attention is paid to periodic tests in the class

2 Which learning structure suits to extrinsic techniques of motivation?
 (a) Signal learning (b) Chain learning
 (c) All of these (d) None of these

3 Which of the following defines nature of learning?
 (a) Learning is adaptation
 (b) Learning is improvement
 (c) Learning is organising experience
 (d) All of the above

4 Learning **[UK BEd 2018]**
 (a) is not affected by a learner's emotions
 (b) has very little connection with emotions
 (c) is independent of a learner's emotions
 (d) is influenced by a learner's emotions

5 The most appropriate meaning of learning is **[DU BEd 2018]**
 (a) modification of behaviour
 (b) inculcation of knowledge
 (c) personal adjustment
 (d) acquisition of skills

6 Which one of the following is central to learning? **[BHU BEd 2018]**
 (a) Conditioning (b) Rote memorisation
 (c) Imitation (d) Meaning-making

7 A conducive learning environment creates **[Bihar BEd 2018]**
 (a) comfortable teaching
 (b) focused students
 (c) improved learning results
 (d) All of the above

8 Learning may be defined as a relatively .... change in behaviour. **[Bihar BEd 2018]**
 (a) temporary (b) permanent
 (c) slow (d) complicated

9 Identify the condition necessary for promoting learning in school. **[Bihar BEd 2018]**
 (a) Neatness (d) Cleanliness
 (c) Sanitation (d) All of these

10 Which of the following statements regarding children and their learning is correct? **[CTET 2019]**
 (a) Children have to be rewarded and punished to make them motivated for learning
 (b) All children are naturally motivated to learn and are capable of learning
 (c) Children's motivation to learn and their capability to learn is pre-determined by heredity only
 (d) Children's socio-economic background determines and limits their motivation and learning capability

11 Learning is **[UK BEd 2019]**
 (a) everything we know is learned
 (b) a relatively permanent influence on behaviour, knowledge and skill
 (c) directly observable and measurable
 (d) limited to particular age level

12 'Learning is the modification of behaviour through experience and training'. This statement was given by
 (a) Gates and Others **[IGNOU BEd 2019]**
 (b) Morgan and Gilliland
 (c) Skinner
 (d) Cronbach

13 Which one of the following classrooms encourages rich learning? **[CTET 2018]**
 (a) A classroom with structured and planned learning driven by textbook content
 (b) A classroom with a variety of material displayed in the class beyond the reach of children so that the material lasts longer
 (c) A classroom with open activity corners and a variety of children's literature in open shelves accessible any time of the day
 (d) A classroom with neatly organised material in cupboards brought out once a week for free play

14 Many educationists and psychologists have defined learning in different ways. According to these, definitions learning is a .... continuous process?

(a) life long   **[UK BEd 2017]**
(b) upto childhood
(c) upto old age
(d) upto adulthood

15 Which of the following describes the change in an individual's behaviour arising from experience?   **[KVS TGT 2017]**

(a) Motivation
(b) Modelling
(c) Learning
(d) Perception

16 Best learning is that which   **[CG BEd 2016]**

(a) is given by a knowledgeable teacher
(b) the pupils learns themselves
(c) is given by using educational technology
(d) None of the above

17 Which of the following is the characteristic of learning?

(a) Learning is a continuous modification of behaviour
(b) Learning is pervasive
(c) Learning is often a change in the organisation of behaviour
(d) All of the above

18 Characteristics of social constructivist approach of learning is   **[CG BEd 2019]**

(a) emphasis on child's cognition for learning
(b) emphasis on processing of information for learning
(c) emphasis on collaboration with others for learning
(d) emphasis on experiences for learning

19 All are the characteristics of learning except   **[UK, CG BEd 2016]**

(a) learning is a progress of the organism
(b) learning is a process related to educating environment
(c) learning is the result of practice
(d) learning reinforces further learning

20 In chain leaning   **[CG BEd 2016]**

(a) opposite words are used
(b) substitution words are used
(c) Both (a) and (b)
(d) None of the above

21 A very useful principle of learning that a new response is strengthened by is

(a) punishment
(b) reinforcement
(c) biofeedback
(d) discriminative stimulus

22 Which of the following is a domain of learning?   **[UK BEd 2018]**

(a) Professional   (b) Experiental
(c) Affective   (d) Spiritual

23 Which of the following is not a key process through which meaningful learning occurs?   **[CTET 2019]**

(a) Exploration and interaction
(b) Memorisation and recall
(c) Repetition and practice
(d) Instruction and direction

24 Which of the following statements about learning is correct from a constructivist perspective?   **[CTET 2019]**

(a) Learning is the process of reproduction and recall
(b) Learning is the process of rote memorisation
(c) Learning is conditioning of behaviours by repetitive association
(d) Learning is the process of construction of knowledge by active engagement

25 Learning is influenced by   **[IGNOU 2019]**

(a) social interactions
(b) interpersonal relations
(c) communication with others
(d) All of the above

26 In the process of learning of child, parents should perform the role of......... .   **[CG BEd 2019]**

(a) negative   (b) frontline
(c) sympathetic   (d) neutral

27 Which one of the following is the most suitable to improve children's learning?   **[CTET 2018]**

(a) Teacher should facilitate children to interact with each other on real-life situations
(b) Regular assessment test should be conducted
(c) Teacher should explain the content using different examples and illustrations
(d) All types of learning material should be there in the class

28 According to Lev Vygotsky, learning is
    (a) a conditioned activity   **[CTET Dec 2019]**
    (b) a social activity
    (c) an individual activity
    (d) a passive activity

29 Which of the given principle of learning helps teachers to provide a desirable change of behaviour in learners?
    [UK BEd 2017]
    (a) Theory of Insight
    (b) Theory of Learning by Trial and Error
    (c) Imitation Theory
    (d) Theory of Learning by Experience

30 Which of the following will be most appropriate to maximise learning ?
    [CG BEd 2019]
    (a) Teacher should identity her cognitive style as well as her student's cognitive style
    (b) Individual difference in students should be smoothened by pairing similar students
    (c) Teacher should focus on only one learning style to bring optimum result
    (d) Students of similar cultural background should be kept in the same class to avoid difference in opinion

31 The lowest level of learning in cognitive domain is   **[BHU BEd 2019]**
    (a) knowledge   (b) synthesis
    (c) analysis   (d) comprehension

32 Students learning occurs when
    (a) there is active teaching   **[BHU BEd 2019]**
    (b) parents are active
    (c) principal is vigilant
    (d) students are made active

33 Which one is not an element of positive learning environment?   **[Bihar BEd 2020]**
    (a) Motivating the learner
    (b) Creation of interest
    (c) Control by force
    (d) Planning activities

34 Which of the following statements is true about 'learning'?   **[IGNOU BEd 2017]**
    (a) Errors made by children indicate that no learning has taken place
    (b) Learning is effective in an environment that is emotionally positive and satisfying for learners
    (c) Learning is not affected by emotional factors at any stage of learning
    (d) Learning is fundamentally a mental activity

35 When the pre-learning does not affect the new horizontal learning approach is called as   **[UK BEd 2017]**
    (a) zero transfer of learning
    (b) irrespective transfer of learning
    (c) positive transfer of learning
    (d) negative transfer of learning

36 What is the most important in the process of learning?   **[UK BEd 2017]**
    (a) Child's heredity
    (b) Techniques of learning
    (c) Examination result of learner
    (d) Economic status of the child

37 Zone of proximal development is
    [KVS TGT 2017]
    (a) mental representation of the external world on the part of the child
    (b) series of actions in which a child undergoes social interactions with peers
    (c) range of tasks that a child is in the process of learning to complete
    (d) sum of own conscious thoughts and feelings introspected by child

38 To start the work, continue and stable, it is called
    (a) motivation   (b) learning
    (c) work   (d) play

39 Which of the following factors is not related to motivation?
    (a) Interest   (b) Objectives of life
    (c) Physical fitness   (d) Mental health

40 Abraham Maslow explained theory of motivation in 1954 in the perspective of
    (a) needs   (b) reward
    (c) expectancy   (d) objectives

41 As soon as the process of motivation stops
    (a) activity of the person also stops
    (b) need of the activity becomes dead
    (c) All of the above
    (d) None of the above

42 Goals of life also become motivating force because
    (a) goals become the need of the person
    (b) goals stimulate internal process of the person involved
    (c) All of the above
    (d) None of the above

43 The theory similar to Maslow theory of motivation is
(a) drive theory
(b) social theory
(c) instinct theory
(d) None of these

44 Which point is taken into account by the teacher while selecting a particular technique of motivation?
(a) Learning-objectives and its level
(b) Learning structure
(c) All of the above
(d) None of the above

45 Motivation technique can work only upto
(a) application level of cognitive objectives
(b) comprehension level of objectives
(c) highest level of cognitive domain
(d) None of the above

46 Techniques of motivation are most useful for realising
(a) cognitive objectives
(b) affective objectives
(c) psychomotor objectives
(d) All of the above

47 With the reference to activities relating to the issue of motivation

Key Elements		Action
1. Intrinsic motivation	A.	Begin with some unconditional positive praise . For example, you did that well
2. Extrinsic motivation	B.	The teacher and/or the pupils reconnect with the lesson overview and specific objectives and with agreed personal goals and targets
3. Expectation for success	C.	Encourage learners to identify their own reasons for taking part in the lesson

Codes

	A	B	C			A	B	C
(a)	2	1	3		(b)	3	1	2
(c)	1	3	2		(d)	1	2	3

48 .... is considered a sign of motivated teaching.
(a) Maximum attendance in the class
(b) Remedial work given by the teacher
(c) Questioning by students
(d) Pin drop silence in the class

49 Which of the following is appropriate for environment conductive to thinking and learning in children?
(a) Allowing students to take some decisions about what to learn and how to learn
(b) Passive listening for long periods of time
(c) Home assignments given sequently
(d) Individual tasks done by the learners

50 A student works hard to clear an entrance test for admission into a medical college. The student is said to be motivated
(a) experientially
(b) intrinsically
(c) extrinsically
(d) individually

51 Which of the following is not necessary while giving homework to pupils?
(a) Motivating the pupils to do the homework properly
(b) Giving clear guidelines how to complete the homework
(c) Explaining the purpose of homework
(d) Giving homework on the basis of current learning

52 Which one of the following optimises motivation to learn?
(a) Tendency to choose very easy or difficult goals
(b) Personal satisfaction in meeting targets
(c) Extrinsic factor
(d) Motivation to avoid failure

53 Rajesh is a voracious reader. Apart from studying the course books, he often goes to library and read books on diverse topics. Rajesh does his project even in the lunch break.

He does not need prompting by his teachers or parents to study texts and seems to truly enjoy learning. He can be best describes as a/an.......... .
(a) internally motivated learner
(b) inci-centre learner
(c) teacher motivated learner
(d) measurement-centred learner

54 The inner force that stimulates and compels a behavioural response provides specific direction to that response is
(a) motive
(b) perseverance
(c) emotion
(d) commitment

55 .... motives deal with the need to reach satisfying feeling states to obtain personal goals.
(a) Effective
(b) Affective
(c) Preservation-oriented
(d) Safety-oriented

56 Making students members of a cleanliness community to motivate them for the same, reflects
(a) socio-cultural conceptions of motivation
(b) behaviouristic approach to motivation
(c) humanistic approach to motivation
(d) cognitive approach to motivation

57 Which one of the following strategies should a primary school teacher adopt to motivate her students?   [CTET Sep 2015]
(a) Use incentives rewards and punishment as motivating factors for each activity
(b) Help children set goals as per their interests and support them in working towards the same
(c) Set standard goals for the entire class and have rigid parameters to assess achievement of those goals
(d) Encourage competition for marks amongst individual student

58 What does motivation do in the process of learning?   [UK BEd 2018]
(a) Sharpens memory of the learner
(b) Differentiates new learning from old learning
(c) Makes learners think undirectionally
(d) Creates interest for learning among young learners

59 To encourage children to put in efforts in their studies, teachers need to   [BHU 2018]
(a) control the child
(b) compare the child with others
(c) motivate the child
(d) scold the child

60 The children in a class can be considered to be motivated if   [CTET 2018]
(a) they ask questions seeking clarification from the teacher
(b) they come to school neatly dressed in uniform
(c) they maintain discipline in the class
(d) all are regular in attendance

61 What should a teacher tell her students to encourage them to do tasks with intrinsic motivation?   [CTET 2016]
(a) "Why can't you be like him? See, he has done it perfectly"
(b) "Complete the task fast and get a toffee"
(c) "Try to do it, you will learn"
(d) "Come on, finish it before she does"

62 How can a teacher encourage her students to be intrinsically motivated towards learning for the sake of learning?   [CTET 2016]
(a) By giving competitive tests
(b) By supporting them in setting individual goals and their mastery
(c) By offering tangible rewards such as toffees
(d) By inducing anxiety and fear

Answers

1. (a)	2. (c)	3. (d)	4. (d)	5. (a)	6. (d)	7. (d)	8. (d)	9. (d)	10. (b)
11. (b)	12. (a)	13. (c)	14. (a)	15. (c)	16. (b)	17. (d)	18. (c)	19. (b)	20. (c)
21. (b)	22. (c)	23. (b)	24. (d)	25. (d)	26. (b)	27. (a)	28. (b)	29. (b)	30. (a)
31. (a)	32. (d)	33. (c)	34. (b)	35. (a)	36. (b)	37. (c)	38. (a)	39. (c)	40. (a)
41. (c)	42. (a)	43. (d)	44. (a)	45. (c)	46. (c)	47. (a)	48. (c)	49. (a)	50. (b)
51. (c)	52. (b)	53. (a)	54. (a)	55. (b)	56. (a)	57. (b)	58. (d)	59. (c)	60. (a)
61. (c)	62. (b)								

School Administration and Supervision

Schools are formal institutions where the young members of the community are exposed to values, skills and attitudes that make them useful to themselves and the society. The Education Commission recommended that schools have to be more accountable for their performance and more transparent in their operation and administration.

School administration and supervision refers to such administrative work system, which creates a learning environment between the teacher and the students. It ensures the availability of necessary materials, manages and makes the teaching method effective by supervising the need.

It does all the work related to education. Along with this, it also plays an important role in the implementation of education system and in the formation of time-table.

This administration is also important in the personality development of students. Seeing the importance of its working method, Weish and Ruffner have said that "educational administration is the process by which the goals of education can be easily achieved. Therefore, education can be made accessible by working at different levels of school and supervision."

School administration and supervision are the important components of the management of the school.

School Administration and Supervision

In the absence of proper administration and supervision in the school, the education system in the school cannot run properly. Education also determines the direction of our life, keeping this in mind the school administration and supervision system is divided into three levels

1. Administration and supervision at the internal level.
2. Administration and supervision at the committee level.
3. Administration and supervision at the departmental level.

Administration and Supervision at the Internal Level

- The administration and supervision of the school at the internal level depends on the nature of the school.
- The headmaster is primarily responsible for the management and operation of all the activities of the school.
- The Principal constitutes the Admission Committee, Curriculum Committee, Academic Counselling Committee and Examination Committee.

- All these committees work in their respective areas. He plays an important role in the activities related to admission to curriculum and examination.
- A teachers' committee is formed, in which Time-Table Committee, Library Committee, Student Support Committee (by 15 to 20 talented students) and Scholarship Committee are formed.
- Apart from all this, many extra-curricular activities are organised in the schools, in which optimum all round development of the personality of the students can be achieved.

Administration and Supervision at Committee Level

Many material resources are arranged under the committee level supervision and administration, which are considered to be the basic needs of the school.

School Premises

- Students should be told about the importance of cleanliness of the school premises by teachers, and many competitions should be organised from time to time regarding cleanliness.
- To make the school environment clean and beautiful, gardens of trees and plants should be planted, so that the environment of the school will be fragrant and pollution free and the health of the students will also remain good.
- CCTV cameras should be installed in the school premises so that every activity of the school can be monitored.
- Students should also cooperate in keeping the school clean, they should not spread garbage anywhere but always put it in the dustbin.
- The environment of the school campus should be such that the student feels safe without any fear.

Classroom

- Classroom is the most important physical resource within the school.
- Children's painting arts and crafts should be displayed on the walls and shelves of the classroom from time to time.
- The physical structure and size of the room should be such that children can sit in small groups or can sit in circles to tell or listen to a story.
- School and classroom spaces can be used for educational resources i.e., blackboard can be made by painting the classroom walls upto a height of 4 feet, so that the child can easily write with chalk.

Library

- The library should be built in a quiet place, which is free from noise.
- The library should have good seating arrangement for the students.
- In addition to the books related to the curriculum in the library, it is also necessary to have stories, poetry, educational novels, sports magazines and contemporary magazines.

Laboratory

- In today's scientific age, the emphasis is on acquiring practical knowledge, skills and attitude.
- Various scientific subjects have an important place in the curriculum of different levels of the school.
- Therefore, there is a need for well-organised and well-equipped laboratories to give practical form to their teaching.
- Through these, the teaching of scientific subjects is also made interesting and accuracy is given to these subjects.
- The child is able to acquire knowledge by doing or investigating himself and adopts the point of view of the investigator.

Computer Lab

- Computer Lab is a place where computer knowledge and services are provided to students and people.
- At present, computer literacy has been made compulsory from primary and upper primary classes along with the implementation of NCERT syllabus in government education.
- Therefore, it is very important to arrange computer labs in the schools for the students to have access to computers.
- It is very important to have adequate amount of computers, internet service, proper seating arrangement for students, etc., in computer lab, as well as there should be trained computer teachers in the school.

Assembly Hall

- Generally every school needs to have a big hall. It is imperative to have this in schools in urban areas.
- The determination of its length and width is based on the number of students in the school.
- It should have a platform on one side, which can be used for resources, used in seminars and other cultural programs.

Playground

- It is an essential part of life and has more importance in students' life.
- It helps a lot in physical and mental development.
- There should be enough grass in the playground, so that no student is injured by falling while playing, as well as there should be a complete arrangement for the spectators in the playground.

Principal Office

In addition to the general office, special rooms, halls, etc., there should be a principal office in the school building, so that the work of school can be done smoothly.

Teachers' Staff Room

There should be a teachers' staff room for the teachers, in which there should be suitable arrangement for their sitting, keeping files and books.

Toilets

- Toilets should be mandatory in every school. There should be separate toilets for boys and girls in schools.
- The arrangement of water in these toilets should be good, as well as soaps or hand wash should also be available.
- There should be a dustbin near the toilet room.

Water Supply

There should be a system of cold water for the students during the summer days. The water tank should be cleaned once a week. There should be good drainage system in the school premises.

Canteen

It is also very necessary to make arrangements for canteen in the school, in which arrangements should be made for lunch or refreshments of children.

Hostel Arrangements

- Hostel arrangements should also be made in schools. Often many students come to study from far away places, they are not able to travel from home to school every day.
- Hostel arrangements should be made for such students, so that their time can be saved and they can make good use of that time.
- In the hostel, there should be arrangement of good and healthy food, clean water for drinking, place to eat and rest.

It is the duty of the headmaster to inspect the hostel from time to time, so that he can know what level of facilities are provided in the hostels and how these can be improved substantially.

Administration and Supervision at the Departmental Level

The role of administration and supervision at the departmental level is considered very important in schools.

The functions of the committees constituted at the departmental level are limited to their department only. Such committees mainly work in a diagnostic manner and solve problems promptly.

Different committees are formed for various functions such as for teaching, classroom, school premises, library, sanitation, computer labs, laboratories, drinking water, hostel, sports, etc. They submit their report to the departmental head. The Head of the Department takes necessary steps as per the report.

The working system of the departmental committee is considered democratic, because the Departmental Committee works according to the instructions of the central or internal committee. The following are responsible for the administration and supervision at the departmental level

Responsibility of Primary Class Teachers The role of primary teachers is important in the administration of the school. The most important task of primary education is to analyse and improve the performance of teachers so that they can teach as per the levels and needs of students.

Responsibility of the Principal The role of the principal is considered important in the school administration. He directly supervises the works. The headmaster of the school is expected to make proper arrangements for teaching courses in the school. Also, it is the primary responsibility of the principal to provide quality leadership to the teaching plan.

Duties of the School Superintendent The school superintendent regularly inspects the schools. He recommends rules, controls and provides special help in the organisation of the school council. He presides over the various meetings of the school council and prepares the regular calendar of the school session.

A superintendent is believed to provide informational and collaborative benefits to teachers. The role of the superintendent is considered to be constructive and creative.

1 School is formal institution that provides
    (a) Values to the learners
    (b) Skills to the learners
    (c) Attitude to the learners
    (d) All of the above

2 Which of the following is true?
    (a) School is a social institution
    (b) School is an agent of social progress
    (c) Social organisations are human structures designed to achieve common goals
    (d) All of the above

3 Which of the following provides direction to our life?
    (a) Social environment
    (b) Education
    (c) Laboratory
    (d) Administrative structure

4 For the smooth functioning of the education system, what is very important to have in the school?
    (a) Administrative system and supervision
    (b) Supervision and educational planning
    (c) Educational environment and planning
    (d) All of the above

5 In how many levels the school administration and supervision system is divided?
    (a) 5   (b) 4
    (c) 3   (d) 2

6 If the size of the school is large, then to whom does the principal entrust the responsibility of supervision and administration?
    (a) Students   (b) Teachers
    (c) Superintendents   (d) All of these

7 Who conducts the administrative work of the whole school?
    (a) Principal
    (b) Teacher
    (c) District Education Officer
    (d) Block Education Officer

8 Who constitutes the committees associated with school administration and supervision at the internal level?
    (a) Teacher
    (b) Department Head
    (c) Principal/Headmaster
    (d) Black Education Officer

9 Which committee does the principal constitute?
    (a) Admission Committee
    (b) Curriculum Committee
    (c) Examination Committee
    (d) All of the above

10 Which committee is formed to plan teaching-learning process?
    (a) Library Committee
    (b) Student Support Committee
    (c) Scholarship Committee
    (d) All of the above

11 How many talented students are included in the Student Support Committee?
    (a) 10-15   (b) 15-20
    (c) 20-25   (d) 30-35

12 Which of the following committees is not constituted to conduct the co-curricular activities?
    (a) Sports Committee
    (b) Publication Committee
    (c) Curriculum Committee
    (d) None of the above

13 Which of the following is not a part of school building?
    (a) Girl's hostel
    (b) Laboratories
    (c) Gymnasium
    (d) National Highway

14 Which institution is the center to increase our daily efficiency?
    (a) Reading room   (b) Playground
    (c) School   (d) Family

15 The benefit of planting trees in school is
(a) It increases tree cover
(b) It provides pollution free environment
(c) Cleanliness
(d) All of the above

16 Suitable infrastructure to make teaching effective is
(a) School ground
(b) School building
(c) Blackboard
(d) All of the above

17 What should be done to keep the school environment fragrant and pollution free?　**[Bihar BEd 2018]**
(a) Do painting
(b) Do gardening
(c) The auditorium should be surrounded
(d) Facility of drinking water should be made

18 To keep control on every activity of the school
(a) Private guard should be appointed
(b) Inspector should be appointed
(c) Police surveillance should be increased
(d) CCTV cameras should be installed

19 School should have classroom
(a) in secret place
(b) under the open sky
(c) under tree
(d) fully ventilated

20 What should be the physical structure and size of the classroom?
(a) Very large
(b) Very small
(c) Of natural size
(d) As per the strength of students in a class

21 The corner of a classroom is used as
(a) for punishing students
(b) for keeping cupboards
(c) to keep study material
(d) for decoration purpose

22 Where is the school library built?
(a) In a quiet place
(b) Next to office
(c) Beside canteen
(d) Next to toilet

23 Which of the following is not an example of physical infrastructure of a school?　**[Bihar BEd 2020]**
(a) Playground　　　　(b) Building
(c) Laboratory　　　　(d) Library

24 Whose arrangement is mandatory near the toilet?
(a) Water　　　　　　(b) Dustbin
(c) Gardening　　　　(d) Both (a) and (b)

25 Why is it necessary to drain water from the school premises?
(a) There should be no stagnation of water
(b) Diseases should not spread
(c) Cleanliness should be maintained
(d) All of the above

26 Which of the following is the greatest problem for school?　**[Bihar BEd 2020]**
(a) Lack of finance
(b) Lack of good infrastructure
(c) Lack of good teachers
(d) Lack of students continuously

27 The main aim of educational supervision is
(a) Promotion of welfare of students
(b) Organisation of teaching working days
(c) Best use of school systems
(d) Best implementation of curriculum

28 The school principal is directly responsible
(a) to the local school board
(b) to the education committee of the school board
(c) to the local superintendent
(d) to the state superintendent

29 Which of the following is necessary for proper management of school's physical resources?　**[Bihar BEd 2018]**
(a) Preparing improvement projects
(b) Finding ways to finance resource management
(c) Getting feedback on management procedure
(d) All of the above

30 Characteristics of human resource management in school are **[Bihar BEd 2018]**
(a) Hiring of school staff
(b) Construction of classrooms
(c) Influence of students in school
(d) All of the above

31 Accurate position descriptions are the backbone of a good   **[Bihar BEd 2018]**
(a) HR system
(b) Staff system
(c) School class system
(d) Training system

32 If you find the administration of the school irregularities are on the rise, which of the following solutions will you follow?
  [MP BEd 2016]
(a) Coordination between managing committee, principal, teachers and students
(b) Solve problems of students
(c) Solve problems of teachers
(d) Impose severe punishment

33 Which of the following is an example of effective school practice?   **[CTET 2018]**
(a) Corporal punishment
(b) Individualised learning
(c) Competive classroom
(d) Constant comprative evaluation

34 Which one is not the quality of a good school?   **[Bihar B Ed 2020]**
(a) Teaching of all subjects
(b) Conduction of debates and essay writing
(c) No organisation of games
(d) Well developed laboratories

35 The educational institution with no barrier of age of study is termed as
  [Bihar BEd 2020]
(a) Free institution of education
(b) Closed institution of education
(c) Evening institution of education
(d) Open education institution

36 Mrs Kapur, a teacher of class III wants her students to enjoy school. She makes few academic or behaviour demands on them. She believes in the importance of giving students autonomy.

In her interaction with students, she tries hard to be a good listener, to emphathise, and to show warmth and affection. She knows that students sometimes take advantage of her, but believes that students will eventually develop a sense of responsibility for their own learning and behaviour.   **[KVS TGT 2017]**

Which of the classroom management style is she practising?
(a) Democratic
(b) Authoritative
(c) Authoritarian
(d) Permissive

37 If remarks are passed by students on you, as a teacher, you will   **[DU BEd 2018]**
(a) punish them
(b) expel them from the college
(c) be impartial at the time of evaluation
(d) take revenge while evaluating internal test copies

38 Classroom discipline can be maintained effectively by   **[DU BEd 2018]**
(a) knowing the cause of indiscipline and handling it with stern hand
(b) by putting on fancy clothes in the classroom
(c) providing a programee which is according to the interest of the pupils
(d) None of the above

39 Which is not desired in schools?
  [Bihar BEd 2020]
(a) Regular attendance
(b) Good conduct
(c) Corporal punishment
(d) Awards

40 The school through its programmes help students to   **[IGNOU BEd 2017]**
(a) assimilate culture
(b) protest culture
(c) ignore other culture
(d) make them cultured

41 Ms. Shailja, a teacher of class V has high expectations from her students in terms of both academic achievement and social personal behaviour. She believes that it is important to create a warm, supportive classroom environment that is sensitive to students needs. She is firm but takes time to provide rationale for various classroom rules. She believes that there must be conseqeunces when students violate the rules, but she tries to invoke penalties that are fair and that dont humiliate students. **[KVS TGT 2017]**

Which of the classroom management style is she practising?
(a) Laissez faire
(b) Authoritarian
(c) Permissive
(d) Authoritative

42 School help students to ...... with its events and programs. **[Bihar BEd 2019]**
(a) cultural intermingle
(b) ignore other cultures
(c) oppose the culture
(d) become cultured

43 The educational environment in a school can be adversely affected if **[Bihar BEd 2019]**
(a) physical punishment is given everytime
(b) the students are encouraged to write wall magazines pamphlet
(c) teachers are left free to try new laws and process
(d) frequent parents teachers association meeting are held

44 According to your point of view, sports activities in a school **[Bihar BEd 2019]**
(a) are important for psychotic development
(b) are generally means to waste time
(c) are not important given the hectic schedule of the school
(d) All of the above

45 The impact of school supervisor should be done according to **[Bihar BEd 2019]**
(a) greater community satisfaction
(b) greater personal satisfaction
(c) decline in misbehaviour in class
(d) greater progress of students towards the goals of education

46 In a democratic country like India, schools should concentrate on **[Bihar BEd 2020]**
(a) development of traits to face the hurdless of daily life
(b) development of traits of a good citizenship
(c) preparation for academic excellence
(d) inculcation of values cherished by country

47 Class discipline is oriented towards **[Bihar BEd 2020]**
(a) social confirmity
(b) personal and social adjustment
(c) self reliance
(d) acceptable class behaviour

Answers

1. (d)	2. (d)	3. (b)	4. (a)	5. (c)	6. (b)	7. (a)	8. (c)	9. (d)	10. (d)
11. (b)	12. (c)	13. (d)	14. (c)	15. (d)	16. (d)	17. (b)	18. (d)	19. (d)	20. (d)
21. (c)	22. (a)	23. (d)	24. (d)	25. (d)	26. (b)	27. (a)	28. (b)	29. (d)	30. (d)
31. (a)	32. (a)	33. (b)	34. (c)	35. (d)	36. (d)	37. (c)	38. (a)	39. (c)	40. (a)
41. (c)	42. (a)	43. (a)	44. (a)	45. (d)	46. (b)	47. (b)			

Chapter 15

Assessment and Evaluation System

Assessment

Assessment is the process by which the information collected is related to the known goal or purpose for which it is designed. Knowledge, skills, attitudes, behaviour and abilities are assessed under assessment. Traditionally, knowledge is measured by various types of examinations.

According to **Dr. Bob**, "It consists the basic assumption that there is a relationship between what a person does and what he knows, determining that relationship is the assessment".

In other words, it can be said that "the method of obtaining, reviewing and using information about a person or something is called assessment".

Evaluation

The term evaluation means, 'to evaluate something'. Evaluation clarifies the need of qualities or characteristics. The evaluation presents an analytical or qualitative description of the qualities present in a person and it tells how suitable or satisfactory he is for a certain purpose/task.

In education how much a child has succeeded in his aims, can only be determined through evaluation. Thus, there is a close relationship between evaluation and aims.

Education is considered as an investment in human beings in terms of development of human resources, skills, motivation, knowledge and so on. Evaluation helps to build an educational programme, assess its achievements and improve upon its effectiveness.

It serves as an in-built monitor within the programme to review the progress in learning from time to time. It also provides valuable feedback on the design and the implementation of the programme. Thus, evaluation plays a significant role in any educational programme.

Evaluation plays an enormous role in the teaching-learning process. It helps teachers and learners to improve teaching-learning process. Thus, evaluation is a continuous process and a periodic exercise.

Definitions of Evaluation

A number of educationists have described evaluation in the following ways

According to **James M. Bradfield**, "Evaluation is the assignment of symbols to phenomenon, in order to characterise the worth or value of a phenomenon, usually with reference to some social, cultural or scientific standards."

According to **C.E. Beeby** "Evaluation is the systematic collection and interpretation of evidence leading as a part of process to a judgement of value with a view to action."

According to **Hanna** "The process of gathering and interpreted evidence changes in the behaviour of all students as they progress through school is called evaluation".

According to **C.V. Goods** "Evaluation is a process of judging the value of something by certain appraisal."

According to **Norman E. Gronlund** and **Robert L. Linn** "Evaluation is a systematic process of collecting, analysing and interpreting information to determine the extent to which pupils are achieving instructional objectives."

Nature of Evaluation

Evaluation is a very broad and multifaceted concept. It is apart from assessing the knowledge of the curriculum and has a vast and broad range of all objectives related to the school curriculum, which is related to the development of the overall personality of students. The three main components of the evaluation process are Teaching Objectives, Assessment Tools and Behaviour Change Tools.

Learning activities are organised in the school to achieve the teaching objectives, in which the behaviour of the students changes and these behavioural changes are compared with the educational objective.

The nature of evaluation can also be expressed by the following facts

- It determines the future programs of students on the basis of quality, value and impact of their results.
- The main purpose of evaluation is to decide about the direction, nature and level of behavioural change.

- It is the process of determining the extent of attainment of the objectives of education.

Objectives of Evaluation

- To know what the child has learnt.
- To know about learning difficulties of children.
- To help in diagnosing weakness of students.
- To help in predicting future achievement.
- To test the development of skills and attitudes of students.
- To familiarise the teacher with nature of pupil learning, development and progress.
- To serve as a means of improving school-community relation.

Steps of Evaluation Process

Purpose For what the evaluation is being conducted.

Audience The audience will determine the type of information collected and reported.

Resources What resources will be needed to conduct the evaluation?

Data Gathering Techniques Multiple techniques are used to increase the validity of the result.

Analysis Different interpretations are used to analyse the outcome of the evaluation.

Reporting An evaluation report is distributed to the identified audience (parents, guardians, etc).

Characteristics of Evaluation in Education

Continuous Process Evaluation is a continuous process. It leads together with teaching- learning process.

Comprehensive Evaluation is comprehensive as it includes everything which can be evaluated.

Child Centered Evaluation is a child-centered process which gives importance to the learning process and not to the teaching process.

Remedial Evaluation is remedial in nature. Evaluation comments on the result which helps in remedial work of students.

Cooperative Process Evaluation is a cooperative process involving students, teachers, parents and peer-groups.

Teaching Methods Effectiveness of teaching method is evaluated in the evaluation process.

Common Practice Evaluation is a common practice among the proper growth of the child mentally and physically.

Multiple Aspects It is concerned with the total personality of students.

Principles of Evaluation

1. **Principle of Continuity** Evaluation is a continuous process, which goes on continuously as long as the student is related to education. Whatever the learner learns, it should be evaluated daily. Only then the learner could have better command in the academic studies.

2. **Principle of Comprehensiveness** By comprehensiveness we means to assess all aspects of the learner's personality. It is concerned with all-round development of the child.

3. **Principle of Objectives** Evaluation should be based on the objectives of education. It should be helpful in finding out where there is a need for redesigning and refraining the learner's behaviour.

4. **Principle of Child Centeredness** In the process of evaluation, child remains in the central part. The behaviour of the child is the central point for assessment. It helps a teacher to know the grasping power of a child and usefulness of teaching material.

5. **Principle of Learning Experience** Evaluation is also related to the learning experiences of the learner. In this process, we don't evaluate only the curricular activities of the learner but his co-curricular activities are also evaluated. Both types of activities are helpful in increasing learners experiences.

6. **Principle of Broadness** Evaluation should be broad enough to cover all the aspects of life.

7. **Principle of Application** Evaluation judges that student is better to apply his knowledge and understanding in different situations in order to succeed in life.

Functions of Evaluation

The main functions of evaluation are as follow

1. **Placement Work** Evaluation helps in the study of the early behaviour of students. Placement assignments can lead to specific instruction for each student. It provides individual instruction to the students. It prepares students for higher education. It prepares the students of higher education for different professions and tasks.

2. **Instructional Work** By adequately planned teaching, the teacher gets an opportunity to choose the right method and technique. Evaluation helps students to choose realistic and appropriate objectives. It helps in choosing the right instructional techniques. It helps in curriculum improvement. It provides opportunities to teachers to improve their teaching methodology and to choose the right teaching technology.

3. **Diagnostic Task** Evaluation reveals the strengths and weaknesses of students, programs and teachers. This gives an opportunity to choose the right remedial methods. It gives opportunity to identify the attitudes, interests and intelligence of the students.

Students have the opportunity to choose specific instruction for the specific needs. With the help of evaluation, information about the progress and shortcomings of weak students is obtained and opportunity is given to overcome their shortcomings.

4. **Administration Work** Evaluation helps in deciding on the right educational policy for the students. Students can be divided into different classes according to their ability. With the help of evaluation system students can be promoted to their next class. In the evaluation, comparative chart of different students can be made. It also functions for formation of right public opinion towards students and education system and building relationships with society.

5. **Guidance Work** Evaluation helps the student to choose his course and career plan. It helps learners to know about the speed and slowness of their learning process. It helps the teacher to know about the students, so that he can give them academic, vocational and personal guidance.

6. **Developmental Work** It helps to provide necessary feedback to students and teachers in the process of learning and teaching. It helps the teachers in improving teaching techniques, so that necessary improvements can be made. It helps to assist in the achievement of educational goals and objectives.

Types of Evaluation

There are three kinds of evaluation usually used in the school education. These are as follow

1. Formative Evaluation

Formative evaluation occurs throughout a class or course, and seeks to improve student achievement of learning objectives through approaches that can support specific student needs. It occurs in the short-term, as learners are in the process of making meaning of new content and integrating it into what they already know.

Formative evaluation also enables the teacher to rethink instructional strategies, activities, and content based on student understanding and performance.

It is the most powerful type of evaluation for improving student understanding and performance.

Its examples include a very interactive class discussion, on-the-spot performance, quiz, etc.

2. Summative Evaluation

This type of evaluation takes place to evaluate student learning, knowledge, proficiency or success at the conclusion of an instructional period, like at the end of a term or a year.

The results are primarily used by teachers and schools to identify strengths and weaknesses of curriculum and instruction, with improvements affecting the next year's/term's students.

Its examples are final exams, major cumulative projects, research projects and performances, etc.

3. Interim Evaluation

This type of evaluation takes place occasionally throughout a larger time period.

Interim evaluation tends to be more formal, using tools such as projects, written assignments and tests. The learners should be given the opportunity to re-demonstrate their understanding once the feedback has been understood and acted upon.

Interim evaluation can help teachers identify gaps in students' understanding and the teachers' instruction.

Its examples are chapter test, extended essay, a project scored with a rubric and so on.

Differences between Summative and Formative Evaluation

Basis	Summative Evaluation	Formative Evaluation
When	It is done at the end of a learning activity.	It is done during a learning activity.
Goal	It aims to make a decision.	It aims to improve learning.
Feedback	It is given as a final judgement.	Its feedback is to return the material.
Frame of Reference	It is sometimes normative (comparing each student against all others) and sometimes criterion.	It is always criterion (evaluating students according to the same criteria).
Example	Final essays	Weekly quizes

Classification of Evaluation Techniques

Evaluation technique is not the end of teaching-learning process, although it is a valid theory that change the thinking and understanding behaviour of the students.

Thus, a standard evaluation indicates the qualitative change in the behaviour of the students.

The evaluation techniques are divided into two i.e. **qualitative** and **quantitative** techniques.

Quantitative Techniques

The quantitative techniques can be categorised into three elements.

(i) **Written Examination** This technique or method is also known as paper-pencil test. It is one of the popular techniques of evaluation in these days. Further, it has four basic components i.e. very short, short, long and essay type question-answers.

(ii) **Oral Examination** This technique is supplementary to the written examination. Test of reading ability and pronunciation is the example of oral examination.

(iii) **Practical Examination** This technique is used for testing the experimental activities of the students as well as manipulative skills of students. It is done in subjects like science, agricultural craft, music and technology.

Qualitative Techniques

Qualitative techniques are focussed on understanding how students make meaning and experience their environment or world.

These techniques can be categorised into following

(i) **Interview** It comprises a number of open-ended questions that result in responses that yield information. It is common to engage in face-to-face verbal interviews with one individual or with a group of students. It is because of the fact that students are usually more willing to talk than write.

(ii) **Observation** It does not require direct contact with the students, rather this type of data collection involves a teacher providing information-rich descriptions of behaviour, conversations, interactions of the students for outcomes of the students' behaviour.

(iii) **Checklist** It does not only give the observer a set of criteria to observe, but it allows the observer to show student progress over time and to correlate a number with a qualitative process.

(iv) **Rating Scale** It is used for applying the expression of opinion or judgement regarding some situation, object, or character.

(v) **Cumulative Records** It is used for knowing the details about students' behaviour. Cumulative records include anecdotal records, cumulative record cards and diaries of students.

School Based Assessment (SBA)

This form of assessment is performed at the school level by teachers and educators. It is done fully in the school based on guidelines by the Board of Education to which the school is affiliated.

The features of SBA are as follow

- It is child-centered and multi-dimensional. Thus, it improves the social, physical, emotional and intellectual development of children.
- Teachers have full authority in SBA without external interference.
- It is more transparent in nature as compared to summative assessment.
- It provides a good idea to teachers about what the children have learnt, how they learn, what difficulties they face, what their interests are and so on.
- The traditional evaluation system used earlier, in which only the School Board exams were the determining factors, suffered from various drawbacks, the most important being that it assessed only the scholastic areas of learning and not the actual capabilities of the learners. It also did not take into consideration the aspects of improvement of children's learning.
- Now, SBA focuses on continuously developing the skills and competencies of children, diagnosing the deficiencies and taking appropriate remedial measures. In this regard, the Central Board of Secondary Education (CBSE) started using SBA in the form of Continuous and Comprehensive Evaluation (CCE) from 2010 onwards.

Characteristics of School Based Assessment

- It is more comprehensive and continuous than the traditional system.
- Its main goal is to help the learner to orient towards planned learning and development.

- It takes care of the needs of the learner as a responsible citizen of the future.
- It is more transparent, predictive and provides a greater scope for collaboration between learners, teachers and parents.
- SBA helps the learner to utilise his potential in a better way. It provides the teachers with a keen eye to find a way, which can prove to be helpful for different learners in solving their problems and difficulties.
- This assessment, apart from being child-centred, is also school-centred, meaning that no outside agency interferes with the evaluation process. It is completely school based and is done by the teacher.
- School based assessment is multi-dimensional. Its multifaceted nature is known from the fact that it acknowledges and takes care of the social, emotional, physical and intellectual growth as well as other areas of development of the learners, which are interrelated and cannot be discussed separately.

Continuous and Comprehensive Evaluation (CCE)

Continuous and Comprehensive Evaluation refers to the system of school based evaluation of students, which covers all aspects of the development of students. This is a child's developmental process in which dual objectives are emphasised. These objectives are based on consistency in assessment on one hand and on evaluation of learning broadly and on the consequences of behaviour on the other.

The meaning of 'continuous' here is to emphasise that the assessment of the identified aspects of student growth and development is a continuous process rather than a one-time programme, which is built into the entire teacher-learning process and is carried over the entire duration of the academic session.

'Comprehensive' means a plan to examine the growth and development of the students by including scholastic and co-scholastic aspects. Since abilities, attitudes and thinking manifest themselves in different ways; the term 'comprehensive' refers to the application of many tools and techniques. It is aimed at evaluating student development in areas of learning, such as knowledge, comprehension, interpretation, application, analysis, evaluation and creativity.

Objectives of CCE

- To support in the development of cognitive, psychomotor and affective skills.
- Emphasising the learning process and not memorising it.
- Making assessment an integral part of the teaching-learning process.
- Using assessment to improve student achievement and teaching-learning strategies followed by remedial instruction based on regular diagnosis.
- Using assessment as a quality control device to maintain desired levels of performance.
- Determining social usefulness, desirability or effectiveness of a program and making appropriate decisions about the students, the learning process and the learning environment.
- To make teaching-learning process a student-centred activity.

Features of CCE

- The 'Continuous' aspect of CCE takes care of the 'Continuous' and 'Periodical' aspects of the evaluation.
- Continuity means assessment of students at the beginning of education (summative evaluation) and assessment during the learning process (formative evaluation), which is done informally, using multiple methods of evaluation.
- Periodicity means the determination of performance, which is done repeatedly at the end of the unit/period (summarisation).
- The 'comprehensive' component of CCE takes care of the assessment of the all-round development of the personality of the child. This includes determining the scholastic as well as co-scholastic aspects of student development.
- Scholastic aspects include curricular areas, while co-scholastic aspects include life skills, co-curricular attitudes and values.
- Assessment in academic fields is carried out informally and formally using multiple methods of assessment, both on a continuous and periodic basis.
- Diagnostic evaluation is done at the end of the unit/examination. In some units, the reasons for poor performance are ascertained using diagnostic tests. Thereafter, appropriate intervention and action is taken and thereafter re-examinations are carried out.
- In order to make assessment comprehensive, both scholastic and co-scholastic areas should be given importance. Simple and manageable methods of evaluating co-scholastic aspects of growth must be included in the comprehensive evaluation scheme.

Functions and Importance of CCE

In the teaching-learning process, evaluation is expected to take care of the scholastic and coscholastic aspects.

If one is weak in any area, diagnostic evaluation should be done and remedial measures adopted. Following are the functions and importance of CCE

- It helps the teacher to organise effective strategies. Continuous evaluation assists regular assessing of the extent of a learner's progress (aptitude and achievement with reference to specific scholastic and co-scholastic areas).

- Continuous evaluation serves to diagnose weaknesses and helps the teacher to find out the strengths and weaknesses of individual learner and his/her needs.
- Through continuous assessment, children can know their strengths and weaknesses. It can motivate children to develop good study habits, rectify mistakes and channelise their activities towards achieving desired goals.
- CCE identifies areas of interest, tendency, attitudes and values. It helps in making future decisions regarding the choice of subjects, courses and careers.
- It gives information about the progress of the students in scholastic and co-scholastic areas and thus, helps in making predictions about the future success of the learner.
- The main emphasis of CCE is on the continuous growth of students and ensuring their intellectual, emotional, physical, cultural and social development and hence, it will not be limited to assessing the student's academic achievements only.
- This assessment can be used as a means of motivating learners for other programs, providing information, feedback and taking follow-up actions to improve learning outcomes in education and presenting a comprehensive picture of learner's description.

1 Assessment is purposeful if   **[CTET 2016]**
(a) it serves as a feedback for the students as well as the teachers
(b) it is done only once at the end of the year
(c) comparative evaluations are made to differentiate between student's achievements
(d) it induces fear and stress among the students

2 Assessment   **[CTET 2019]**
(a) should be based on objective type written tasks
(b) should be undertaken as a separate activity
(c) should be a part of the teaching-learning process
(d) should be done only in term of marks

3 Assessment   **[CG BEd 2018]**
(a) is a good strategy to label and categorise children
(b) should actively promote competitive spirit among children
(c) should generate tension and stress to ensure learning
(d) is a way to improve learning

4 Which of the following statements about assessment are correct?   **[MP, UK BEd 2017]**
A. Assessment should help students to see their strengths and gaps and help the teacher to fine-tune her teaching accordingly.
B. Assessment is meaningful only if comparative evaluations of students are made.
C. Assessment should assess not only memory but also understanding and application.
D. Assessment cannot be purposeful if it does not induce fear and anxiety.
(a) A and B   (b) B and C
(c) B and D   (d) A and C

5 Teacher can utilise both assessment for learning and assessment of learning to   **[CTET 2018]**
(a) monitor children's progress and set appropriate goals to fill their learning gaps
(b) know children's progress and achievement level

(c) know learning needs of child and select teaching strategy accordingly

(d) assess child's performance at periodic intervals and certify his/her performance

6 Primary objective of assessment should be **[CTET 2019]**

(a) assigning rank to students

(b) understanding children's clarity and confusions about related concepts

(c) labelling students as per their score

(d) marking pass or fail on the report cards

7 Evaluation

(a) should actively promote competitive spirit among children

(b) should generate tension and stress to ensure learning

(c) is a good strategy to label and categorise children

(d) is a way to improve learning

8 Evaluation is helpful to a teacher in which of the following ways?

(a) It opens new avenues for action researches

(b) A teacher can categorise his pupil into different groups

(c) A teacher can give immediate feedback to his pupils

(d) All of the above

9 The main purpose of conducting evaluation is

(a) to label children as either slow learners or gifted

(b) to identify children who need remediation

(c) to diagnose learning difficulties and problem areas

(d) to provide feedback on the extent to which we have been successful in imparting education for a productive life

10 The evaluation of students can be used by teachers in teaching to develop insight into

(a) changing the teaching approach to meet students needs

(b) creating groups of 'bright' and 'weak' students in the class

(c) identifying the students who need to be promoted to the higher class

(d) not promoting those students who do not meet school standards

11 Who said that "Evaluation is a process of judging the value of something by certain appraisal"?

(a) C. V. Goods   (b) Hanna

(c) Norman E. Gronlund   (d) Robert L. Linn

12 Which one of the following statements would be the most effective way of conducting evaluation?

(a) Evaluation should be done by an external agency and not by the teacher

(b) Evaluation should be done at the end of the session

(c) Evaluation is an inbuilt process in teaching-learning

(d) Evaluation should be done twice in an academic session at the begining and at the end

13 In the learning evaluation is essential for

(a) motivation

(b) grades and marks

(c) screening test

(d) fostering the purpose of segregation and ranking

14 The objective of evaluation is to

(a) know what the child has learnt

(b) know about learning difficulties of child

(c) establish that learning has actually been achieved

(d) All of the above

15 Which of the following is the step of evaluation process?

(a) Audience

(b) Purpose

(c) Data gathering techniques

(d) All of the above

16 Which of the following is/are the characteristic(s) of evaluation in education?

(a) It is a continuous process

(b) It is comprehensive

(c) It is a child-centered process

(d) All of the above

17 Which of the following is not a characteristic of evaluation?

(a) It is done at the end of the task

(b) It is a comprehensive process

(c) It is a systematic process going in the direction of pre-determined objective

(d) It is a purposeful activity fulfilling the requirement of the teacher

18 Which of the following is the Principle of Evaluation?
(a) Principle of Continuity
(b) Principle of Comprehensiveness
(c) Principle of Objectives
(d) All of the above

19 Which of following statements is true?
(a) Evaluation is a term used interchangeably with measurement
(b) Evaluation is completely different from measurement
(c) Evaluation is component of measurement
(d) Evaluation is an extension of measurement

20 Evaluation is purposeful if
(a) it induces fear and stress among the students
(b) comparative evaluations are made to differentiate between the student's achievement
(c) it serves as a feedback for the student's as well as for the teachers
(d) it is done only once at the end of the year

21 Which one of the following types of evaluation assesses the learning progress to provide continuous feedback to both teachers and students during instruction?
(a) Placement evaluation
(b) Interim evaluation
(c) Formative evaluation
(d) Summative evaluation

22 Formative assessment may be a
(a) pre-test
(b) post-test
(c) Both (a) and (b)
(d) Neither (a) nor (b)

23 Which of the following is not a tool to be used in formative assessment in the scholastic domain?
(a) Open-ended questions
(b) Projects
(c) Classroom activity
(d) Conversational skill

24 Which one of the following is not a suitable formative evaluation task?
(a) Observation
(b) Project
(c) Open-ended questions
(d) Ranking the students

25 Which of the following is not a type of evaluation?
(a) Summative
(b) CCE
(c) Norms
(d) Formative

26 Which of the following statements is correct?
(a) Summative evaluation is not as comprehensive as formative evaluation
(b) Formative evaluation can be summative also
(c) There is hardly any difference between formative evaluation and summative evaluation
(d) All of the above

27 Which of the following is not associated with criterion referenced evaluation?
(a) Evaluation results show the level of performance expected at a particular stage of development
(b) Learners' measurement of some explicit objectives
(c) Evaluation measures the taught content during a specific time
(d) Individual progress is measured by evaluation

28 A collection of a student's work in an area showing growth, self-reflection and achievement is known as
(a) Cumulative record
(b) Judgement
(c) Assessment
(d) Interim evaluation

29 School Based Assessment (SBA) allows teachers to
(a) evaluate students without giving them feedback
(b) evaluate students in each semester
(c) not evaluate students
(d) engage regularly with the learners

30 Which of the following indicates evaluation?
(a) Mohan got 38 percent marks in maths
(b) Vishal got 70 marks out of 100
(c) Ravi secured first division in final examination
(d) All of the above

31 SBA focuses on
(a) taking appropriate remedial measures
(b) diagnostic the deficiencies in learners
(c) continuously developing the skills and competencies of learners
(d) All of the above

32 SBA is primarily based on the principle that
(a) students should at all costs get high grades
(b) schools are more efficient than external bodies of examination
(c) teachers know about their learners capabilities better than external examiners
(d) assessment should be very economical

33 SBA
(a) helps all students learn more through diagnosis
(b) makes students and teachers non-serious and casual
(c) hinders achieving Universal National Standards
(d) dilutes the accountability of Boards of Education

34 SBA was introduced to
(a) ensure the holistic development of all the students of the country
(b) decentralise the power of boards of school education in the country
(c) encourage schools to excel by competing with other schools in their area
(d) motivate teachers to make record of all the activities of students for better interpretation of their progress

35 Teachers who work under SBA
(a) need to assign project work in each subject to individual student
(b) observe students minutely on a daily basis to assess their values and attitudes
(c) feels a sense of ownership for the system
(d) are overburdened because they need to take frequent tests besides Monday tests

36 CCE stands for
(a) Continuous Curricular Examination
(b) Curricular and Co-curricular Examination
(c) Compulsory Comprehensive Evaluation
(d) Continuous and Comprehensive Evaluation

37 Which of the following statements is not true about CCE?
(a) It uses grades instead of marks
(b) It is a school based evaluation
(c) It increases the burden on teachers
(d) It reduces stress among learners

38 Continuous and Comprehensive Evaluation emphasises
(a) how learning can be observed, recorded and improved upon
(b) redundancy of the board examination
(c) fine-tuning of tests with the teaching
(d) continuous testing on a comprehensive scale to ensure learning

39 By which of the following methods the true evaluation of the students is possible?
(a) Evaluation at the end of the course
(b) Continuous evaluation
(c) Evaluation twice in a year
(d) Formative evaluation

40 According to Continuous and Comprehensive Evaluation in Sciences at least some formative assessments should be based on **[KVS TGT 2017]**
(a) project work in groups
(b) conversation skills
(c) experiments and lab activities
(d) writing skills

41 Logical base for sustainable and comprehensive evaluation is **[UK BEd 2017]**
(a) evaluation of more than one side in learning
(b) overrun of opportunity of evaluation
(c) overall nature of human's personality
(d) overload on teacher

42 Which one of the following is related to Continuous and Comprehensive Evaluation? **[CTET 2018]**
(a) It is useful to label children as slow, poor or intelligent
(b) It has been mandated by the Right to Education Act of India
(c) It is an integral part of teaching-learning process
(d) It focuses on child's achievement in different learning areas

43 What are the characteristics of Continuous and Comprehensive Evaluation? **[UK BEd 2018]**
1. It increases the workload on students by taking multiple tests
2. It replaces marks with grades

3. It evaluates every aspect of the student

4. It helps in reducing examination phobia

Select the correct answer by using the codes given below.
(a) 2, 3 and 4
(b) 1, 2 and 3
(c) 2 and 4
(d) 1, 2, 3 and 4

44 Evaluation for learning takes into account the following except
(a) learning styles of subjects
(b) needs of students
(c) learning styles of students
(d) strength of students

45 Sometimes tests are taken without notice. What is their use?
(a) These tests can be taken when teacher has not prepared a lesson/topic
(b) They compel the students to study regularly
(c) Surprise tests help in correct evaluation of student's knowledge
(d) All of the above

46 Good evaluation of written material is not based on which of the following?
(a) Logical presentation
(b) Ability to write what is read
(c) Linguistic expression
(d) Comprehension of subject

47 After preparing a question paper, a teacher checks whether the question paper tests the specific learning objectives planned for the course. The teacher is concerned with which of the following?
(a) Objectivity of the test
(b) Validity of the test
(c) Reliability of the test
(d) Content coverage

48 Which one of the following evaluation technique will nurture the best capacity of a child? **[UK BEd 2017]**
(a) When students has repeated the facts through multiple choice question evaluation
(b) When positive cooperation takes place between students and marks in examination
(c) When conceptual change and optional solutions of students has been evaluated through different methods
(d) When marks and place are the only standard to evaluate students in class

49 Which is the best technique to evaluate the student's achievement? **[UK BEd 2017]**
(a) Class division on the basis of marks obtained
(b) Using grade technique
(c) Comparative analysis
(d) All of the above

50 Distributing grade system according to the sustainable and comprehensive evaluation, which one of the percentage mark obtain has been kept as best rank? **[UK BEd 2017]**
(a) 90%-100%   (b) 56%-74%
(c) 75%-89%   (d) 35%-55%

Answers

1. (a)	2. (c)	3. (d)	4. (d)	5. (b)	6. (b)	7. (d)	8. (c)	9. (d)	10. (a)
11. (a)	12. (c)	13. (a)	14. (d)	15. (d)	16. (d)	17. (a)	18. (d)	19. (d)	20. (c)
21. (c)	22. (c)	23. (d)	24. (d)	25. (c)	26. (a)	27. (a)	28. (d)	29. (d)	30. (d)
31. (d)	32. (c)	33. (a)	34. (a)	35. (c)	36. (d)	37. (c)	38. (a)	39. (b)	40. (c)
41. (a)	42. (b)	43. (a)	44. (b)	45. (c)	46. (d)	47. (b)	48. (c)	49. (b)	50. (a)

Chapter 16

Research Aptitude

Research is composed of two words 'Re' and 'Search' which means to 'search again' or to search for new facts or modify older ones in any branch of knowledge. Research is the process of discovering new knowledge.

In other words, "Research is a systematic investigation (i.e. the gathering and analysis of information) designed to develop or contribute to generalisable knowledge."

Research aptitude is an attitude of inquiry/search /investigation, a scientific and objective effort made to uncover facts, hence requires the application of scientific methods.

The use of 'systematic investigation' in the formal definition represents how research is normally conducted. For it a hypothesis is formed, appropriate research methods are designed, data is collected and analysed, and research results are summarised into one or more 'research conclusions'.

These research conclusions are then shared with the rest of the scientific community to add to the existing knowledge and serve as evidence to form additional question that can be investigated.

Definitions of Research

Definitions given by some scholars are as follow

According to **Redman** and **Mory**, "Research is a "systematic effort to gain new knowledge."

According to **Webster**, "Research is a studious inquiry or examination, critical and exhaustive investigation or experimentation, having its aim for discovery of new facts and their correct interpretation".

According to **J W Best**, "Research is considered to be the more formal, systematic, intensive process of carrying on the scientific methods of analysis. It involves a more systematic structure of investigation, usually resulting in some sort of formal record of procedures and report of results or conclusions."

According to **John Creswell**, "Research is a process of steps used to collect and analyse information to increase our understanding of a topic or an issue."

According to **Morley**, "Research is a process of arriving at dependable solutions to problems through the planned and systematic collection, analysis and interpretation of data."

Objectives of Research

Objectives are the goals, researcher set out to attain in their study. They inform the reader what the researcher wants to accomplish through the research work.

The objectives of research can be catagorised as

1. **Theoretical Objectives** They lead to the formulation of new theories and basic

knowledge by exploring the association between different variables.

2. **Factual Objectives** Studies of such objectives which aim at finding new facts.

3. **Application Objectives** Such objectives suggest the use of already existing theories to new situations.

4. **Variable Objectives** In fact they are philosophical in nature in which the final result is obtained on the basis of philosophy.

5. **Practical Objectives** These objectives are categorised as developmental research and in order to achieve them functional research is undertaken.

Research objectives are the results sought by the researcher, to achieve at the end of the research study. Though, each research has its own specific purpose, research objectives vary with its achievement.

Characteristics of Research

- Research is directed towards the solution of a problem.
- Research is based upon observable experience or empirical evidence.
- Research demands accurate observation and description.
- Research involves gathering new data from primary sources or using existing data for a new purpose.
- Research activities are characterised by carefully designed procedures.
- Research requires expertise i.e., skill necessary to carry out investigation, search related to literature to understand and analyse the data gathered.
- Research involves the quest for answers to unsolved problems.
- Research requires courage.
- Research needs patience.
- Research is carefully recorded and reported.

Requirements of Educational Research

Educational research is an important point of education and teaching. Its need can be understood by the following points

- **To find the answer to the fundamental questions** Those questions related to education which are still unanswered, their correct answers are known only through research.
- **To solve the educational problems** Whatever problems come in the field of education we get their solutions only through educational research.
- **To evaluate the principles of pedagogy and to formulate new theories** The principles which lose their importance over time are evaluated and in their place new theories are presented only through educational research.
- **For smooth classroom teaching** There is a need for continuous research on how the classroom environment is good, effective presentation, solving the problems of students and teachers.
- **For the evaluation of textbooks and curriculum** Designing the textbooks and curriculum according to the times and needs of students is also possible through academic research.
- Educational research is needed to evaluate the importance and usefulness of media.

Nature of Educational Research

- The main basis of educational research is the philosophy of education.
- Educational research is based on understanding and imagination.
- Interdisciplinary approach is used in educational research.
- Deductive reasoning is used in educational research.

- Educational research is based on the cause and effect relationship. It is not necessary to be an expert for academic research. Teachers can also do this.
- Educational research is subjective rather than objective.
- Educational research is less accurate than other research, because the sample does not fully represent the population.
- Educational research cannot be made mechanical. It is less expensive.

Types of Research

Types of research are as follow

Objective Based Research

1. **Descriptive Research** This research systematically describes a situational problem and provides information about various subjects like living condition of a community.

   It consists of surveys and fact-finding enquiries. In this research the researcher has no control over the variables, he/she can only report what has happened or what is happening.

   The descriptive research has its sub-types such as ex-post facto research, historical research, analytical research, survey studies and correlational studies.

2. **Correlational Research** This research measures the level of association between two or more variables. In correlational research the independent and dependent variables are quantitative. It is important to stress that correlation refers to measures of association and do not necessarily indicate causal relationship between variables.

   Correlational research aims to find out whether there is

   (i) **Positive correlation** In this research, both variables change in the same direction. E.g., as height increases, weight also increases.

   (ii) **Negative correlation** In this research, the variables change in opposite direction. E.g., as coffee consumption increases, tiredness decreases.

   (iii) **Zero correlation** In this research there is no relationship between the variables. E.g., coffee consumption is not correlated with height.

3. **Explanatory Research** Explanatory research is conducted for those problems which have not been researched before. The purpose of explanatory research is to explain why certain events occur and to build, elaborate, extend or test theory. Explanatory research allows the researcher to test and verify specific theories and make amendments to those theories.

   For example, to analyse the effects of re-branding initiatives on the levels of customer loyalty.

4. **Exploratory Research** Exploratory research is conducted for such problems which have not been clearly defined.

   It is flexible and can address research questions of all types (what, why, how). This research is often used to generate formal hypothesis.

   For example alcoholism (drinking) is a serious issue in Indian society, but this behaviour is not clearly defined as it has some medical concern also. At the end of research the researcher explored numerous reasons of alcoholism and developed a hypothesis that alcohol is consumed by people for relaxation of body.

   It is exploratory research because there is still scope open for further research on this problem.

5. **Experimental Research** Experimental research is a systematic and scientific approach to research, in which the researcher manipulates one or more variables. This research also controls and changes the other

variables. The purpose of experimental research is to study the cause and effect relationship.

For example, education, a high degree of skill, sectors and experiences all are independent variables, which separately influence salary of an individual. If any of these variable is higher, the salary of an individual will be higher.

Application Based Research

This research seeks to solve daily practical problems. It has following types

1. **Basic/Fundamental Research** This research involves the process of collecting and analysing data to develop theory. It supports theories which explain how things operate, what makes things happen, why social relations have a certain way and why society changes.

   For example, a study looking at how caffeine consumption impacts the brain.

2. **Applied Research** It is conducted to solve a specific practical problem related to medicine, business and education of an individual, group or society.

   It uses the data directly from real world application. Its ultimate goal is to improve the human condition.

   For example, finding out the best way to approach and treat diseases like anxiety/depression, etc.

Logic Based Research

1. **Deductive Research** It is a research which moves from more general to more specific level. In this research the researcher studies what others have done, reads existing theories and then tests hypothesis that emerge from those theories.

For example, in a study which explains the impact of classroom environment on a child's mental state, a researcher deducted that lack of basic supplies are associated with the behavioural issues of children in a classroom.

2. **Inductive Research** In this research, a researcher collects the data that is relevant to his/her topic of interest.

   For example, a researcher collected data about depression and aggression among teenagers. He finds out that after declaration of board exams result, a number of teenagers became depressed or aggressive.

   Now, the researcher developed a theory that over expectation of parents from their child is the main reason of depression among them.

Formation/Inquiry Based Research

This type of research is based on the direct or indirect interaction of researcher, with a set of people. It has the following types

1. **Unstructured Research** In unstructured research the problem which has to be investigated is not pre-determined, rather they are spontaneous. In this type of research, the researcher is free to explore nature of problem, issue or phenomenon without quantifying it.

   For example, study of the diversity of food pattern in different parts of India.

2. **Structured Research** It is also known as systematic observation. It is a data collecting method. In this research, researcher gather data without direction involvement with the participants. It uses coding method for data collection.

   For example, if Indian Standards Institution wants to gather data about a popularity of a certain food product. It will use structured research methodology to sort the data to find a quantitative outcome.

Concept Based Research

1. **Conceptual Research** This type of research is generally used by philosophers and thinkers to develop new concepts or the reinterpret the existing concepts.
2. **Empirical Research** The empirical research relies on experiences or observation alone. It is a data based research coming up with conclusions that are capable of being verified by observation or experiment.

Process Based Research

1. **Qualitative Research** In this type of research the main objective is to develop an understanding of human beings / social science to know what people feel and think. It seeks to obtain information, and description of complex and dynamic processes using holistic, naturalistic and non-manipulative methods.

   In this research no statistical tests are required.

2. **Quantitative Research** It is mostly related to the positivist or post-positivist paradigm. It involves collecting and converting data into numerical form.

   It is deductive in nature as it tests theories which have already been proposed. This research is based more directly on its original plans and its results are more readily analysed and interpreted.

3. **Mixed Research** This type of research involves collecting, analysing and intergrating quantitative (e.g. experiments surveys) and qualitative (e.g. focus groups, interviews) research.

Importance of Research

The importance of research is increasing day by day in the present educational system, because research has been compulsorily included in every teacher institution and curriculum. The importance of research can be seen through the following points

- It is helpful in expanding and improving research knowledge.
- Research gives impetus to the intellectual thinking and development of a person.
- It proves helpful in eliminating any kind of bias.
- Research proves helpful in achieving any objective.
- Spreads new knowledge and ideas in the society.
- Research provides scientific methods to achieve some objective.
- It is used in presenting a solution to a problem.

Steps/Process of Research

A research involves a systematic process that focuses on being objective and gathering a multitude of information for analysis, so that the researcher can come to a conclusion.

Formulating Research Problem

⇓

Reviewing the Research Structure

⇓

Conducting the Literature Review

⇓

Developing the Hypothesis

⇓

Preparation of Research Design

⇓

Collection of Data

⇓

Analysis and Interpretation of Data

⇓

Concluding the Data and Formal Write-up of the Research Report

Methods of Research

Research actually presents a scientific solution to a problem of a particular nature. Therefore, the method of research is determined according to the nature of the problem. Scholars have classified research methods in many ways. But the classification given by Best and Kahn is considered the best. According to them, six main methods of research have been considered, which are as follow

1. **Historical Research Method** According to **John W. Best**, "Historical research is concerned with the scientific analysis of historical problem. Its various verses create a new understanding in relation to the past, which is related to the present and the future." Scientific study is done about any object, idea, event, community, society through historical research. Historical evidence is required in this method.

2. **Descriptive Research Method** Under this, the work on a clearly defined problem is done. It can be of many types like specific, simple and very difficult. It explains about what a particular problem is. Under this, we get useful information to solve the problem. For this, imaginative planning is necessary. This research can be both numerical and qualitative.

   This requires imaginative planning. In this research method, the present situation is described and analysed. It is also called Applied Research.

3. **Experimental Research Method** In this method, the researcher is always searching for new facts and it helps in increasing the knowledge of the researchers. In this method, the researcher studies the casual relationship between the independent variable and the dependent variable. It is a method of testing a hypothesis and it is said that this method describes and analyses the facts about what will happen.

4. **Action Research Method** Generally, the above three methods of research (historical, descriptive and experimental) have been described by scholars, but it was not possible to solve the problems of higher educational institutions with these methods. Therefore, the Principle of Action Research Method was adopted to solve the problems of educational institutions. It offers solutions to business problems rather than seeking theoretical knowledge.

5. **Quantitative Research Method** Under Quantitative Research Method, the hypothesis is determined first as the principles have already been determined. Being based on research and data, its conclusion is also determined by the data itself. This research is devoid of any sense. In this research the information is obtained statistically. This research is the collection of data from structured interviews, observations, review of records and reports.

6. **Qualitative Research Method** The purpose of this research is to understand human behavior and the reasons that control it. Under this method, questions like what, where, when, why and how, etc., are analysed. Hypothesis is not used in this research. This research is based on personal experiences instead of quantitative.

Research Paper

Research paper is a detailed article, on the basis of which the researches are molded in public form. In this whole process the researcher is introduced to scholars, intellectuals and the whole world. Research paper is a paper through which the researcher presents the facts, data, perspectives and conclusions of his entire research.

In this whole process, the researcher has to resort to two types of sources, which are called primary sources and secondary sources. In the course of writing research papers, the difference between facts and ideas has to be kept in mind, we accept the fact as truth. Evidence is not needed to prove them. Many ideas and observations are presented in the research paper. In this it is necessary that the researcher should not mix facts and ideas, because in doing so the level of any form falls.

Research Paper Writing Process

Many points are followed in the writing process of any research paper; like

- First of all, the topic of research is selected.
- The literature related to the subject matter is surveyed.
- After that the objective of the research is decided. After setting the objectives, the research concepts are determined.
- This is followed by research samples of designs to complete the research, for example, jurisprudence, tools and statistical techniques.
- Jurisprudence is needed for reduction in research expenditure, increase in efficiency and accuracy of results.
- Various methods in research in the process of writing research papers are used; for example, historical, experimental and descriptive.
- After all this the available data is analysed.
- After the analysis of the data, the conclusion of the research is drawn.
- At the end a list of reference books is presented.
- The research paper actually brings to the fore the theoretical side of the research, in which the researcher basically uses inductive and deductive tasks to establish his ideas.

Essentials of Research Article

- It is compulsory to have some important facts in any research article.
- It is mandatory to have a hypothesis and a proposed question in any research article.

- It is necessary to have some suggestions for research.
- Research articles should be such that, along with the description of the topics, the conclusion of the entire research article should be there.
- The list of research related topics is mandatory in the article.
- It must be kept in mind in the research article that there should not be newspaper articles.
- It should be compulsorily followed in the research paper that the researcher should not mix facts and ideas because this leads to research at a lower level.

Errors in Research

- The error may arise due to some confusion in selecting the research methodology, data collection or data interpretation.
- Errors can also be due to biases and prejudices that the researcher introduce into the research analysis.
- Small errors can occur due to research writers that go unnoticed during proofreading of the manuscript.
- Errors can also result due to research questions that does not prove to be well-defined and researchable.

Suggestions to Remove Errors in Research

- Choose research methodology very carefully.
- Use objectivity in research. It means to avoid bias in the research process which is considered unethical.
- Proofreading of the research manuscript should be done carefully.
- Use or formulate well-defined and researchable questions.
- The researchers must know who they should survey.

Exercise

1 Research means
(a) finding solution to any problem
(b) searching again and again
(c) working in a scientific way to search for truth of any problem
(d) None of the above

2 Who said that "Research is a systematic effort to gain new knowledge" ?
(a) JW Best
(b) Redman and Mory
(c) Webster
(d) None of the above

3 Who said that "Research is a process of steps used to collect and analyses information to increase our understanding of a topic or an issue"?
(a) Creswell
(b) JW Best
(c) Morley
(d) Keringer

4 Which of the following is/are the nature of research?
(a) It is scientific in nature
(b) It is logical in nature
(c) It is objective and factual
(d) All of the above

5 A good research aims at
(a) solving routine problems
(b) betterment of the society
(c) developing generalisations, theories and principles
(d) None of the above

6 In what ways the objectivity of the research can be enhanced?
(a) Through its validity
(b) Through its reliability
(c) Through its impartiality
(d) All of the above

7 Which of the following is the objective of research?
(a) To determine the frequency with which sometime occurs
(b) To describe, unexplained horizon of knowledge
(c) To gain familiarity with phenomena and achieve new insight into it
(d) All of the above

8 Which is the main objective of research?
(a) To summarise what is already known
(b) To review the literature
(c) To discover new facts or to make fresh interpretation of known facts
(d) None of the above

9 Which of the following is/are correct?
(a) Objectives are to be stated in chapter I of the thesis
(b) In research objective can be worded in question form
(c) In research objectives can be worded in statement form
(d) All of the above

10 A research is conducted to fulfil which of the following?
(a) Generate new knowledge
(b) Obtain research degree
(c) Reinterpret existing knowledge
(d) All of the above

11 The quality of research can be judged by the
(a) methodology adopted in conducting the research
(b) relevance of research
(c) experience of researcher
(d) depth of research

12 Sine qua non (essential elements) of good research is
(a) a good research supervisor
(b) a well formulated hypothesis
(c) adequate library
(d) a well formulated problem

13 Which of the following show(s) the charatericstics of a research?
(a) It is directed towards the solution of a problem
(b) It is based upon observable experience or empirical evidence
(c) It demands accurate observation and description
(d) All of the above

14 Which of the following is true about research?

(a) It involves gathering new data from primary sources or using existing data for a new purpose
(b) Research activities are characterised by carefully designed procedures
(c) It involves the quest for answers to unsolved problems
(d) All of the above

15 Research can be classified as

(a) quantitative and qualitative research
(b) philosophical, historical, survey and experimental research
(c) basis, applied and action research
(d) Both (a) and (b)

16 Which type of research systematically describes a situational problem and provides information about various subject like living condition of a community?

(a) Correlational research
(b) Descriptive research
(c) Experimental research
(d) Exploratory research

17 In which research the researcher has no control over the variables, she/he can only report what has happened or what is happening?

(a) Correlational research
(b) Experimental research
(c) Descriptive research
(d) Exploratory research

18 Which of the following is most appropriate about ex-post facto research?

(a) The research is carried out along prior to the incident
(b) The research is carried out after the incident
(c) The research is carried out prior to the incident
(d) The research is carried out keeping in mind the possibilities of an incident

19 Which type of research concerns itself with cause effect relationship?

(a) Analytical research
(b) Correlational research
(c) Ex-post facto research
(d) Explanatory research

20 Which research is conducted for those problems which have not been researched before?

(a) Exploratory research
(b) Explanatory research
(c) Analytical research
(d) Historical research

21 Which research measures the level of association between two or more variables?

(a) Descriptive research
(b) Correlational research
(c) Experimental research
(d) Exploratory research

22 Correlational research aims to find out which of the following?

(a) Negative correlation
(b) Positive correlation
(c) Zero correlation
(d) All of the above

23 "To search measures to reduce the absentee rate among employees of a company" is the example of which type of research?

(a) Explanatory research
(b) Ex-post facto research
(c) Analytical research
(d) Correlational research

24 Which research is conducted for such problems which have not been clearly defined?

(a) Experimental research
(b) Basic / Fundamental research
(c) Exploratory research
(d) None of the above

25 Which of the following is/are type(s) of field studies?

(a) Hypothesis testing
(b) Exploratory testing
(c) Both (a) and (b)
(d) None of the above

26 Which research is primarily concerned with finding out 'what is' or 'what was' ?

(a) Descriptive research
(b) Correlational research
(c) Explanatory research
(d) None of the above

27 The experimental studies are based on
(a) conceptual parameters
(b) the manipulation of the variables
(c) survey of literature
(d) conceptual parameters

28 Which research has a purpose to study the cause and effect relationship?
(a) Exploratory research
(b) Explanatory research
(c) Experimental research
(d) None of the above

29 The research that applies the laws at the time of field study to draw more and more clear ideas about the problem is
(a) Action research
(b) Experimental research
(c) Applied research
(d) None of the above

30 Which of following is the example of basic/fundamental research?
(a) A study, looking at how family environment influence the socialisation of a child
(b) A study assessing whether men and women are likely to suffer from depression
(c) A study looking at how caffeine consumption impacts our brain
(d) All of the above

31 Which research has an ultimate goal to improve the human condition?
(a) Basic research   (b) Applied research
(c) Inductive research (d) Deductive research

32 Which research moves from more general to more specific level?
(a) Inductive research
(b) Deductive research
(c) Structured research
(d) Unstructured research

33 Which of the following is the type of logic based research?
(a) Inductive research

(b) Deductive research
(c) Structured research
(d) Both (a) and (b)

34 Which of the following is also known as systematic observation?
(a) Unstructured research
(b) Structured research
(c) Mixed research
(d) Quantitative research

35 Empirical research is based on
(a) direct observation of researcher
(b) direct experience of researcher
(c) writing skill of researcher
(d) Both (a) and (b)

36 In which research no statistical test is required?
(a) Empirical research
(b) Conceptual research
(c) Qualitative research
(d) None of the above

37 Which research is mostly related to the positivist or post-positivist paradigm?
(a) Qualitative research
(b) Quantitative research
(c) Empirical research
(d) Mixed research

38 Which research involves collecting, analysing and integrating quantitative and qualitative research?
(a) Empirical research
(b) Conceptual research
(c) Mixed research
(d) None of the above

39 Which of the following is the suggestion to remove errors in research?
(a) Proofreading of the research manuscript should be done carefully
(b) Choose research methodology very carefully
(c) Use objectivity in research
(d) All of the above

Answers

1. (c)	2. (b)	3. (a)	4. (d)	5. (c)	6. (d)	7. (d)	8. (c)	9. (c)	10. (d)
11. (d)	12. (b)	13. (d)	14. (d)	15. (d)	16. (b)	17. (c)	18. (d)	19. (a)	20. (c)
21. (b)	22. (d)	23. (a)	24. (c)	25. (b)	26. (c)	27. (c)	28. (c)	29. (b)	30. (a)
31. (b)	32. (b)	33. (d)	34. (b)	35. (c)	36. (c)	37. (b)	38. (c)	39. (d)	

Chapter 17

Communication and Interpersonal Relationship

Communication

Communication is fundamental to the existence and survival of humans as well as to an organisation.

Communication is simply the act of transferring information from one place, person or group to another. The term 'Communication' has been derived from the Latin word 'Communicare' which means to share, or to make common.

It is the process of sharing ideas, concepts, imaginations, feelings, behaviours and written content among the people to reach a common understanding.

Every communication involves at least one sender, a message and a recipient. The process of education is not possible without communication, because in education and teaching, teachers reveal their ideas to the students which leads to their all round development.

Definitions of Communication

According to **Keith Davis**, "Communication is the process of passing information and understanding from one person to another."

According to **Carl Howland**, "Communication is the process by which an individual transmits stimuli to modify the behaviour of the other individuals."

According to **Millet**, " The underlying aim of communication is the meeting of minds on common issue".

According to **Oxford Dictionary**, "Communication is transferring or conveying of meaning".

According to **Berlo**,"Communication as S-R Model or Sender-Receiver Model, where 'sender' stands for 'stimulus' and 'receiver' stands for 'response'. This was later extended to S-M-C-R Model that stands for Sender-Message-Channel-Receiver .

It is the basic communication process. Thus, the above definitions make it clear that "the essence of communication is understanding the information, not transmitting the information."

Importance of Communication

- Communication develops interaction between students and teachers.
- Communication helps to develop relation among people.
- Communication provides subject-matter for knowledge.
- Communication provides the way to achieve success.
- Communication determines personality of an individual.

- Communication helps in making a person social.
- Communication makes the people literate and employed in a society.
- Communication helps in bringing change in the society.
- Communication increases morale of a group.
- Communication provides a good environment for an individual to develop.
- Communication encourages people for establishing coordination.
- Communication inspires people of an organisation to work effectively.
- Communication facilitates access to the vital information required to take decisions.
- Communication provides a platform for people to communicate with each other.

Elements of Communication Process

Communication is a continuous process which mainly involves three elements i.e. sender, message and receiver. The elements involved in the communication process are explained below

1. **Sender** The sender or the communicator generates the message and conveys it to the receiver. He is the source and the one who starts the communication.
2. **Message** It is the idea, information, view, fact, feeling etc., that is generated by the sender and is then intended to be communicated further.
3. **Encoding** The message generated by the sender is encoded symbolically such as in the form of words, pictures, gestures, etc. before it is being conveyed.
4. **Media** It is the manner in which the encoded message is transmitted. The message may be transmitted orally or in writing.

   The medium of communication includes telephone, internet, post, fax, e-mail, etc.

The choice of medium is decided by the sender.

5. **Decoding** It is the process of converting the symbols encoded by the sender. After decoding, the message is received by the receiver.
6. **Receiver** Receiver is the person who is last in the chain and for whom the message was sent by the sender.

   Once the receiver receives the message and understands it in proper perspective and acts according to the message, only then the purpose of communication is successful.
7. **Feedback** Once the receiver confirms to the sender that he has received the message and understood it, the process of communication is completed. Feedback is a listener's verbal or non-verbal response to a message.
8. **Noise** It refers to any obstruction that is caused by the sender, message or receiver during the process of communication. For e.g. bad telephone connection, faulty encoding, faulty decoding, inattentive receiver, poor understanding of message due to prejudice or inappropriate gesture, etc.

Nature of Communication

Nature of communication can be understood through the following points

- Communication is a two-way process of understanding between two or more persons i.e. sender and receiver. A person cannot communicate with himself.
- Communication is a continuous process. Exchange of ideas and opinion amongst people is an ongoing process. Continuous interaction promotes understanding and exchange of information relevant for decision-making.
- It is a dynamic process that keeps changing in different situations. Communication between sender and receiver takes different forms and

medium depending upon their moods and behaviour.

- Communication is a pervasive activity. It takes place at all levels (top, middle and low) in all functional areas like production, finance, personnel and sales of a business organisation.

- A minimum of two persons i.e. sender and receiver must be present for communication to take place. It may be between superiors, subordinates and peer groups.

- Communication involves exchange of ideas and opinions. People interact and develop understanding for each other.

- Though words are active carriers of information, gestures can sometimes be more powerful than words. Facial expressions, sounds, signs and symbols are the non-verbal forms of communication.

- Communication is goal-oriented. Unless the receiver and sender know the purpose they intend to achieve through communication, it has little practical utility.

- Communication is effective when sender and receiver develop mutual understanding of the subject. Messages conveyed should be understood by the receiver in the desired sense.

Effective Communication

Effective communication is defined as the ability to convey information to another effectively and efficiently. It takes place when both the sender and receiver derive a common meaning from a meassage.

There must be a mutual understanding and a common language between the sender and the receiver for the transmission of ideas or information. Listening is an important part of communication. Therefore, the receiver of information should be a good listener just as the sender should be a good communicator.

Types of Effective Communication

The types of effective communication are given below

Verbal Communication

It refers to the form of communication in which message is transmitted, verbally i.e. by the use of sounds and words. Use of language in both spoken and written form is part of verbal communication.

In this type of communication, one has to remember the acronym KISS (Keep It Short and Simple). Verbal communication is further divided into two categories

(i) Oral Communication

It includes face-to-face conversation, speech, telephinic conversation, video, TV, radio, internet, etc. Spoken words are also used in oral communication.

Oral communication is influenced by pitch, volume, speed and clarity of speaking. They all are termed as para language.

Advantages

- It brings quick feedback.
- It is voluntary and natural, easy for others to understand.
- It establishes a close relationship between speaker and listener.
- It also supports non-verbal communication.
- By reading facial expression and body language, one can guess whether one should trust, what is being said or not.

Disadvantages

- The delivered words are temporary.
- What is heard is often forgotten.
- User is unable to think about what he is delivering.

(ii) Written Communication

The communication which is performed through any written document is called written communication. Written language, signs, symbols are used to communicate in this communication.

Message can be trasmitted, via e-mail, letter, report, memo, etc. Therefore, written communication is the process of communication in which messages or information is exchanged or communicated within sender and receiver through written form.

Vocabulary, grammar, writing style, precision, clarity of the language, etc., influence messages, which are sent by the sender.

Written communication is the most common form of communication in business firms. Thus, it is considered as core among the business skills.

Advantages

- Message can be revised and edited many times before being sent, thus there is less chance of error.
- It provides record for every message sent and can be saved for later study.
- A written message enables receiver to fully understand it.
- Written message sends appropriate feedback.

Disadvantages

- It does not bring instant feedback.
- It takes more time in composing a written message.
- Not everyone is good at writing.

Non-Verbal Communication

The non-verbal communications are those communications where the sending or receiving of messages is done through the wordless messages. It means that communication is established other than oral and written. It is all about the body language of the speaker and does not make use of words.

There are three distnct areas involved in this type of communication. They are

(i) **Audio Sign** It plays a very crucial role in non-verbal communication. Audio signs communicate the intended emotions in the from of sounds that are different for varying emotions.

For example, bell in a school, fire alarms, drumbeats, work shift alarms in factories and so on.

(ii) **Body Language** It is that aspect of non-verbal communication which speaks without use of words.

Each part of human body responds to different situation in a varied manner. It includes all actions i.e. physical or physiological postures, facial expressions, gestures and other body movements.

Our body movement includes our head, eyes, shoulders, lips, eyebrows, legs, arms and hands. All these can convey if we are uncomfortable, friendly, anxious or nervous.

(iii) **Visual Sign** It is the act of using photographs, art, drawings, sketches, charts and graphs to convey information. For example, signed light (Red, Green and Blue).

Advantages

- Information can be easily presented in non-verbal communication.
- This type of communication helps illiterate people to communicate with others by using gestures, facial expressions, eye contact, proximity, touching, etc.
- The message of non-verbal communication reach the receiver very fast. Thus, it reduces the time of both communicator and receiver.
- In this communication, people can repeat the verbal messages according to their need. For example, point in a direction while stating directions.

Disadvantages

- Non-verbal communication is quite vague and imprecise.
- In this type of communication, long conversation and necessary explanations are not possible.

- As gestures and facial expressions are used in this communication, so it is difficult to understand quickly and requires a lot of repetitions to clarify the meaning of something.
- Non-verbal communication does not follow any rules, formality or structure like other communication.

Intercultural Communication

This communication takes place between people of different cultures. Basically, 'inter' is a prefix that means 'between' and 'cultural' means 'from a culture'.

In this communication, we study about the communication across different cultures and social groups or how culture affects communication. Each culutre has its own beliefs, values, rituals and morals which gets reflected in the people of that culture.

So, in inter-cultural communication, cultural values get shared when people of different cultures interact with each other. However, absence of a common language can be a barrier in this type of communication.

This type of communication plays a great role in understanding various disciplines of Social Sciences such as cultural studies, anthrophology, linguistics, psychology and communication studies.

Advantages

- It is important to establish and maintain positive intergroup relations.
- It can increase cultural knowledge and awareness, communication skills and tolerance.

Disadvantages

- Sometimes, foreign students experience feelings of uncertainty and anxiety about how to integrate into their host society.
- It also creates incompatibility among students, intercultural conflicts and social alienation.

Group Communication

Group communication is the exchange of information and ideas between individuals using interpersonal skills.

In group communication, team members have to effectively participate for an effective communication.

It provides an opportunity for people to come together to discuss and exchange views of common interest. It includes collective decision-making, self-expression, increasing one's effect and elevating one's status. In group communication, there will be more resources, knowledge and ideas.

Advantages

- In group communication, people have chances to gain more information and knowledge.
- Through group communication, many goals can be achieved, like collective decision-making, self-expression, increasing one's effect, elevating one's status and relaxation and so on.
- By group communication, people eliminate all the biases that are generally introduced due to individual decision-making. It also reduces the unreliability of individual decisions.

Disadvantages

- In group communication, group interaction is time consuming and often inefficient, especially in an emergency.
- In group communication, imbalances in status, skills and goals, may distort the process and the outcome sharply.

Classroom Communication

Classroom communication is the interaction between the teacher and the students in a classroom setting. It involves teacher who provides information, shares knowledge and experiences.

In such communication, there are students who grasp these information. Effective classroom communication takes place when there is a two way flow of information.

For this, a teacher should be a good speaker so that he/she is able to communicate properly. Students should be active listeners, they should be open to ask their queries and raise doubts.

Classroom communication takes place effectively when teacher uses teaching aids like charts, maps, slides, models, projectors, etc. Various methods of classroom communication can be adopted for effective interaction such as lecturing, discussion, debate, dialogues, demonstrations, etc.

Advantages

- Classroom communication gives chance to both students and teachers to interact with each other.
- It improves the relationship between students and teachers.
- It helps to exchange different ideas, views, feeling, expression in the classroom.
- It improves the monotonous environment of the classroom.

Disadvantages

- It is not beneficial, if it is one way flow of information i.e. from the teacher only.
- Long duration of classroom communication may affect the decorum of the classroom teaching- learning process.
- Long conversation with students creates noise in the classroom.

Interpersonal Relationship

Close relationships are sometimes called interpersonal relationships. The closest relationships are most often found with family and a small circle of peer group. Interpersonal relationships are formed in the context of social, cultural and other influences.

The role of the teacher within the classroom appears to be the single most important factor in our educational setting. Although the majority of studies in the field of interaction analysis have focused on the relationship of teaching techniques to academic achievement, there is an increasing interest in the interpersonal relationships between teacher and students.

Interpersonal interaction skills revolve around the ability of the teacher to provide certain core conditions which are essential in creating a positive educational setting. These conditions consist of warmth, empathy, respect, genuineness, concreteness, self-disclosure, immediacy and confrontation.

Importance of Interpersonal Relationship between Teacher and Students

- Interpersonal relationships between teacher and students are important for overall physical and emotional development of students.
- These relationships help to develop mutual trust between teachers and students.
- These relationships provide students chance to express their feelings, thoughts and views in the classroom setting.
- These relationships give chance to students to develop their thoughts as children in school are not empty bodies to be filled with an endless number of facts.
- These provide chance to make choices and share in the process of decision-making.
- Mutual interpersonal relationship between students and teacher is essential in developing a working relationship within the classroom.
- Good interpersonal relationship between students and teacher encourages student-centered classroom, where the student is an active participant who shares in the responsibility of planning and implementing learning activities. In such classroom, the

teacher's role is that of a facilitator of learning experiences where she/he motivates and guides student activities rather than dictating them.

Types of Interpersonal Relationship

These are the most common types of interpersonal relationship

1. **Family** Family can include our parents, siblings, grandparents, aunts, uncles, cousins and guardians. These are the first relationships we ever form. These bonds can last a lifetime. Sometimes we hold different values or ideals than family members do.

   But it's essential to maintain open and respectful communication. In some cases, personal differences can't be overcome and the interpersonal relationships with family members might become strained or non-existent.

2. **Friendship** Some friendships are even more important than family connections. Friends may highlight different aspects of our personality.
   Some of these relationships may only last a little while, but other bonds will stand the test of time.

3. **Work** We may see our co-workers more than we see our own family, so it's normal to form strong bond with our co-workers. Our shared experiences can create relationships that impact the workplace dynamic.

We don't always agree with colleagues, even if they're a friend, but it's important to maintain respectful interpersonal relationship to ensure both work and friendship are valued.

Ways to Build Up Good Teacher-Students Interpersonal Relationships

The establishment of harmonious relationships largely dependent on teachers. Following are the points which may help to build up good teacher-students interpersonal relationship

- Teachers' rich knowledge and amiable personality is the basis of a harmonious relationship between teachers and students.
- Teachers should treat students as friends, showing teachers' love and concern, which will cause students to love them in return.
- Teachers should treat students like their children when talking to them.
- Teachers shouldn't criticise their students in front of their peers to let them lose 'face'. If necessary they should sit down privately and have a talk with them.
- Teachers should have more personal interactions and communication with students, having an open ear to students' personal troubles.
- Teachers should show their positive attitude towards their students.

1 The English word 'communication' is derived from the word
(a) commune   (b) communalism
(c) common sense   (d) communicare

2 Communication is the process of sharing
(a) ideas, feelings
(b) concepts, behaviour
(c) imaginations, written content
(d) All of the above

3 Communication means
(a) transferring or conveying thoughts, views, emotions or information through specific signals and symbols
(b) radio, TV, cinema, etc
(c) telephone, telegram, fax, radio
(d) None of the above

4 Communication is the process of passing information and understanding from one person to another is given by
(a) Carl Hovland
(b) Keith Davis
(c) David Berlo
(d) Harold D. Lasswell

5 "Communication is transferring or conveying of meaning" is given by
(a) Millet   (b) Oxford Dictionary
(c) Berlo   (d) Carl Howland

6 In the SMCR Model, 'S' stands for
(a) Select   (b) Sender
(c) Service   (d) System

7 Who gave the S-R Model?
(a) Millet   (b) Carl Howland
(c) Berlo   (d) Keith Davis

8 Which of the following signifies the importance of communication?
(a) Communication develops interaction between students and teachers
(b) Communication helps to develop relations among people
(c) Communication provides subject matter for knowledge
(d) All of the above

9 Which one of the following is correct?
(a) Communication is not a mere transmission, it aims at understanding
(b) Efficient communication minimises time and cost involved in the exchange process
(c) Communication is a process involving a sender who sends a meassage, a channel through which a message is transmitted and a receiver
(d) All of the above

10 Which of the following is the most fundamental component of the manager's job?
(a) Directing
(b) Testing
(c) Communicating
(d) Managing

11 The essence of communication is
(a) transmitting information
(b) shorting information
(c) imparting knowledge
(d) sharing and understanding information

12 The transmission of the message from sender to recipient can be affected by
(a) our emotions
(b) cultural situation
(c) medium used to communicate
(d) All of the above

13 Which of the following is not true about communication?
(a) Communication provides the way to achieve success
(b) Communication does not determine personality of an individual
(c) Communication helps in making a person social
(d) All of the above

14 Communication helps
(a) in making a person social
(b) in bringing change in the society
(c) in increasing morale of a group
(d) All of the above

15 Which of the three components are parts of human communication process?
(a) Message, Noise, Feedback
(b) Feedback, Message, Critquing
(c) Message, Recording, Feedback
(d) Noise, Feedback, Jargon

16 The process of communication runs through
(a) a sender
(b) a receiver
(c) a channel
(d) All of these

17 In the process of communication, which one of the following is in the chronological order?
(a) Communicator, Medium, Receiver, Effect, Message
(b) Medium, Communicator, Meassage, Receiver, Effect
(c) Communicator, Message, Medium, Receiver, Effect
(d) Message, Communicator, Medium, Receiver, Effect

18 "The sender of information experesses his ideas into words, symbols or signs to convey the message." This is known as
(a) decoding
(b) encoding
(c) communication channel
(d) None of the above

19 In the communication process, to encode means to
(a) block a pathway between the sender and receiver of a message
(b) translate ideas into a code
(c) speak to large group of people
(d) ubteroret a code

20 Which of the following stages of communication process includes the conversion of symbols into a meaningful information?
(a) Encoding
(b) Decoding
(c) Receiving
(d) Channelising

21 It is the process which translates the message into a form that can be understood by the receiver is called
(a) encoding
(b) receiver
(c) decoding
(d) feedback

22 To decode a message is to
(a) translate ideas into code
(b) interpret a message
(c) evaluate a message
(d) reject a message

23 Which of the following is/are the stage(s) of communication process?
(a) Encoding
(b) Decoding
(c) Both (a) and (b)
(d) None of the above

24 In circular communication, the encoder become a decoder when there is
(a) noise
(b) audience
(c) criticality
(d) feedback

25 Feedback is a listener's
(a) acceptance of a message
(b) aversion to a message
(c) verbal critique of your message
(d) verbal or non-verbal response to a message

26 Which of the following cen hamper the process of communication?
(a) Channel
(b) Encoder
(c) Noise
(d) Pollution

27 Anything that interferes with a message in communication is known as
(a) Context
(b) Noise
(c) Decoding
(d) Feedback

28 In the classroom, the teacher sends the message either in words or images. The students are really
(a) encoders
(b) decoders
(c) agitators
(d) propagators

29 Communicating the message to each individual personally rather through a message hung on a board will be
(a) effective communication
(b) best communication
(c) bi-directional communication
(d) final communication

30 Each type of communication is affected by its
(a) Reception
(b) Transmission
(c) Non-regulation
(d) Context

31 Where accuracy of a communication is important then which communication type is desirable?
(a) One way communication
(b) Two way communication
(c) Both (a) and (b)
(d) None of the above

32 Use of language in both spoken and written forms is part of
(a) non-verbal communication
(b) intercultural communication
(c) verbal communication
(d) None of the above

33 Break-down in verbal communication is described as
(a) short circuit   (b) contradiction
(c) unevenness   (d) entropy

34 The term 'KISS' (Keep It Short and Simple) is almost used in which communication?
(a) Verbal   (b) Non-verbal
(c) Intercultural   (d) Group

35 Verbal classroom communication includes
[Bihar BEd 2018]
(a) Directions are given in written
(b) Body language is used
(c) Teacher or student speak a loud
(d) None of the above

36 Which of the following is the advantage of oral communication?
(a) It brings quick feedback
(b) It is voluntary and natural, easy for others to understand
(c) It establishes a close relationship between speaker and listeners
(d) All of the above

37 Which of the following is/are the advantage(s) of having written communication?
(a) Message can be revised several times
(b) It is a permanent record that can be saved
(c) Receiver has more time to analyse the message
(d) All of the above

38 In written communication, message can be transmitted through
(a) e-mail   (b) letter
(c) report   (d) All of these

39 Which of the following influences messages which are sent by the sender?
(a) Grammar   (b) Vocabulary
(c) Gestures   (d) Both (a) and (b)

40 In business firms which of the following is the most common form of communication?
(a) Oral communication
(b) Non-verbal communication
(c) Written communication
(d) Intercultural communication

41 Which of the following best signifies the written communication?
(a) Message can be revised and edited many times
(b) It provides record for every message sent and can be saved for later study
(c) A written message enables receiver to fully understand it
(d) All of the above

42 Learning to communicate with others is the key to
(a) never being misunderstood
(b) winning the approval of everyone around you
(c) eliminating all of your listener's physiological noise
(d) establishing rewarding relationship

43 Which of the following is/are correct in respect to non-verbal communication?
I. It helps illiterate people to communicate with others easily.
II. In this communication, people can repeat the verbal messages according to their need.
III. In this communication, there is a great possibility in distortion of information.
Select the correct answer from the codes given below.
(a) Only I   (b) I and II
(c) II and III   (d) All of these

44 When gesture are used, then it is
[Bihar BEd 2018]
(a) verbal communication
(b) non-verbal communication
(c) written-communication
(d) All of the above

45 Audio sign, body language and visual signs are part of
(a) verbal communication
(b) non-verbal communication
(c) intercultural communication
(d) group communication

46 Which of the following is the barrier in intercultural communication?
(a) Lack of knowledge
(b) Area/location
(c) Views of people
(d) Absence of a common language

47 Intercultural communication plays a great role in understanding which of the following disciplines of social sciences?
(a) Cultural studies   (b) Anthropology
(c) Psychology   (d) All of these

48 Which of the following is true about intercultural communication?
I. It is important to establish and maintain positive intergroup relations.
II. It can increase cultural knowledge and awareness, communication skills and tolerance.
III. It also creates incompatibility among students, intercultural conflicts and social alienation.
Codes
(a) I and II   (b) II and III
(c) Only III   (d) All of these

49 In group-communication there is/are
(a) Self-expression
(b) Common interest
(c) Decision-making
(d) All of the above

50 Which of the following is correct about Group Communication?
I. In this communication, people have chances to gain information and knowledge.
II. Through this communication, many goals can be achieved like collective decision-making, self-expression, etc.

III. In this communication, group interaction is time consuming.
Select the correct answer from the codes given below.
(a) I and II   (b) II and III
(c) Only I   (d) All of these

51 Classroom communication of a teacher rests on the Principle of
(a) Infotainment
(b) Edutainment
(c) Entertainment
(d) Power Equation

52 Which of the following principles is a useful guide for establishing effective classroom communication?
(a) Principle of Teachers
(b) Principle for Selection of Instructional Methods and Media
(c) Principle of Creating Conducive Learning Environment
(d) All of the above

53 The type of communication that the teacher has in the classroom, is termed as
(a) interpersonal communication
(b) mass communication
(c) group communication
(d) face-to-face communication/classroom communication

54 Classroom communication can be described as
(a) exploration
(b) institutionalisation
(c) unsignified narration
(d) discourse

55 Which of the following is true about classroom communication?
I. It gives chance to both students and teachers to interact with each other.
II. It improves the relationship between students and teachers.
III. It improves the monotonous environment of the classroom.
Codes
(a) I and II   (b) II and III
(c) Only III   (d) All of these

56 Positive classroom communication leads to
                                            [UK BEd 2018]
  (a) coercion   (b) submission
  (c) confrontation   (d) persuasion

57 What are the barriers to effective
communication?   **[UK BEd 2018]**
  (a) Moralising, being judgemental and
      comments of consolation
  (b) Dialogue, summary and self-review
  (c) Use of simple words, cool reaction and
      defensive attitude
  (d) Personal statements, eye contact and
      simple narration

58 Interpersonal relationship is an
association which may be based on
  (a) inference   (b) love
  (c) solidarity   (d) All of these

59 Which of the following is true about
interpersonal relationship?
  I. It is important for overall physical and
      emotional development of students.
  II. It helps to develop mutual trust
      between teachers and students.
  III. It provides chance to make choices
      and share in the process of decision-
      making.
  Codes
  (a) Only I   (b) I and II
  (c) II and III   (d) All of these

60 Which of the following is a type of
interpersonal relationship?
  (a) Friendship   (b) Family
  (c) Work   (d) All of these

Answers

1. (d)	2. (d)	3. (a)	4. (b)	5. (b)	6. (b)	7. (c)	8. (d)	9. (d)	10. (c)
11. (d)	12. (d)	13. (b)	14. (d)	15. (a)	16. (d)	17. (c)	18. (b)	19. (b)	20. (b)
21. (c)	22. (b)	23. (c)	24. (d)	25. (d)	26. (c)	27. (b)	28. (b)	29. (a)	30. (d)
31. (b)	32. (c)	33. (d)	34. (a)	35. (c)	36. (d)	37. (d)	38. (d)	39. (d)	40. (c)
41. (d)	42. (d)	43. (d)	44. (b)	45. (b)	46. (d)	47. (d)	48. (d)	49. (d)	50. (d)
51. (b)	52. (d)	53. (d)	54. (d)	55. (d)	56. (d)	57. (a)	58. (d)	59. (d)	60. (d)

Chapter 18

School Education System, Policies and Administration

Education is a power which plays an important role in the development of human resources of a nation. Its importance has been realised since time immemorial and continuous right up to today. Education is both acquisition of knowledge and experiences as well as the development of skills, value, habits and attitudes which help to lead a worthwhile life in this world.

Education is generally given in both formal and informal forms. The formal education system includes primary, secondary and higher education. Therefore, there are three levels of education in the education system of India.

Under this many policies have been made from time to time to improve the three levels of education and to add contemporary subjects, while education is included in the Concurrent List.

Therefore, the role of the center and the states in its administrative system is found in both separate and combined forms. Thus, the detailed information of India's education system, policies and administration are as follows

Primary Education System

Primary education is the first stage of formal education. The main objective of primary education is to develop knowledge of the rules of society, development of good habits and language development in the students. Provision has been made to make primary education free and compulsory in India.

By the 86th Constitutional Amendment Act, 2002, a provision has been made regarding free and compulsory education to all children upto the age of 6-14 years under Article 21 (A). This Act has come into force with effect from 1st April, 2010.

Primary education is a child-centred education. India's primary education is from class I to VIII, with basic primary education from class I to V, while upper primary education runs from class VI to VIII. Under the Millennium Development Goals (MDGs) announced in the year 2000, India had set a target of universal primary education by the year 2015. Under the Sustainable Development Goals, we now have to achieve the goal of universal primary education by the year 2030.

The National Education Policy aims at universal enrollment for children upto the age of 14 and improving the quality of education.

Secondary Education System

Secondary education system helps to develop historical and national outlook in secondary education students. It is only through this that students become aware of their constitutional rights and duties. At the same time, their logical thinking develops.

Students become familiar with various subjects such as science, humanities, social sciences and vocational faculties only through secondary education. Secondary education is divided into two parts, Secondary and Higher Secondary. Secondary classes are IX and X and Higher Secondary classes are XI and XII.

The secondary curriculum in India consists of subjects like language, science, mathematics, social science, arts, technology and physical education. Based on the performance of the first two years of secondary school, students have an opportunity to opt for teaching streams like science, commerce and arts/humanities in higher secondary schools.

The examination in secondary education is conducted by the State Board, Central Board of Secondary Education, etc.

Secondary Education Commission

The Secondary Education Commission was constituted on September 23, 1952 under the chairmanship of Dr. Laxman Swami Mudaliar, hence this commission is also called Mudaliar Commission.

Its aim is to examine the prevailing secondary education in the country, to suggest measures for the restructuring and revision of secondary education in the context of its aims, organisation, relationship of primary and higher education, and correlation of different types of secondary schools. The Mudaliar Commission recommended that there should be two types of institutions of teacher education, which are as follow

1. Primary teacher training institutions under a separate board, whose objective was to train all those candidates who have passed S.L.C. (Matriculation) or Higher Secondary class, which is of 2 years.

2. Secondary teacher training institutions, which are university recognised and affiliated to the courts whose objective was to train the graduates for a period of one year.

Criteria of Curriculum

The Secondary Education Commission also recommended diversification of the curriculum, adding an intermediate level and introducing three-tier undergraduate courses, etc., which should be

- Three years of secondary and four years of higher education.
- Multi-purpose schools and Vocational Training Centers should be established.
- Objective Test Method should be adopted and instead of giving institutional marks, indicative marks should be given.
- General knowledge, art and music should be made compulsory in the curriculum of high school and higher secondary level of education.

Higher Education System

The tertiary level of education which comes after Primary and Secondary education is known as Higher Education system.

The major changes in the traditional style of Higher Education were brought by the Europeans starting from 1600 AD. The British successfully controlled much part of India and established formal system of Higher Education which continues till date.

India's higher education system is the world's third largest in terms of number of students, next to China and the United States. It is largest in the world in terms of number of educational institutions.

India's Higher Education sector has witnessed a tremendous increase in the number of

Universities/University level Institutions and Colleges since independence.

The involvement of private sector in higher education has seen drastic changes in the field. At present over 60% of higher education institutions in India are promoted by the private sector.

Tertiary education is of many types such as general, vocational, professional or technical. Higher education is provided by universities, colleges and institutes of technology.

There are three levels of higher education

1. Graduate level
2. Post-Graduate level
3. Research level which includes research in Ph.D., fellowship for post Doctorate

Higher Education in Modern India

Major changes in the traditional style of higher education were started by the Europeans in 1600 AD.

The British successfully controlled much part of India by the 1800 AD under the East India Company and established formal system of higher education, which continues till date.

The English Higher Educational Institution in India was started in Calcutta in 1817 AD. It started with the establishment of Hindu College.

On the basis of the advice of the Viceroy Lord Macaulay, Calcutta, Bombay and Madras universities were established on the style of the University of London (British style) in 1857 AD.

In the year 1918, the Nizam of Hyderabad established Osmaniya University, in which Urdu was made the medium of higher education. Between 1913 and 1921, six residential and teaching integrated universities were established.

The Aligarh Muslim Anglo Oriental College established by Sir Syed Ahmed in the year 1875. It became Aligarh Muslim University in the year 1920.

It is noteworthy that in the year 1925, the name of the Inter University Board was changed to 'Union of Indian Universities' and under this, information regarding educational, cultural and related fields started being exchanged among all the universities.

Emergence Acquisition of Higher Education in Pre. Independence Period

Lord Macaulay's Minute, 1835

- In 1835 under Lord William Bentinck, it was decided to introduce English as the medium of instruction.
- Macaulay's Minute refers to his proposal of education for the Indians. It focused upon English education instead of traditional Indian learning, he told oriental culture was 'defective' and 'unholy'.
- He believed in educating a few upper and middle class students. Ultimately, education would trickle down to the masses. This was called Infiltration Theory.
- He wished to create a class of Indians who were Indian in colour and blood but English in taste and affiliation.
- In this way, he played an important role in building the modern education.

Wood's Despatch, 1854

- In 1854, Charles Wood prepared a despatch on the educational system for India.
- Considered the Magna Carta of English education in India, this document was the first comprehensive plan for spreading of education in India.
- In 1857, universities at Calcutta, Bombay and Madras were setup and later, departments of education were setup in all provinces.
- The Bethune School founded by J.E.D Bethune at Calcutta in 1849, was the first school to educate women.

- An agriculture Institute at Pusa (Bihar) and an Engineering Institute at Roorkee were also started.

Emergence of Higher Education in Post-Independence Period

After attaining independence in 1947, the main task of the Government of India was to have a rapid socio-economic development and reconstruction of Indian society. The Government realised and recognised the important role of education in achieving its objective. The development of higher education after independence can be traced through the following commissions and committees

Radha Krishnan Commission, 1948

Also known as University Education Commission. This Commission was set up to report on university education in the country.

Its recommendations proved to be of immense significance in establishing an educational system for independent India.

It recommended the following

- There should be 12 years of pre-university educational course .
- Higher education should have three main objectives namely; central education, liberal education and occupational education.
- A university degree should not be considered essential for administrative services.
- University education should be placed in 'Concurrent List'.
- A University Grants Commission (UGC) should be set up to look after university education in the country.
- English as the medium of instruction for higher studies should not be removed in haste.

Kothari Education Commission, 1964-66

A Commission was set up under Dr DS Kothari by Government of India to advise on the national pattern of education. Titled as 'Education and National Development' report, it was a very progressive report. Its recommendation included the following

- Free, universal and compulsory education up to the age of 14.
- A three language formula i.e, Mother tongue, Hindi and English and also development of regional languages.
- An Independent Regulatory Authority for Higher Education (IRAHE) should be formed.
- The UGC should focus on disbursement of grants and maintaining public institutions of higher learning.

Subramanian Committee on New Education Policy, 2016

Under T.S.R Subramanian a committee for Evolution of the New Education Policy (NEP) was constituted by the Ministry of Human Resource Development (MHRD) in October, 2015. It submitted its report on 7th May, 2016. The committee proposed some important features for the development of education.

Some of the important features are given below

- An Indian Education Service (IES) should be established as an All India Service.
- The outlay on education should be raised to atleast 6% of GDP without further loss of time.
- There should be minimum eligibility condition with 50% marks at graduate level for entry to B.Ed courses and Teacher Entrance Test (TET) should be made compulsory for recruitment of teachers.
- Compulsory certification should be made mandatory for teachers in government and private with provision for renewal in every 10 years based on independent external testing.
- It is also recommended in this committee that the top 200 foreign universities should

be allowed to open campuses in India and give the same degree which is acceptable in the home country of the said university.

Other recommendations of the committee include ICT in Education, the Right To Education (RTE) Act, 2009, National Higher Education Promotion and Management Act (NHEPMA), Early Childhood Care (ECCE) and so on.

Structure of Higher Education in India

The structure of Higher Education in India is given below

University Grants Commission (UGC)

The University Grants Commission (UGC) was formally inaugurated by Late Shri Maulana Abul Kalam Azad, the then Minister of Education, on 28th December, 1953.

It was formally established in November 1956 as a statutory body of the Government of India through an Act of Parliament.

The functions of UGC are as follow

- Promoting and coordinating university education.
- Determining and maintaining standards of teaching, examination and research in universities.
- Framing regulations on minimum standards of education.
- Monitoring developments in the field of collegiate and university education, disbursing grants to the universities and colleges.
- Serving as a vital link between the Union and State Governments and institutions of higher learning.
- Advising the Central and State Governments on the measures necessary for the improvement of university education.

Inter University Centres (IUCs)

The UGC establishes autonomous Inter University Centres within the university system under Clause 12(CCC) of the UGC Act.

It provides common advanced centralised facilities/services for universities which are not able to invest in infrastructure and other inputs. It also plays a vital role in offering the best expertise in each field to teachers and resources across the country.

The Nuclear Science Centre at New Delhi (now called Inter University Accelerator Centre) was the first research centre established in 1994. As of now, six inter-university centres are functioning within the university system. They are as follows

- Inter University Accelerator Centre (IUAC), New Delhi
- Inter University Centre for Astronomy and Astro-physics (IUCAA), Pune
- UGC-DAE Consortium for Scientific Research (UGC-DAECSR), Indore
- Information and Library Network (INFLIBNET), Ahmedabad
- Consortium for Educational Communication (CEC), New Delhi
- National Assessment and Accreditation Council (NAAC), Bangalore

The University Level Institutions

The university-level institutions in the Indian higher education system are basically of the following types

Central Universities are tertiary-level institutions that are established through Act of Parliament or State Legislatures. They are almost entirely funded by Governments.

The universities that are established by Acts of Parliament are funded by the Central Government and are commonly referred to as

Central Universities. For example, Aligarh Muslim University, University of Delhi and Jawaharlal Nehru University.

Deemed Universities are institutions that are deemed–to–be–universities for the purposes of the University Grants Commission Act, 1956. The Deemed University status is conferred by the Central Government, on the advice of the University Grants Commission for work of high quality in specialised academic fields.

For example Manipal Academy of Higher Education, Manipal and Tata Institute of Social Sciences, Mumbai. Tamil Nadu is the state with most deemed universities, (28 universities). The Indian Institute of Science, Bangalore and Indian Agricultural Research Institute, Delhi were the first two institutes to be granted a deemed status in 1958.

Institutions of National Importance are institutions established or so designated, by Acts of Parliament that undertake teaching and research in areas that are critical to national development.

For example, Seven Indian Institutes of Technology, and Sree Chitra Tirunal Institute for Medical Sciences and Technology, Trivandrum.

State Universities are public universities run by the State Government of each of the states and union territories of India, and are usually established by a local Legislative Assembly Act.

For example, Dr. B.R. Ambedkar University (Andhra Pradesh), Nalanda Open University (Bihar), Indira Gandhi Delhi Technical University for Women (Delhi). Uttar Pradesh has the most State Universities in India.

Private Universities are established through the State or Central Act by a sponsoring body including a registered company, a trust or a registered society under Section 25 of the Companies Act, 1956.

Educational Policies

Policies can be understood as a course of action which are directed towards goals. Some of the important policies on education are as follows

National Policy on Education (NPE), 1968

- It was the first Education Policy of India which was based on the recommendation of the Kothari Commission (1964-66).
- The three language formula proposed in this policy was very important from the point of view of national integration.
- It emphasised the need for raising the standards of education at all levels.
- It emphasised on the strengthening of post-graduate teaching and research as well as of centers of advanced study.

National Policy on Education (NPE), 1986

- In 1986, Rajiv Gandhi the then Prime Minister of India introduced a new National Policy on Education.
- It provided for a common educational structure like $10 + 2 + 3$.
- It suggested strengthening of adult education, vocational education, gradual replacement of affiliating system by autonomous colleges, setting up of Open University and rural university system and fortifying technical and management education.

National Policy on Education (NPE), 1992

- The NPE, 1986 was modified by the P.V Narasimha Rao Government in 1992. It was adopted in 2005 which was recognised as "Common Minimum Programme".

- It implemented All India Bases Common Entrance Examination for admission in all professional and technical programmes in India.
- The Indian Government laid down a Three Exam Scheme for admission to Engineering and Architecture/Planning programmes such as JEE, AIEEE at the National Level and SLEEE State Level Engineering Entrance Examinations.
- In this policy, State Level Institutions have option to join AIEEE.

National Policy on Education (NPE), 2016

- The draft of this policy was released by the MHRD.
- The focus of the policy is to address gender discrimination, creation of educational tribunals, and a common curriculum for Science, Mathematics and English.
- Keeping in view of special importance of Sanskrit, facilities for teaching Sanskrit at the school and university levels will be offered on more liberal scale.
- An independent mechanism for administering the National Higher Education Fellowship Programme will be put in place.
- A quality assurance mechanism for accreditation of all universities/institutions offering ODL/MOOCS will be put in place to ensure quality, promote innovation and reshape and modernise the ODL/MOOCs courses and programmes.
- In order to promote innovation, creativity and entrepreneurship, 100 more incubation centres will be established in HEIs over a period of next 5 years.

New Policy on Education (NPE), 2020

On 26th August, 2020, the Central Government cleared the New Education Policy (NEP) based on the report of former ISRO scientist Dr K Kasturirangan.

The latest policy is the Third Education Policy to be implemented in the country and will replace the erstwhile policy of 1986.

The salient features of NEP are given below

- The Ministry of Human Resource Development has been renamed as Ministry of Education.
- In context of school education, it provides for a "5 + 3 + 3 + 4" design corresponding to the age groups 3-8 years (foundational stage), 8-11 (preparatory), 11-14 (middle), and 14-18 (secondary). Apart from providing continuity to school education, it will bring pre-school under the ambit of school education.
- In higher education, following reforms has been suggested
  - Replacing UGC and AICTE with the Higher Education Commission of India (HECI).
  - Allowing reputed Foreign Institutions to open their campuses.
  - Re-introduction of four – year multi-disciplinary Bachelors' program, with exist option.
  - Discontinuation of M. Phil program.
  - Constitution of National Research Foundation (NRF) to enhance the pace of research in the country.
  - Flexibility to Institutions to offer different design for Master's program.
  - Phasing out of all institutions offering single streams and all universities and colleges must aim to become multi-disciplinary by 2040.

Administration of Higher Education System

Education is listed in the Concurrent List of Seventh Schedule of the Indian Constitution.

Thus, both the centre and state have the authority to make legislations on it. If any dispute occurs the upper hand goes to the centre.

There is another body called CABE that plays an important role in educational governance. The responsibilities that each of these bodies have are as follows

Central Government

The Government of India has controlled the education through following functions

- It lays down the National Policy on Education.
- It provides grants to UGC.
- It establishes Central Universities and Institutions of national importance.
- It declares an educational institution as deemed university on the recommendation of the UGC.

State Government

The State Government performs the following functions

- States have also set up state councils and advisory boards to provide guidelines for proper functioning of higher education institutions in the states.
- These state councils coordinate the roles of government, universities and apex regulatory agencies for higher education within the state.

Central Advisory Board of Education (CABE)

- It is the highest advisory body to advise the Central and State Governments in the field of education.
- It was established in 1920 and its present form is continued from 1994.
- It plays a pivotal role in reviewing educational development, determining the changes required to improve the system and monitoring the implementation.

Suggestions for Improving the Higher Education System

- There is a need to implement innovative and transformational approach from Primary to Higher education level to make Indian educational system globally more relevant and competitive.
- In higher educational institutes Industrial co-operation must be there for the development of curriculum, organising expert lectures, internships, live projects, career counselling and placements.
- Higher educational institutes need to improve quality, reputation and establish credibility through student exchange, faculty exchange programs, and other collaborations with high-quality national and international higher educational institutes.
- Government must promote collaboration between Indian higher education institutes and top International institutes.
- There is a need to focus on the graduate students by providing them such courses in which they can achieve excellence, gain deeper knowledge of subject and good jobs.

1 The formal education system of India includes which of the following?
(a) Primary Education System
(b) Secondary Education system
(c) Tertiary/Higher Education System
(d) All of the above

2 The provision regarding free and compulsory education to all children upto age of 6-14 years came into force in which year?
(a) 2002   (b) 2005
(c) 2008   (d) 2010

3 The Secondary Education Commission was constituted in which year?
(a) 1952   (b) 1961
(c) 1971   (d) 1981

4 According to the Right to Education Act, 2009, children with special needs should study   **[BHU, BEd 2018]**
(a) in special schools created exclusively for them
(b) at home with their parents and care givers providing necessary support
(c) in inclusive education set ups with provisions to cater to their individual needs
(d) in vocational training centres which would prepare them for life skills

5 Right of Children to Free and Compulsory Education Act, 2009 stipulates that learning should be   **[UK BEd 2018]**
(a) through activities in a child-friendly manner
(b) support by extra coaching
(c) restricted to co-scholastic subjects
(d) carefully monitored by frequent testing

6 Tertiary level of education is also known as
(a) Vocational education
(b) Professional education
(c) Higher education
(d) None of the above

7 The major changes in the traditional style of higher education were brought by
(a) Dutch   (b) Portuguese
(c) British   (d) None of these

8 Which higher education system is the world's third largest in terms of number of students?
(a) USA   (b) Australia
(c) India   (d) China

9 Which higher education system is the world's largest in terms of number of educational institutions?
(a) USA   (b) China
(c) India   (d) Britain

10 At present, how much higher education institutions in India are promoted by the private sector?
(a) 40%   (b) 50%
(c) 60%   (d) 70%

11 Tertiary Education System includes which of the following education system?
(a) Vocational education
(b) Professional education
(c) General education
(d) All of the above

12 The English higher educational institution in India was started in
(a) Madras
(b) Calcutta
(c) Mumbai (Bombay)
(d) None of the above

13 Which university was based on the British style in 1857?
(a) Bombay   (b) Madras
(c) Calcutta   (d) All of these

14 Who established Osmaniya University in the year 1918?
(a) Sir Syed Ahmed
(b) Raja Ram Mohan Roy
(c) Nizam of Hyderabad
(d) None of the above

15 In which year Lord William Bentinck introduced English as the medium of instruction for Indians?

(a) 1801   (b) 1815
(c) 1825   (d) 1835

16 Which of the following is known as the 'Magna Carta of English education in India, which was the first comprehensive plan for spreading of education in India?

(a) Radha Krishnan Commission
(b) Lord Macaulay's Minute
(c) Wood's Despatch
(d) None of the above

17 In which year the University Grants Commission was established?

(a) 1953   (b) 1944
(c) 1948   (d) 1960

18 Which of the following is the function of UGC?

(a) Promoting and coordinating university education
(b) Determining and maintaining standards of teaching, examination and research in universities
(c) Framing regulations on minimum standards of education
(d) All of the above

19 The University Grants Commission was established with which of the following aims?

(a) Identifying and sustaining institutions of potential learning
(b) Capacity building of teachers
(c) Providing autonomy to each and every higher educational institution of India
(d) All of the above

20 Higher education is important because

(a) it contributes to the national development through dissemination of specialised knowledge and skills
(b) it gives a person opportunity to succeed in today's global economy
(c) it provides people with opportunity to reflect on the critical, social, economic, cultural and moral issues faced by humanity
(d) All of the above

21 Which of the following institutions are empowered to confer or grant degrees, under the UGC Act, 1956?

A. A university established by an Act of Legislature.
B. A university established by an Act of Parliament.
C. An institution which is deemed to be university.
D. A university/institution established by a linguistic minority.

Select the correct answer from the codes given below.

(a) A and B   (b) A, B and C
(c) A, B and D   (d) All of these

22 Most of the Universities in India are funded by

(a) the Central Government
(b) the State Government
(c) the University Grants Commission
(d) Private bodies and individuals

23 Which of the following are Central Universities?

A. University of Delhi
B. Aligarh Muslim University
C. JNU
D. Kurukshetra University

Codes

(a) A, B and C   (b) B, C and D
(c) A and B   (d) All of these

24 Which of the following statements are correct about Central University?

A. The Central University is established under an Act of Parliament.
B. The President of India Act as the visitor of the University.
C. The President has the power to nominate some members to the Executive.
D. The President occasionally presides over the meeting of the Executive Committee or Court.

Select the correct answer from the codes given below.

(a) A, B and D   (b) A, C and D
(c) A, B and C   (d) A, B, C and D

25 Universities having central campus for imparting education are called
(a) State Universites
(b) Central Universites
(c) Deemed Universites
(d) Open Universites

26 Which of the following institutions was the first to be granted a deemed status in 1958?
(a) Indian Agriculture Research Institute, Delhi
(b) Delhi University
(c) Indian Institute of Science
(d) Both (a) and (c)

27 Deemed Universities declared by UGC under Section 3 of the UGC Act, 1956, are not permitted to
(a) given affiliation to any institute of higher education
(b) offer programmes in higher education and issue degrees
(c) offer distance education programmes without the approval of the Distance Education Council
(d) open off campus and offshore campus anywhere in the country and overseas respectively without the permission of the UGC

28 The difference between the University and the Deemed University is that the former
(a) is much bigger in size
(b) is established by the Act of Legislature
(c) looks after only affiliated colleges
(d) is established by the Central Government

29 Which of the following is/are the institution(s) of national importance?
(a) Seven Indian Institutes of Technology
(b) Sree Chitra Tirunal Institute for Medical Sciences and Technology
(c) Manipal and Tata Institute of Social Sciences
(d) Both (a) and (b)

30 Which State has most number of Deemed Universities in India?
(a) Maharashtra
(b) Karnataka
(c) Gujarat
(d) Tamil Nadu

31 The state with most State Universities is
(a) Uttar Pradesh
(b) Tamil Nadu
(c) West Bengal
(d) Rajasthan

32 Which of the following is the example of Private University?
(a) Sikkim Manipal University
(b) O. P. Jindal Global University
(c) Mohammad Ali Janhar University
(d) All of the above

33 Which National Policy on Education (NPE) emphasised on strengthening of post-graduate teaching and research?
(a) NPE, 1968
(b) NPE, 1986
(c) NPE, 1992
(d) NPE, 2016

34 National Policy on Education, 1968 was which education policy of India?
(a) First
(b) Second
(c) Third
(d) Fourth

35 'Operation Black Board' was the outcome of **[IGNOU, BEd 2019]**
(a) Kothari Commission
(b) National Curriculum Framework, 2005 (NCF, 2005)
(c) National Policy on Education, 1986 (NPE, 1986)
(d) National Curriculum Framework, 2000 (NCF, 2000)

36 Which government modified NPE, 1986 in 1992?
(a) Atal Bihari Vajpayee
(b) P. V. Narsimha Rao
(c) Charan Singh
(d) Rajiv Gandhi

37 The review of NPE, 1986, Programme of Action was done by
(a) Yashpal Committee
(b) Sapru Committee
(c) Rama Murti Committee
(d) National Commission for Teachers

38 Which National Policy on Education suggested strengthening of adult education, vocational education and setting up of open university and rural university?
(a) NPE, 1968
(b) NPE, 1986
(c) NPE, 1992
(d) NPE, 2016

39 Which National Policy on Education was recognised as "Common Minimum Programme"?
(a) NPE, 1968 (b) NPE, 1986
(c) NPE, 1992 (d) NPE, 2016

40 Which policy had the focus to address gender discrimination?
(a) NPE, 1968
(b) NPE, 1986
(c) NPE, 1992
(d) NPE, 2016

41 Which is the third Education Policy to be implemented in India?
(a) NPE, 1986
(b) NPE, 1968
(c) NPE, 2020
(d) None of the above

42 Education is listed in the Concurrent List of which Schedule of the Indian Constitution?
(a) Sixth Schedule (b) Fifth Schedule
(c) Seventh Schedule (d) Eighth Schedule

43 With respect to the constitutional provisions, education is the subject of
[KVS BEd 2017]
(a) Union List (b) Central List
(c) State List (d) Concurrent List

44 Why education is considered important?
(a) It plays an important role in economic, cultural and social development
(b) It helps in the holistic development of child personality
(c) It helps in the development of skills attitudes, habits and values
(d) All of the above

Answers

1. (d)	2. (d)	3. (a)	4. (c)	5. (a)	6. (c)	7. (c)	8. (c)	9. (c)	10. (c)
11. (d)	12. (b)	13. (d)	14. (c)	15. (d)	16. (c)	17. (a)	18. (d)	19. (d)	20. (d)
21. (c)	22. (c)	23. (a)	24. (c)	25. (b)	26. (d)	27. (a)	28. (c)	29. (d)	30. (d)
31. (a)	32. (d)	33. (a)	34. (a)	35. (c)	36. (b)	37. (c)	38. (b)	39. (b)	40. (d)
41. (c)	42. (c)	43. (d)	44. (d)						

Practice Set 01

1. Which of the following is the most important single factor in underlying the success of beginning a teacher?
   (a) Scholarship
   (b) Communicative ability
   (c) Organisational ability
   (d) Personality and its ability to relate to the class and to the pupils

2. A teacher ....
   (a) should have command over his subject
   (b) should introduce the lesson before he starts teaching
   (c) should have command over his language
   (d) All of the above

3. If remarks are passed by students on you, as a teacher, you will
   (a) punish them
   (b) expel them from the college
   (c) be impartial at the time of evaluation
   (d) take revenge while evaluating internal test copies

4. Classroom discipline can be maintained effectively by
   (a) knowing the cause of indiscipline and handling it with stern hand
   (b) by putting on fancy clothes in the classroom
   (c) providing a programme which is according to the interest of the pupils
   (d) None of the above

5. The most appropriate meaning of learning is
   (a) modification of behaviour
   (b) inculcation of knowledge
   (c) personal adjustment
   (d) acquisition of skills

6. Gifted children are best catered to by educational programmes that
   (a) emphasise mastery of knowledge by recall
   (b) make use of gifts and rewards to motivate them to perform according to minimum standards of learning
   (c) stimulate their thinking and give them opportunities to engage in divergent thinking
   (d) control their aggressive behaviour

7. An effective teacher in a classroom, where students come from diverse backgrounds, would
   (a) focus on their cultural knowledge to address individual differences among the group
   (b) push students from deprived backgrounds to work hard, so that they can match up with their peers
   (c) ignore cultural knowledge and treat all his students in a uniform manner
   (d) create groups of students with those from the same economic background put together

8. Which of the following statements about assessment are correct?
   I. Assessment should help students see their strengths and gaps and help the teacher fine-tune her teaching accordingly.
   II. Assessment is meaningful only if comparative evaluations of students are made.
   III. Assessment should assess not only memory but also understanding and application.
   IV. Assessment cannot be purposeful if it does not induce fear and anxiety.
   Codes
   (a) I and II   (b) II and III
   (c) II and IV   (d) I and III

9. "Reasoning of child is not logical and is based on intuition rather than on systematic logic." According to Piaget, this stage of cognitive development is called
   (a) sensory motor period
   (b) preparations period
   (c) concrete operations period
   (d) formal operations period

10. Learning is
(a) everything we know is learned
(b) a relatively permanent influence on behaviour, knowledge and skill
(c) directly observable and measurable
(d) limited to particular age level

11. The child is raised in isolation from human contact often show extreme, long-lasting language deficits that are rarely entirely overcome by later exposure to language. This evidence support to which aspect of language development?
(a) Environmental   (b) Biological
(c) Interactionist   (d) Pragmatic

12. A teacher can address diversity in her class by
  I. Accepting and valuing differences.
  II. Using socio-cultural background of children as a pedagogic resource.
  III. Accommodating different learning styles.
  IV. Giving standard instruction and setting uniform benchmarks for performance.

Select the correct answer using the codes given below.
(a) I, II and IV   (b) I, II, III and IV
(c) II, III and IV   (d) I, II and III

13. Bloom's taxonomy is a hierarchical organisation of ....
(a) achievement goals
(b) curricular declarations
(c) reading skills
(d) cognitive objectives

14. According to Vygotsky, why do children speak to themselves?
(a) Children use their speech to attract the attention of adults to them
(b) Children are very talkative by nature
(c) Children are egocentric
(d) Children use speech to guide their actions

15. The domains of development such as physical, cognitive, social and emotional are developed in which one of the following process?
(a) Distinctly
(b) Partially
(c) Randomly
(d) Integrated and holistically

16. The term 'inclusion' means educating child with special need in the regular classroom for
(a) sometime
(b) most of the time
(c) full time
(d) during social activities in the school

17. In an inclusive classroom with diverse learners, cooperative learning and peer-tutoring
(a) should be actively discouraged and competition should be promoted
(b) should be used only sometimes, since, it promotes comparison with classmates
(c) should be actively promoted to facilitate peer-acceptance
(d) should not be practised and students should be segregated based on their abilities

18. Which of the following statements about cognition and emotions is correct?
(a) Cognition and emotions are processes independent of each other
(b) Cognition and emotions are interwined and affect each other
(c) Cognition affects emotions but emotions do not affect cognition
(d) Emotions affect cognition but cognition does not affect emotions

19. Which of the following parenting styles is most effective for development of children's social competence?
(a) Authoritarian   (b) Neglectful
(c) Authoritative   (d) Indulgent

20. A child who is high and low in a characteristic (such as anxiety or sociability) will remains so at later ages. This statement streeses on the importance of
(a) hereditary
(b) environment
(c) hereditary and environment
(d) maturation

21. Characteristics of social constructivist approach of learning is
(a) emphasis on child's cognition for learning
(b) emphasis on processing of information for learning
(c) emphasis on collaboration with others for learning
(d) emphasis on experiences for learning

22. Which of the following is a significant fact about development?
(a) It does not follow a predictable pattern
(b) It is a product of the interaction of hereditary and environment
(c) All individuals have similar rates of development
(d) Development proceeds from specific to general

23. In NCF 2005, the objective of including art education in school is
(a) to appreciate cultural heritage
(b) to develop student's personality and mental health
(c) Only (a)
(d) Both (a) and (b)

24. According to Vygotsky, a range of task too difficult for the child to do alone, but possible with the help of adults and more skilled peers, is called
(a) Guided participation
(b) Scaffolding
(c) Zone of proximal development
(d) Inter subjectivity

25. Two students read the same passage yet construct entirely different interpretations of its meaning. Which of the following is true about them ?
(a) It is possible because the teacher has not explained the passage
(b) It is not possible and the students need to re-read the passage
(c) It is possible because different factors affect learning of individuals in varied ways
(d) It is not possible because learning is not meaning making

26. Which of the following strategies of teaching-learning is obstacle in developing creativity?
(a) Help students to think in flexible ways
(b) Encourage students to take risk
(c) Overcontrol students during teaching learning
(d) Guide students to be persistent and delay gratification

27. What is the correct sequence of memory process?
  I. Encoding
  II. Storage
  III. Attention
  IV. Retrieval
Select the correct answer using codes below
(a) III, I, II, IV
(b) II, III, I, IV
(c) I, III, II, IV
(d) III, II, I, IV

28. The main role of education according to Plato was
(a) to strengthen the state
(b) to develop the personality of each individual
(c) to develop the power of contemplation
(d) All of the above

29. Which of the following will be most appropriate to maximise learning?
(a) Teacher should identify her cognitive style as well as of her student's cognitive style
(b) Individual difference in students should be smoothened by pairing similar students
(c) Teacher should focus on only one learning style to bring optimum result
(d) Students of similar cultural background should be kept in the same class to avoid difference in opinion

30. An inclusive school reflects on all the following questions except
(a) do we believe that all students can learn
(b) do we work in teams to plan and deliver learning enabling environment
(c) do we properly segregate special children from normal to provide better care
(d) do we adopt strategies catering for the diverse needs of students

31. Learning disabilities may occur due to all of the following except
(a) teachers way of teaching
(b) prenetal use of alcohol
(c) mental retardation
(d) meaningitis during infancy

32. Murray created the history by constructing a test, what is that?
(a) Ink Blot Test
(b) Sentence Completion Test
(c) Thematic Apperception Test
(d) Rating Scale

33. Match the following principles of development with their correct descriptions.

Principle		Description
A. Proximodistal trend	(i)	Different children develop at different rates.
B. Cephalocaudal trend	(ii)	Head to toe sequence.
C. Inter-individual differences	(iii)	In a single child, the rate of development can vary from one domain of development to the other.
D. Intra-individual differences	(iv)	From the centre of body to outwards.
	(v)	Progression from simple to complex.

Codes

	A	B	C	D
(a)	(ii)	(iv)	(i)	(iii)
(b)	(v)	(ii)	(i)	(iii)
(c)	(ii)	(iv)	(iii)	(i)
(d)	(iv)	(ii)	(i)	(iii)

34. In order to understand the maladjustment and frustration of children and also to treat them effectively the teacher gets good support from the
(a) Study of child psychology
(b) Friendly treatment of children
(c) Parents/guardians of the children
(d) Principal of the school

35. Maladjustment in children is
(a) a result of frustration
(b) another name of frustration
(c) a reason of frustration
(d) All of the above

36. Intelligence is
(a) a set of capabilities
(b) a singular and generic concept
(c) the ability to imitate others
(d) a specific ability

37. Which of the following is not a product of learning?
(a) Knowledge
(b) Concepts
(c) Attitudes
(d) Maturation

38. Which of the following is the most influential agent of socialisation?
(a) Family
(b) Peers
(c) Media
(d) Teacher

39. A teacher can help the children to process a complex situation by
(a) encouraging competition and offering a high reward to the child who completes the task first
(b) not offering any help at all so that children learn to help on their own
(c) giving a lecture on it
(d) breaking the task into smaller parts and writing down instructions

40. Strut, stride and trudge are words that describe a manner of
(a) riding
(b) walking
(c) galloping
(d) running

41. 'Micro teaching' is
(a) teaching by observing minute behaviour of students
(b) organised practice teaching
(c) micro managing the routine of students in the school
(d) teaching students in small groups

42. Assessment
(a) is a good strategy to label and categorise children
(b) should actively promote competitive spirit among children
(c) should generate tension and stress to ensure learning
(d) is a way to improve learning

43. Arrange the following in chronological order.
   I. Sensorimotor stage
   II. Pre-operational stage
   III. Concrete operational stage
   IV. Formal operational stage
(a) I, II, IV, III
(b) II, III, IV, I
(c) IV, I, III, II
(d) II, I, III, IV

44. Which of the following statements is true about ability grouping?
(a) Students learn better in homogeneous groups
(b) For smooth and effective teaching, a class should be homogeneous
(c) Children are intolerant and do not accept differences
(d) Teacher may use multilevel teaching to cater to different ability groups

45. Kindergarten System (KG) of education was propounded by
(a) Dewey   (b) Froebel
(c) Plato   (d) Spencer

46. Roli is unable to pronounce the words 'study' and 'society' clearly. As her teacher what will you do?
(a) Humiliate Roli by isolating her and asking her to repeat the words
(b) Asking the entire class to repeat the words and appreciating Roli when she repeats them correctly
(c) You will just ignore it
(d) You will ask the class to laugh at her

47. Effective teaching, by and large, is a function of
(a) teacher's scholarship
(b) teacher's honesty
(c) teachers making students learn and understand
(d) teachers liking for the job of teaching

48. It is said that 'Development is never ending process'. Which of the following defines it?
(a) Principle of interaction
(b) Principle of continuity
(c) Principle of interrelation
(d) Principle of integration

49. Students can be promoted
(a) by giving example
(b) by giving suitable record
(c) by giving direction
(d) None of the above

50. The main objective of a test in class is
(a) to repeat whatever is taught till now
(b) to gauge educational achievement
(c) students are trained to give reply after thinking
(d) to give practice of writing notes

51. Which of the following is a feature of progressive education?
(a) Flexible time table and sitting arrangement
(b) Instruction based solely on prescribed textbooks
(c) Emphasis on scoring goods marks in examinations
(d) Frequent tests and examinations

52. Most psychologists believe that development is due
(a) largely to nature
(b) largely to nurture
(c) to nature and nurture acting separately
(d) to an interaction of nature and nurture

53. Hyperactive children need
(a) special attention in the classroom
(b) separate classroom
(c) special teachers
(d) special curriculum

54. To enable students to make conceptual changes in their thinking, a teacher should
(a) offer rewards for children who change their thinking
(b) discourages children from thinking on their own and ask them to just listen to a teacher and follow that
(c) offer an explanation in a lecture mode
(d) make clear and convincing explanations and have discussions with the students

55. Which of the following is not a component of human development?
(a) Continuity
(b) Sequentiality
(c) Differentiality
(d) None of the above

56. Which of the following situations is illustrative of child-centred classroom?
(a) A class in which the teacher dictates and the students are asked to memorise the notes
(b) A class in which the textbook is the only resources the teacher refers to
(c) A class in which the students are sitting in groups and the teacher takes turns to go to each group
(d) A class in which the behaviour of students is governed by the rewards and punishments the teacher would given them

57. According to Vygotsky, children learn
(a) when reinforcement is offered
(b) by maturation
(c) by imitation
(d) by interacting with adults and peers

58. Which years are globally recognised as the most critical years for the life long development of a child?
(a) 1-3 years   (b) 1-6 years
(c) 6-8 years   (d) 12-16 years

59. Which statement from the following does not suit a teacher?
(a) really interested in students
(b) able to direct and discipline his students
(c) enthusiastic about the work that the teachers do
(d) reluctant to adapt himself to new situations

60. Children are most creative when they participate in an activity
(a) to escape their teacher's scolding
(b) under stress to do well in front of others
(c) out of interest
(d) for rewards

Answers

1. (d)	*2. (d)*	*3. (c)*	*4. (a)*	*5. (a)*	*6. (c)*	*7. (c)*	*8. (d)*	*9. (b)*	*10. (b)*
11. (c)	*12. (d)*	*13. (d)*	*14. (d)*	*15. (d)*	*16. (b)*	*17. (c)*	*18. (b)*	*19. (c)*	*20. (c)*
21. (c)	*22. (b)*	*23. (d)*	*24. (c)*	*25. (c)*	*26. (c)*	*27. (a)*	*28. (b)*	*29. (a)*	*30. (c)*
31. (a)	*32. (c)*	*33. (d)*	*34. (a)*	*35. (a)*	*36. (a)*	*37. (a)*	*38. (a)*	*39. (d)*	*40. (b)*
41. (b)	*42. (d)*	*43. (d)*	*44. (d)*	*45. (b)*	*46. (b)*	*47. (c)*	*48. (b)*	*49. (b)*	*50. (b)*
51. (a)	*52. (d)*	*53. (a)*	*54. (d)*	*55. (d)*	*56. (c)*	*57. (d)*	*58. (d)*	*59. (c)*	*60. (c)*

Practice Set 02

1. Creative writing should be an activity planned for
   - (a) only those children reading on grade level
   - (b) only those children who can spell and also, can write cohesive sentences
   - (c) only those children who want to write for the newspaper of the class
   - (d) All children

2. Kohlberg has given
   - (a) the stages of cognitive development
   - (b) the stages of physical development
   - (c) the stages of emotional development
   - (d) the stages of moral development

3. Child-centred pedagogy means
   - (a) giving moral education to the children
   - (b) asking the children to follow and imitate the teacher
   - (c) giving primacy to children's voices and their active participation
   - (d) letting the children be totally free

4. Which audio-visual aid is simple, easy to use and not expensive?
   - (a) Slides
   - (b) Transparencies
   - (c) Cassettes
   - (d) Compact discs

5. Which of the following is not a technique for problem solving?
   - (a) Alogrithms
   - (b) Heuristics
   - (c) Experimentation
   - (d) Means-end-analysis

6. Pary school is a term used for which class level?
   - (a) Class I-VIII
   - (b) Class I-X
   - (c) Class I-V
   - (d) Nursery class

7. The best way to teach a concept to students is to proceed from ....
   - (a) Difficult to simple
   - (b) Known to unknown
   - (c) Unknown to known
   - (d) Abstract to concrete

8. The duration of secondary education in India is ...... year.
   - (a) 02
   - (b) 04
   - (c) 06
   - (d) 05

9. The most potent reason of student indiscipline in schools is ......
   - (a) Absenteeism of teachers
   - (b) Absenteeism of students
   - (c) Non-completion of course
   - (d) Non-involvement of students in activities

10. Which one is most important for a teacher?
    - (a) Expertise in subject content
    - (b) Expertise in teaching skills
    - (c) Rapport with students
    - (d) Good health

11. A semester consists of ..... month duration.
    - (a) 04
    - (b) 03
    - (c) 06
    - (d) 05

12. Which one is not an element of positive learning environment?
    - (a) Motivating the learner
    - (b) Creation of interest
    - (c) Control by force
    - (d) Planning activities

13. N.C.C. belongs to which of the following in school?
    - (a) Curricular activity
    - (b) Co-curricular activity
    - (c) Army activity
    - (d) Service activity

14. Which one is not a literary activity?
    - (a) Essay writing
    - (b) N.S.S.
    - (c) Debate
    - (d) Quiz

15. If students make noise in the class, they should be ....
    - (a) punished
    - (b) beaten
    - (c) sent out
    - (d) engaged in activities

16. Which of the following is the greatest problem for a school?
(a) Lack of finances
(b) Lack of good infrastructure
(c) Lack of good teachers
(d) Lack of students continuously

17. Which is the greatest quality of student for learning?
(a) Good memory
(b) Good communication ability
(c) Hard word to learn
(d) Curiosity to learn

18. Which one is not the quality of a good school?
(a) Teaching of all subjects
(b) Conduction of debates and essay writing
(c) No organisation of games
(d) Well developed laboratories

19. Which of the following is not an example of physical infrastructure of a school?
(a) Playground
(b) Building
(c) Laboratories
(d) Librarian

20. The educational institution with no barrier of age of study is termed as ......
(a) Free institution of education
(b) Closed institution of education
(c) Evening institution of education
(d) Open education institution

21. Which of the following is major cause of decreasing ethical standards in the society?
(a) Educational policy failure
(b) Poverty
(c) Lack of schools
(d) Lack of good teachers

22. Which is not part of 3Rs?
(a) Speaking
(b) Reading
(c) Writing
(d) Arithmetic

23. Which is related to education of deaf and dumb?
(a) Braille
(b) Sign language
(c) Brailler
(d) All of the above

24. Which new term has been coined for students who are deaf and dumb, blind or lack some abilities?
(a) Special need
(b) Divyang
(c) Inclusive children
(d) None of these

25. Which one should be followed by a good teacher in a class?
(a) Teach fast learners
(b) Teach mediocre learners
(c) Teach slow learners
(d) Teach (a), (b) and (c) together

26. What is the duration of higher secondary education?
(a) 4 years
(b) 3 years
(c) 2 years
(d) 1 year

27. Which is not desired in schools?
(a) Regular attendance
(b) Good conduct
(c) Corporal punishment
(d) Awards

28. Which is a responsible cause of growing indiscipline in schools?
(a) Economic difficulty
(b) Lack of leadership by teachers
(c) Intervention by parents
(d) Growing aspirations

29. Which of the following is most effective for promotion of learning among school students?
(a) Lecture
(b) Dictation
(c) Guided activities
(d) Pictures

30. Which is not the part of co-curricular activities in schools?
(a) Debates
(b) Music and song competitions
(c) Class lecture
(d) Drama

31. In a democratic class, a teacher's work is to
(a) allow the students for complete autonomy of choices without any advice and interference
(b) tell the students, which of the option among the different ones, is an intelligent choice
(c) make students more capable of choosing from the growing list of options
(d) let students choose for themselves

32. A student has a problem, who then asks his/her teacher "What should I do"? The teacher needs to
(a) tell the student the course of process, keeping in mind his own capacity
(b) tell the student if he was in his place what would he do
(c) ask the student such question which provide him/her useful information to take meritorious decision
(d) ask the student to identify oneself so that he/she can identify his/her own ability to solve

33. The best expressed opinion of planning group is
(a) it encourages the initiative and leadership of a person
(b) it puts an end on the personal conflicts
(c) it encourages the children for making optimum use of their capabilities
(d) more investigation is to be done before accepting or rejecting it

34. The impact of school supervisor should be done according to
(a) greater community satisfaction
(b) greater personal satisfaction
(c) decline in misbehaviour in class
(d) greater progress of students towards the goals of education

35. The most important work of a teacher is
(a) complete focus on development of students
(b) to provide remedial aid whenever needed
(c) to provide effective education
(d) to maintain order and discipline in the class

36. As applicable to the classroom, the teacher's role in motivation is essentially subject of
(a) awakening the needs in the students
(b) channelising the energies of aware and conscious students in a creative direction
(c) inculcating new interests
(d) providing attractive incentives that are accessible to the students

37. The chief responsibility of the teachers is
(a) planning educational experiences
(b) enhancing relations with parents
(c) using the novel techniques of teaching
(d) implementing the administrative policies

38. Class discipline is oriented towards
(a) social confirmity
(b) personal and social adjustment
(c) self-reliance
(d) acceptable class behaviour

39. Which of the following statements prove that schools should be the leaders in social upliftment?
(a) General work of school
(b) Progressive work of school
(c) Conservative work of school
(d) Reactionary work of school

40. Which of the following statement is not true?
(a) Schools essentially affect the societal changes
(b) Schools are a powerful factor in social change.
(c) Schools are a strong factor of disintegration
(d) Schools are social medium for cultural diffusion

41. Which of the following is against the spirit of equality of educational opportunities?
(a) Government School
(b) Government Aided School
(c) Aashram School
(d) Navodaya School

42. School help students to ...... with its events and programs.
(a) cultural intermingle
(b) ignore other cultures
(c) oppose the culture
(d) become cultured

43. The primary aim of classroom teaching should be
(a) increasing the self-confidence of learners
(b) to train the learners in few professions
(c) to prepare them for higher classes
(d) to make learning easier

44. The educational environment in a school can be adversely affected if,
(a) physical punishment is given everytime
(b) the students are encouraged to write
(c) teachers are left free to try new laws and processes
(d) frequent parents teachers association meetings are held

45. According to your point of view, sports activities in a school,
(a) are important for psychotic development
(b) are generally means to waste time
(c) are not important given the hectic schedule of the school
(d) All of the above

46. A teacher can become more effective if,
(a) student score higher marks
(b) teacher uses good quality supporting study material
(c) he helps the learners achieve proficiency in studies
(d) he helps students in raising questions

47. What shall be done from the following to address the incorrect answer of any student?
(a) The subject matter needs to be explained again
(b) The students must be told that their answer is wrong
(c) Other student shall be asked to tell the correct answer
(d) Explaining and asking to answer again

48. A teacher shall keep his voice in ...... in a class.
(a) high tone
(b) slower voice
(c) louder voice
(d) normal voice

49. 'Scientific approach' can be developed effectively in the learners
(a) by teaching science
(b) by teaching them acceptance
(c) by making them follow the elders
(d) by accepting the facts only after investigating it

50. We can evade the unwanted psychological stresses arising due to annual examination system by using
(a) only recurring tests
(b) research parameters with recurring tests
(c) testing by teachers of another school
(d) no test at all

51. Aptitude test is used to
(a) measure success
(b) measure proficiency
(c) to indicate success in any task
(d) measure the capacity/capability

52. Why is it recommended to provide grades in place of marks?
(a) It is easier to provide grades
(b) It will make teaching-learning easier
(c) It will enhance the qualities of education
(d) It will reduce the mistakes committed during corrections and evaluations

53. Information sharing in a classroom will become more effective if,
(a) the sender uses the same code as the one, used by receiver to decodify the information
(b) the observer proceeds slowly, but orderly
(c) the receiver is willing to receive
(d) it is done in favourable atmosphere/conditions

54. The main objective of education is to
(a) make students become capable of earning
(b) prepare students for jobs
(c) help students acquire knowledge
(d) enable all-round development of students

55. A teacher's work is to
(a) help students in self-studies
(b) motivate students for studies
(c) enable friendly environment for studies
(d) tell the students their mistakes

56. Which of the following is not a part of procedure for management of resources?
(a) Making a survey of resources
(b) Analysing the resources
(c) Preparing improvement projects
(d) Collecting funds from public

57. Which of the following is necessary for proper management of school's physical resources?
(a) Preparing improvement projects
(b) Finding ways to finance resource management
(c) Getting feedback on management procedure
(d) All of the above

58. What should be done to make school environment pollution free and aesthetic?
(a) Building gardens and parks
(b) Whitewashing
(c) Constructing compound walls
(d) Constructing toilets

59. Why should we display a political map of India around the blackboard?
(a) To encourage students for travelling
(b) To write something on the map
(c) To help students in examination
(d) To teach students

60. Which is the worst form of discipline teaching technique?
(a) Time-in
(b) Time-out
(c) Punishment
(d) Consequences

Answers

1. (d)	2. (d)	3. (c)	4. (a)	5. (c)	6. (a)	7. (b)	8. (a)	9. (d)	10. (b)
11. (c)	12. (c)	13. (c)	14. (b)	15. (d)	16. (b)	17. (d)	18. (c)	19. (d)	20. (d)
21. (a)	22. (a)	23. (b)	24. (b)	25. (d)	26. (c)	27. (c)	28. (b)	29. (c)	30. (c)
31. (a)	32. (d)	33. (c)	34. (d)	35. (a)	36. (b)	37. (c)	38. (b)	39. (b)	40. (c)
41. (c)	42. (d)	43. (a)	44. (a)	45. (a)	46. (d)	47. (d)	48. (d)	49. (d)	50. (b)
51. (c)	52. (d)	53. (d)	54. (d)	55. (c)	56. (d)	57. (d)	58. (a)	59. (d)	60. (c)

Practice Set 03

1. Name the disciple technique in which a child is removed from the situation in case of not coping well with the same.
   - (a) Time-out
   - (b) Time-in
   - (c) Consequence
   - (d) Punishment

2. Name the leadership style in which a leader takes care of the opinion and views of the group while making decisions.
   - (a) Autocratic
   - (b) Laissez Faire
   - (c) Monarchic
   - (d) Democratic

3. Verbal classroom communication includes
   - (a) Direction are given in written
   - (b) Body language is used
   - (c) Teacher or student speak aloud
   - (d) None of the above

4. When gestures are used, then it is
   - (a) verbal communication
   - (b) non-verbal communication
   - (c) written communication
   - (d) All of the above

5. If teacher asks students to stop talking, which type of classroom communication is this?
   - (a) Teacher student communication
   - (b) Student teacher communication
   - (c) Student class communication
   - (d) Teacher class communication

6. The motivation under which a person tends to act without any specific identifiable goal is called
   - (a) affiliation
   - (b) power
   - (c) curiosity
   - (d) achievement

7. Punishment is a
   - (a) negative reinforcer
   - (b) positive reinforcer
   - (c) not a reinforcer at all
   - (d) None of the above

8. Activity based questions make social science lessons
   - (a) joyful
   - (b) debatable
   - (c) lengthy
   - (d) comprehensive

9. Doing activities with children will be effective only if
   - (a) the teacher conducts them to complete her 'Lesson Plan'
   - (b) the teacher does them as a pretense to obey her principal's directions for activity-based learning
   - (c) she believes that activity-based education will help the child in understanding the concepts
   - (d) the teacher does not know why she is doing it

10. While teaching 'poverty' which strategy would be most appropriate?
    - (a) Engage students in debate and discussion
    - (b) Ask students to read from the textbook and explain the difficult words
    - (c) Prepare notes and deliver a good lecture
    - (d) Give hand-outs to students and explain

11. Co-curricular activities must be held
    - (a) during school timings
    - (b) outside school timings
    - (c) either during or after school timings
    - (d) should not be held at all

12. Which of the following statements is correct?
    - (a) Curricular activity is formal while co-curricular is informal
    - (b) Curricular activity is informal while co-circular is formal
    - (c) Both are formal
    - (d) Both are informal

13. A conducive learning environment creates
    - (a) comfortable teaching
    - (b) focused students
    - (c) improved learning results
    - (d) All of the above

14. Learning may be defined as any relatively ...... change in behaviour.
(a) temporary
(b) permanent
(c) slow
(d) complicated

15. Identify the condition necessary for promoting learning in school.
(a) Neatness
(b) Cleanliness
(c) Sanitation
(d) All of these

16. Which of the following is not a visual aid of teaching?
(a) Radio
(b) Television
(c) Computer
(d) Drama

17. HRM is a process of making the efficient and effective use of
(a) human resources
(b) student
(c) teaching material
(d) human capital

18. Characteristic(s) of human resource management in school is/are
(a) hiring of school staff
(b) construction of classrooms
(c) to influence students in school
(d) All of the above

19. Accurate position descriptions are the backbone of a good
(a) HR System
(b) Staff system
(c) School class system
(d) Training system

20. Classroom discipline can be maintained effectively by
(a) handling the cause of indiscipline strictly
(b) providing a programme which is according to interest of pupils
(c) by giving corporal punishment
(d) by involving students on blackboard

21. While delivering lecture, if there is some disturbance in the class, then a teacher should
(a) keep quiet for a while and then go on
(b) leave the class
(c) punish those causing disturbance
(d) no bother of what is happening in the class

22. The lowest level of learning in cognitive domain is
(a) knowledge
(b) synthesis
(c) analysis
(d) comprehension

23. NIEPA is mainly concerned with
(a) Educational Practice
(b) Educational Supervision
(c) Educational Planning and Administration
(d) Educational Measurement

24. In which of the following stages the concept of sex has been developed in children?
(a) Infancy
(b) Childhood
(c) Adolescence
(d) Adulthood

25. Play therapy is adopted in the education of children in order to
(a) make the educational process joyful
(b) make education more activity centered
(c) highlight the importance of play activity in education
(d) to understand the inner motives and complexes of children

26. What a teacher should do to take care of genius students in his/her class?
(a) keep teaching slow
(b) should not take special care of those students
(c) teach very fast
(d) provide enrichment programmes

27. Teaching style is primarily related with
(a) 'How' of teaching
(b) 'What' of teaching
(c) 'Why' of teaching
(d) 'When' of teaching

28. Which quality is most important for students?
(a) Good behaviour
(b) Independent thinking
(c) Obedience
(d) Hard work

29. Which statement is true for a cooperative class?
(a) Pupils compete among themselves
(b) Pupils are allowed to present their ideas and discuss freely with one another
(c) Large amount of teacher guidance is required
(d) Pupils work independently

30. You want to ensure participation of more students in class. Which of the following methods of teaching would you adopt?
(a) Role play
(b) Recitation
(c) Discussion
(d) Demonstration

31. .... is the quality of a good teacher.
(a) Sense of humour
(b) Physical strength
(c) Control over emotions
(d) Good command over the subject

32. To encourage children to put in efforts in their studies teachers need to
(a) control the child
(b) compare the child with others
(c) motivate the child
(d) scold the child

33. Children with learning disability
(a) have confusion between letters and alphabets that look alike
(b) easily recognise and comprehend sight words
(c) have retarded mental development
(d) have low IQ

34. In an effective classroom
(a) the children look up to the teacher for guidance and support to facilitate their learning
(b) the children are always anxious and kept on their toes since the teacher keeps on giving regular tests
(c) the children fear the teacher since the teacher uses verbal and physical punishment
(d) the children don't have any regard for the teacher and do as they please

35. Teachers can encourage children to think creatively by
(a) asking them to memorise answers
(b) asking them recall-based questions
(c) giving them multiple choice questions
(d) asking them to think of different ways to solve a problem

36. Which one of the following is central to learning?
(a) Conditioning
(b) Rote memorisation
(c) Imitation
(d) Meaning-making

37. According to the Right to Education Act, 2009, children with special needs should study
(a) in special schools created exclusively for them
(b) at home with their parents and care givers providing necessary support
(c) in inclusive education setups with provisions to cater to their individual needs
(d) in vocational training centres which would prepare them for life skills.

38. According to the National Curriculum Framework, 2005, learning is .... and .... in its character.
(a) passive, simple
(b) active, social
(c) passive, social
(d) active, simple

39. Language .... thought process.
(a) totally governs our
(b) has an influence on our
(c) cannot determine the
(d) does not influence the

40. If a student is rude to you, which strategy would you adopt as a teacher?
(a) Punish the student
(b) Argue with the student
(c) Express shock at such behaviour
(d) Remind the student of classroom rules

41. ...... tests measure the extent of students learning in a given content area.
(a) Aptitude
(b) Diagnostic
(c) Readiness
(d) Achievement

42. Which of the following is Doordarshan's Educational Television channel?
(a) Vidya
(b) Gurukul
(c) Gyan Bharati
(d) Gyan Darshan

43. .... is the apex institution involved in the planned and coordinated development of teacher education system in the country.
(a) UGC
(b) NCTE
(c) NCERT
(d) None of these

44. If a teacher wants her students to acquire problem solving skills, the students should be engaged in activities that involve
(a) recall, memorisation and comprehensions
(b) structured worksheets containing multiple choice questions
(c) drill and practice
(d) inquiring, reasoning and decision making

45. Which one of the following is a correctly matched pair?

(a)	Good boy and good girl orientation	One earns approval by being nice
(b)	Law and order orientation	Ethical principles are self-chosen on the basis of the value of human rights
(c)	Social contract orientation	Physical Consequences of an action determine whether it is good or bad
(d)	Punishment and obedience orientation	Laws are not fixed but can be charged for the good of society

46. Multiple choice questions assess the child's ability to
(a) construct the correct answer
(b) explain the correct answer
(c) recognise the correct answer
(d) recall the correct answer

47. Role of a teacher in a class is to
(a) follow the time table strictly and stick to the course
(b) provide authentic learning situations and facilitate independent thinking in students
(c) fill the students with his/her own knowledge and prepare them for examinations
(d) transmit knowledge in a straight fashion and prepare students for right answers

48. Process of socialisation does not include
(a) acquiring values and beliefs
(b) genetic transmission
(c) learning the customs and norms of a culture
(d) acquisition of skills

49. Questions encouraging students to voice their individual opinions on issues and reflections while giving reasons for the same, promote
(a) standardised assessment of children
(b) analytical and critical thinking
(c) convergent thinking
(d) recall of information

50. Being a teacher what should be your goal?
(a) Develop knowledge and skills in all areas of development

(b) Help children learn
(c) Understand individual differences and learning styles
(d) All of the above

51. Irfan dismantles toys to explore their components. What would you do?
(a) Never let Irfan play with toys
(b) Always keep a close watch
(c) Encourage his inquisitive nature and constructively channelise his energy
(d) Make him understand that toys are delicate and should not be broken

52. The theory of constructivism states
(a) to memorise the information and testing through recall
(b) to focus on the role of imitation
(c) to smphasise on the dominant role of the teacher
(d) to emphasise the role of the learner in constructing his own view of the world

53. Being a teacher what should be your role in meeting the individual differences?
(a) Try to know the abilities, capacities, interests and aptitude of pupils
(b) Try to adjust the curriculum as per needs of individuals
(c) All of the above
(d) None of the above

54. What will you do as teacher if the students do not attend your class?
(a) Keep quiet considering the present attitude of students
(b) Blame the students for their absence
(c) Think of using some other interesting methods of teaching
(d) Know the reasons and try to remove them

55. Which of the following is the most important quality of a good primary teacher?
(a) Enthusiasm of teaching
(b) Patience and determination
(c) Efficiency in the knowledge of subjects
(d) Efficiency in teaching methods

56. Which of the following is not the sense organ of human being?
(a) Neck   (b) Nose
(c) Eye   (d) Tongue

57. In order to help educationally backward child, it is necessary for a teacher
(a) to find out the cause of backwardness
(b) to refer him to other competent teacher
(c) to skip such students
(d) None of the above

58. A teacher told the students to write their class work 5 times. Which of the following law is related to this situation?
(a) Law of effect
(b) Law of exercise
(c) Law of readiness
(d) None of the above

59. Hyperactive children need
(a) special attention in the classroom
(b) separate classroom
(c) special teachers
(d) special curriculum

60. Which of the following way would you adopt for the best remedy of student's problems related to learning?
(a) Suggestion for hard work
(b) Supervised study in library
(c) Suggestion for private tuition
(d) Diagnostic teaching

Answers

1. (b)	2. (d)	3. (c)	4. (b)	5. (c)	6. (c)	7. (c)	8. (d)	9. (c)	10. (a)
11. (a)	12. (a)	13. (d)	14. (d)	15. (d)	16. (a)	17. (a)	18. (a)	19. (a)	20. (b)
21. (a)	22. (a)	23. (c)	24. (b)	25. (d)	26. (d)	27. (a)	28. (b)	29. (b)	30. (c)
31. (d)	32. (c)	33. (a)	34. (a)	35. (d)	36. (d)	37. (c)	38. (b)	39. (b)	40. (d)
41. (d)	42. (d)	43. (b)	44. (d)	45. (a)	46. (c)	47. (b)	48. (b)	49. (b)	50. (d)
51. (c)	52. (d)	53. (c)	54. (d)	55. (b)	56. (a)	57. (a)	58. (b)	59. (a)	60. (d)

Practice Set 04

1. Teacher uses teaching aids for
   - (a) making teaching interesting
   - (b) making teaching understandable to students
   - (c) making students attentive
   - (d) only for the sake of using

2. Which type of nature will you prefer in your class to increase the process of socialisation?
   - (a) Strict
   - (b) Loving and sympathetic
   - (c) Normal
   - (d) None of the above

3. A good teacher is one who can
   - (a) make difficult subject easy
   - (b) say that I do not know everything
   - (c) keep on updating his information
   - (d) All of the above

4. Effectiveness of teacher depends on
   - (a) qualification of teacher
   - (b) personality of teacher
   - (c) handwriting of teacher
   - (d) subject understanding of teacher

5. Which of the following is not a technique for problem solving?
   - (a) Algorithms
   - (b) Heuristics
   - (c) Experimentation
   - (d) Means-end analysis

6. Restriction of the movement of the limbs or any other body part refers to which impairment?
   - (a) Locomotor
   - (b) Mental
   - (c) Visual
   - (d) Learning

7. Teachers in order to complete their lessons quickly expect answers from a preferred group of students. This
   - (a) requires skills to identify the students who can answer the questions more often
   - (b) is necessary to keep going in the class to cover syllabus
   - (c) deprives the other students of equal opportunity
   - (d) supports the students who take interest and become teacher's choice

8. In …… stage, child learns to use language and to represent object by image and words.
   - (a) formal operational
   - (b) concrete operational
   - (c) pre-operational
   - (d) any stage

9. Right of Children to Free and Compulsory Education Act, 2009 stipulates that learning should be
   - (a) through activities in a child-friendly manner
   - (b) support by extra coaching
   - (c) restricted to co-scholastic subjects
   - (d) carefully monitored by frequent testing

10. Which is the first stage in the learning of a child?
    - (a) Teacher
    - (b) School
    - (c) Family
    - (d) Friends

11. Which of the following is not regarded as the tool for formative assessment?
    - (a) Oral questions
    - (b) Multiple choice questions
    - (c) Projects
    - (d) Assignments

12. Which of the following is feature of a case study?
    - (a) Based-on valid data
    - (b) Continuous
    - (c) Systematic
    - (d) All of the above

13. Being a teacher your classroom behaviour should be good because
    - (a) it will set an example
    - (b) students will be more attentive
    - (c) environment would be conducive to learning
    - (d) students will appreciate it

14. Developing moral values among students is very important. What would you do to develop the same?
(a) Encourage moral value related works
(b) Organise classes on moral values
(c) Display stories on moral values
(d) Present yourself as a role model

15. ...... intelligence gives one the ability to manipulate and create mental images.
(a) Bodily
(b) Spatial
(c) Personal
(d) Linguistic

16. Which of the following motivation is considered primary motives?
(a) Physiological motives
(b) Psychological motives
(c) Social motives
(d) Educational motives

17. Why is flexibility in curriculum essential?
(a) To meet the needs of every child
(b) To meet the needs of teachers
(c) To meet the needs of the government
(d) None of the above

18. Human development is divided into which of the following domain?
(a) Physical, spiritual, cognitive and social
(b) Physical, cognitive, emotional and social
(c) Emotional, cognitive, spiritual and social-psychological
(d) Psychological, cognitive, emotional and physical

19. The emphasis from teaching to learning can be shifted by
(a) focusing on examination results
(b) adopting child-centred pedagogy
(c) encouraging rote learning
(d) adopting frontal teaching

20. The most important factor in effective teaching process is
(a) payment of time displayed by teachers and students
(b) teacher subject matter
(c) teacher-student dialogues
(d) completion of courses on time

21. Teacher's main responsibility
(a) to create and teach a text plan
(b) conducting as many activities as possible
(c) maintaining strict discipline
(d) providing learning opportunities according to different learning style of students

22. Activity based teaching emphasises on
....
(a) disciplined class
(b) to complete the activity in a fixed time period
(c) active participation by all students
(d) to take the exam after the end of the activity

23. Which of the following should be considered the most important feature in a teacher at the primary level?
(a) Eagerness to teach
(b) Patience and perseverance
(c) Proficiency in knowledge of teaching methods and topics
(d) The efficiency of reading in a very standard language

24. The learning disability can be caused due to the following reasons except ....
(a) teacher's teaching style
(b) alcohol consumption by mother before birth
(c) insipidness
(d) brain fever during childhood

25. Imitative learning technique is considered as
(a) skill
(b) theatrical method or technique
(c) game method
(d) None of the above

26. What is the difference between teaching methods and teaching strategies?
(a) Text material
(b) Objectives
(c) Format
(d) The Acts

27. The emphasis is laid on ......, to fulfil the psychomotor objective of education.
(a) theory and concept
(b) action and experimentation
(c) school management
(d) None of the above

28. While teaching students, teacher should concentrate on ....
(a) class size
(b) teaching method and direction
(c) on the classification of children
(d) All of the above

29. In 1st class of primary school, main emphasis is on ......
(a) reading
(b) writing
(c) word structure
(d) arithmetic

30. The best place for a child's cognitive development is
(a) playground
(b) auditorium
(c) home
(d) school and class environment

31. The purpose of education should be
(a) developing business skills in students
(b) developing social awareness in students
(c) preparing students for examination
(d) preparing students for practical life

32. Which of the following is done in psychological schools?
(a) Control
(b) Direction
(c) Teaching
(d) All of these

33. Who had written the first book in history of psychology?
(a) William James
(b) RS Woodworth
(c) William Mcdugal
(d) NL Mann

34. 'Mapping the mind' is related to
(a) with the understanding of technology to improve understanding
(b) action plan of courageous work
(c) to increase the mapping in mind
(d) research on the activity of the mind

35. Which of the following is not a sign of exceptional child?
(a) Creativity in ideas
(b) Fight with other
(c) Incompetence in expression
(d) Curiosity

36. In the process of child's learning, parents should perform the role of ....
(a) negative
(b) frontline
(c) sympathetic
(d) neutral

37. The Insight Theory of Learning is promoted by
(a) Gestalt Theorists
(b) Pavlov
(c) Jean Piaget
(d) Vygotsky

38. Which of the following is the most important for teachers?
(a) Maintaining good discipline
(b) To solve the difficulties of students
(c) Punctuality
(d) Have a good time

39. Which quality you consider the most important among students?
(a) Expressing views independently
(b) Modesty
(c) Obedience
(d) Hard working

40. The purpose of TET is to measure which of the following?
(a) Intelligence
(b) Aptitude
(c) Attitude
(d) Values

41. Which of the following is the most subjective method of educational psychology?
(a) Introspection
(b) Extrospection
(c) Observation
(d) Experimentation

42. Find the odd one.
(a) TAT
(b) 16-PF
(c) Raven's test
(d) Draw-a-Man test

43. Giving the meaning to sensation on the basis of past experience is called
(a) sensation
(b) perception
(c) motivation
(d) imagination

44. Five years old Mohan has mental age of eight. What is his IQ?
(a) 150
(b) 160
(c) 140
(d) 135

45. Which IQ range is called trainable IQ level of mentally retarded children?
(a) 70-79
(b) 50-69
(c) 36-49
(d) 35 and above

46. Which among the following is different from the characteristic of a good test?
(a) Reliability
(b) Validity
(c) Objectivity
(d) Aptitude

47. Failure in retention and recall of learnt content is
(a) forgetting
(b) memory
(c) retention
(d) thinking

48. A college wants to give training in use of Statistical Package for Social Sciences (SPSS) to researchers. For this the college should organise
(a) conference   (b) seminar
(c) workshop   (d) lecture

49. A researcher divides his population into certain groups and fixes the size of the sample from each group. It is called
(a) stratified sample   (b) quota sample
(c) cluster sample   (d) All of these

50. Gifted children are best catered to by educational programmes that
(a) emphasise mastery of knowledge by recall
(b) make use of gifts and rewards to motivate them to perform according to minimum standards of learning
(c) stimulate their thinking and give them opportunities to engage in divergent thinking
(d) control their aggressive behaviour

51. Which of the following statement(s) about assessment are correct?
  I. Assessment should help students see their strengths and gaps and help the teacher fine-tune her teaching accordingly.
  II. Assessment is meaningful only if comparative evaluations of students are made.
  III. Assessment should assess not only memory but also understanding and application.
  IV. Assessment cannot be purposeful if it does not induce fear and anxiety.
(a) I and II   (b) II and III
(c) II and IV   (d) II and IV

52. "Reasoning of child is not logical and is based on intuition rather than on systematic logic." According to Piaget, this stage of cognitive development is called
(a) sensory motor period
(b) preparations period
(c) concrete operations period
(d) formal operations period

53. Learning is
(a) everything we know is learned
(b) a relatively permanent influence on behaviour, knowledge and skill
(c) directly observable and measurable
(d) limited to particular age level

54. The facial expressions of students relate to which element of the communication process?
(a) Message   (b) Receiver
(c) Channel   (d) Sender

55. A teacher can address diversity in her class by
  I. Accepting and valuing differences.
  II. Using socio-cultural background of children as a pedagogic resource.
  III. Accommodating different learning styles.
  IV. Giving standard instruction and setting uniform benchmarks for performance.

Select the correct answer using the codes given below.
(a) I, II and IV
(b) I, II, III and IV
(c) II, III and IV
(d) I, II and III

56. In an inclusive classroom with diverse learners, cooperative learning and peer-tutoring
(a) should be actively discouraged and competition should be promoted
(b) should be used only sometimes, since, it promotes comparison with classmates
(c) should be actively promoted to facilitate peer-acceptance
(d) should not be practised and students should be segregated based on their abilities

57. Which of the following parenting styles is most effective for development of children's social competence?
(a) Ahthoritarian
(b) Neglectful
(c) Authoritative
(d) Indulgent

58. A child who is high and low in a characteristic (such as anxiety or sociability) will remains so at later ages. This statement stresses on the importance of
(a) hereditary
(b) environment
(c) hereditary and environment
(d) maturation

59. Which of the following is a significant fact about the development?
(a) It does not follow a predictable pattern
(b) It is a product of the interaction of heredity and environment
(c) All individuals have similar rates of development
(d) Development proceeds from specific to general

60. In NCF 2005, the objective of including art education in school is
(a) to appreciate cultural heritage
(b) to develop students' personality and mental health
(c) Only (a)
(d) Both (a) and (b)

Answers

1. (b)	2. (b)	3. (c)	4. (d)	5. (c)	6. (a)	7. (c)	8. (c)	9. (a)	10. (c)
11. (b)	12. (d)	13. (c)	14. (d)	15. (b)	16. (a)	17. (a)	18. (d)	19. (b)	20. (d)
21. (d)	22. (c)	23. (b)	24. (a)	25. (b)	26. (b)	27. (b)	28. (d)	29. (a)	30. (d)
31. (d)	32. (b)	33. (a)	34. (d)	35. (b)	36. (b)	37. (a)	38. (b)	39. (a)	40. (b)
41. (a)	42. (c)	43. (b)	44. (b)	45. (d)	46. (d)	47. (a)	48. (c)	49. (b)	50. (c)
51. (d)	52. (b)	53. (b)	54. (a)	55. (d)	56. (c)	57. (c)	58. (c)	59. (b)	60. (d)

Practice Set 05

1. Which of the following strategies of teaching-learning is obstacle in developing creativity?
(a) Help students to think in flexible ways
(b) Encourage students to take risk
(c) Overcontrol students during teaching-learning
(d) Guide students to be persistent and delay gratification

2. What is the correct sequence of memory process?

I. Encoding   II. Storage
III. Attention   IV. Retrieval

Select the correct answer using codes below
(a) III, I, II, IV   (b) II, III, I, IV
(c) I, III, II, IV   (d) III, II, I, IV

3. Which of the following is not a characteristic of Dyslexia ?
(a) Problems with reading accuracy, speed and comprehension
(b) Certainty as to right or left handedness
(c) Slow rate of writing
(d) Difficulty in learning and remembering printed words

4. An inclusive school reflects on all the following questions except
(a) do we believe that all students can learn
(b) do we work in teams to plan and deliver learning enabling enviornment
(c) do we properly segregate special children from normal to provide better care
(d) do we adopt strategies catering for the diverse needs of students

5. Defacto School Segregation is primarily a result of
(a) residence pattern of the community
(b) discriminatory zoning of a local school board
(c) guidelines issued by the state commissioner of education
(d) Federal education law

6. Bloom's taxonomy is a hierarchical organisation of ....
(a) achievement goals
(b) curricular declarations
(c) reading skills
(d) cognitive objectives

7. According to Vygotsky, why do children speak to themselves?
(a) Children use their speech to attract the attention of adults to them
(b) Children are very talkative by nature
(c) Children are egocentric
(d) Children use speech to guide their actions

8. A child reasons, 'You do this for me and I'll do that for you'. In which stage of Kohlberg's moral reasoning would this child fall?
(a) The 'good boy-good girl' orientation
(b) The 'social-contract' orientation
(c) The 'instrumental purpose' orientation
(d) The 'punishment and obedience' orientation

9. Watching her grand-daughter arguing with her father for going on a school trip, the grandmother says, "Why can't you be obedient like a good girl? Who will marry you if you behave like a boy?" This statement reflects which of the following?
(a) Gender stereotypes about attributes of girls and boys
(b) Gender constancy
(c) Improper gender identification of the girl
(d) Difficulties faced by families in child rearing

10. The interaction between a teacher and students creates a zone of proximal
(a) confusion   (b) development
(c) distortion   (d) difference

11. Child-centred pedagogy means
(a) giving moral education to the children
(b) asking the children to follow and imitate the teacher

(c) giving primacy to children's voices and their active participation

(d) letting the children be totally free

12. Positive classroom communication leads to

(a) coercion
(b) submission
(c) confrontation
(d) persuasion

13. What are the characteristics of continuous and comprehensive evaluation?

I. It increases the workload on students by taking multiple tests.

II. It replaces marks with grades.

III. It evaluates every aspect of the student.

IV. It helps in reducing examination phobia.

Select the correct answer using the codes given below

(a) II, III and IV
(b) I, II and III
(c) II and IV
(d) I, II, III and IV

14. Which of the following does not belong to a projected aid?

(a) Overhead projector
(b) Blackboard
(c) Epidiascope
(d) Slide projector

15. Learning

(a) is not affected by a learner's emotions
(b) has very little connection with emotions
(c) is independent of a learner's emotions
(d) is influenced by a learner's emotions

16. Effectiveness of teaching has to be judged in terms of

(a) course coverage
(b) student's interest
(c) learning outcomes of students
(d) use of teaching aids in the classroom

17. What are the barriers to effective communication?

(a) Moralising,being judgemental and comments of consolation
(b) Dialogue summary and self-review
(c) Use of simple words, cool reaction and defensive attitude
(d) Personal statements, eye contact and simple narration

18. A child says, 'Clothes dry faster in the Sun.' She is showing an understanding of

(a) symbolic thought
(b) egocentric thinking
(c) cause and effect
(d) reversible thinking

19. All of the following are applicable in good motivation except that it

(a) Should be relevant to the pupils
(b) Should be related to the lesson that follows
(c) Need not always come at the beginning of the lesson
(d) Should always come from the teacher

20. Human personality is the result of which of the following?

(a) Only heredity
(b) Upbringing and education
(c) Interaction between heredity and environment
(d) Only environment

21. The purpose of value education is best served by focusing on

(a) cultural practices prevailing in the society
(b) norms of conduct laid down by a social group
(c) concern for human values
(d) religious and moral practices and instructions

22. Which of the following is the highest level of cognitive ability?

(a) Knowing
(b) Understanding
(c) Analysing
(d) Evaluating

23. A teacher can help the children to process a complex situation by

(a) encouraging competition and offering a high reward to the child who completes the task first
(b) not offering any help at all so that children learn to help on their own
(c) giving a lecture on it
(d) breaking the task into smaller parts and writing down instructions

24. Children are most creative when they participate in an activity

(a) to escape their teacher's scolding
(b) under stress to do well in front of others
(c) out of interest
(d) for rewards

25. 'Mind Mapping' refers to
   (a) a technique to enhance comprehension
   (b) a plan of action for an adventure
   (c) drawing the picture of mind
   (d) researching the function of mind

26. In the context of education, socialisation means
   (a) always following social norms
   (b) creating one's own social norms
   (c) respecting elders in society
   (d) adapting and adjusting to social environment

27. The term 'curriculum' in the field of education refers to
   (a) methods of teaching and content to be taught
   (b) overall programmes of the school which students experience on a day- to - day basis
   (c) evaluation process
   (d) text material to be used in the class

28. A teacher makes use of variety of tasks to cater to the different learning styles of her learners. She is influenced by
   (a) Piaget's Cognitive Development Theory
   (b) Kohlberg's Moral Development Theory
   (c) Gardner's Multiple Intelligence Theory
   (d) Vygotsky's Socio-cultural Theory

29. Human Development is divided into which of the following domain?
   (a) Physical, spiritual, cognitive and social
   (b) Physical, cognitive, emotional and social
   (c) Emotional, cognitive, spiritual and social-psychological
   (d) Psychological, cognitive, emotional and physical

30. Which of the following is not considered a sign being gifted?
   (a) Creative ideas
   (b) Fighting with others
   (c) Novelty in experience
   (d) Curiosity

31. Which of the following is the first step in the scientific method of problem-solving?
   (a) Formation of hypothesis
   (b) Verification of hypothesis
   (c) Problem of awareness
   (d) Collection of relevant information

32. Which of the following is a domain of learning?
   (a) Professional
   (b) Experiental
   (c) Affective
   (d) Spiritual

33. Who said this statement, "Children actively construct their understanding of the world"?
   (a) Jean Piaget
   (b) Pavlov
   (c) Kohlberg
   (d) Skinner

34. Effective teaching by and large is a function of
   (a) teacher's scholarship
   (b) teacher's honesty
   (c) teachers making students learn and understand
   (d) teachers liking for the job of teaching

35. 'Dyslexia' is associated with
   (a) Reading disorder
   (b) Behavioural disorder
   (c) Mental disorder
   (d) Language disorder

36. Student A and Student B ask and answer questions to complete a worksheet. This is
   (a) an information gap activity
   (b) controlled interview
   (c) an information transfer activity
   (d) a role play

37. What is the main purpose of 'Operation Blackboard'?
   (a) Improvement of school facilities
   (b) Making education result-oriented
   (c) Making teaching effective
   (d) Making teaching accountable for results

38. Intelligence and creativity are
   (a) positively related
   (b) negatively related
   (c) not related with each other
   (d) to be creative atleast a normal threshold

39. What does motivation do in the process of learning?
   (a) Sharpens memory of the learner
   (b) Differentiates new learning from old learning
   (c) Makes learners think undirectionally
   (d) Creates interest for learning among young learners

40. Being a teacher what should you learn to understand the nature of children?
(a) Social Science
(b) Physics
(c) Child Psychology
(d) Geography

41. Our emotional experience depends upon
(a) perception of the world
(b) perception of other emotional experiences
(c) perception of our own bodily symptoms
(d) None of the above

42. Being a primary teacher you should keep the pitch of the voice
(a) high enough
(b) moderate
(c) low
(d) sometime low and sometime high

43. Which is not the factor of obstruction in the mental health of children?
(a) Strict discipline
(b) Family struggle
(c) His caste
(d) Sympathetic nature

44. Right of Children to Free and Compulsory Education Act, 2009 stipulates that learning should be
(a) through activities in a child-friendly manner
(b) support by extra coaching
(c) restricted to co-scholastic subjects
(d) carefully monitored by frequent testing

45. In a diverse classroom, learner find it difficult to speak and write good English and often uses their mother tongue. It is because
(a) they do not have the ability to learn English
(b) they are low learners
(c) they are not motivated to learn
(d) they lack enough competence and the structures of the two languages are different

46. Who gave the theory of sociocultural development?
(a) Erikson   (b) Skinner
(c) Piaget   (d) Vygotsky

47. IQ score of mentally retarted ranges
(a) 35-50   (b) 20-35
(c) 70 or below   (d) 50-70

48. Which of the following is not a component of human development?
(a) Continuity   (b) Sequentiality
(c) Differentiality (d) None of these

49. Nitu was absent from school for six months. After coming again to school, what kind of difficulty will she face?
(a) Friendship difficulty
(b) Learning difficulty
(c) Teacher difficulty
(d) No difficulty

50. In your class, a student is constantly rubbing his eyes and is inattentive during blackboard work he is having
(a) adjustment problem
(b) hearing problem
(c) visual problem
(d) All of the above

51. Which of the following statements is true about ability grouping?
(a) Students learn better in homogeneous groups
(b) For smooth and effective teaching, a class should be homogeneous
(c) Children are intolerant and do not accept differences
(d) Teachers may use multilevel teaching to cater to different ability groups

52 Which among the following also known as the toy age?
(a) Infancy
(b) Early childhood
(c) Middle childhood
(d) Adolescence

53. .....intelligence gives one the ability to manipulate and create mental images.
(a) Bodily   (b) Spatial
(c) Personal   (d) Linguistic

54. Who founded the principle of 'the age of moral development'?
(a) Piaget   (b) Kohlberg
(c) Skinner   (d) Vygotsky

55. Which is included in the mental reaction of the thought?
(a) Imagination
(b) Guess
(c) Memory
(d) All of these

56. If a child sitting on the last bench stands, sees the blackboard and sits repeatedly. What inference would you draw in this case?
(a) The child is short height as compared to his classmates
(b) The blackboard is under shining effect of light
(c) The child has defective vision
(d) Both (a) and (c)

57. Concept of curriculum flexibility was introduced to benefit
(a) Disabled children
(b) Madarsas and Maktabs
(c) Scheduled Castes and Scheduled Tribes
(d) All of the above

58. 'Every child is different from himself'. Which is the most responsible factor for this?
(a) Physical atmosphere
(b) Social atmosphere
(c) Heredity
(d) All of the above

59. Gardner formulated a list of seven intelligence. Which among the following is not one of them?
(a) Logical-mathematical intelligence
(b) Spatial intelligence
(c) Bodily - Kinesthetic intelligence
(d) Emotional intelligence

60. In which of the following activities, potential for nurturing creative and critical thinking is relatively greater?
(a) Participation in research conference
(b) Participation in a workshop
(c) Preparing research summary
(d) Presenting a seminar paper

Answers

1. *(c)*	2. *(a)*	3. *(b)*	4. *(c)*	5. *(a)*	6. *(d)*	7. *(d)*	8. *(c)*	9. *(a)*	10. *(b)*
11. *(c)*	12. *(d)*	13. *(a)*	14. *(b)*	15. *(d)*	16. *(c)*	17. *(a)*	18. *(c)*	19. *(d)*	20. *(c)*
21. *(c)*	22. *(d)*	23. *(d)*	24. *(c)*	25. *(d)*	26. *(d)*	27. *(b)*	28. *(c)*	29. *(d)*	30. *(b)*
31. *(d)*	32. *(c)*	33. *(a)*	34. *(c)*	35. *(a)*	36. *(c)*	37. *(a)*	38. *(a)*	39. *(d)*	40. *(c)*
41. *(c)*	42. *(a)*	43. *(a)*	44. *(a)*	45. *(d)*	46. *(d)*	47. *(c)*	48. *(d)*	49. *(b)*	50. *(c)*
51. *(d)*	52. *(b)*	53. *(b)*	54. *(b)*	55. *(d)*	56. *(a)*	57. *(d)*	58. *(d)*	59. *(d)*	60. *(a)*

Printed by Libri Plureos GmbH in Hamburg,
Germany